The Politics of Exclusion

The Politics of Exclusion

The Failure of Race-Neutral Policies in Urban America

Leland T. Saito

Stanford University Press
Stanford, California

Stanford University Press
Stanford, California

Printed in the United States of America on acid-free, archival-quality paper

Library of Congress Cataloging-in-Publication Data

Saito, Leland T., 1955–
  The politics of exclusion : the failure of race-neutral policies in urban America / Leland T. Saito.
    p. cm.
  Includes bibliographical references and index.
   ISBN 978-0-8047-5929-8 (cloth : alk. paper) — ISBN 978-0-8047-5930-4 (pbk. : alk. paper)
     1. Race discrimination—Government policy—United States—Case studies.
     2. Minorities—Government policy—United States--Case studies.   3. United States—Race relations—Political aspects—Case studies.   4. Political planning—United States—Case studies.   I. Title.
   E184.A1S254 2009
   305.800973--dc22

                         2008041321

Typeset by Bruce Lundquist in 10/14 Minion

To my parents, Clara and George Saito

Contents

Illustrations

Figures

Maps

Tables

Preface

WHEN I BEGAN RESEARCHING THIS BOOK on race and public policy, I expected that people with strong and explicit racial biases would be one of the central themes of the story. In fact, this was absolutely not the case. Instead, I encountered people such as Beverly Schroeder, a senior planner for the San Diego Centre City Development Corporation (CCDC), an agency in charge of planning and implementing redevelopment projects in downtown San Diego. My long-term experience working with Schroeder during the decade I spent in my roles as a member of the CCDC Asian Pacific Thematic Historic District Advisory Committee and as a researcher collecting data challenged my assumptions about people involved in economic redevelopment and historic preservation in San Diego. Always professional in demeanor and action, extremely skilled and knowledgeable, Schroeder went out of her way to help me, and my student assistants, in my work as a CCDC committee member and researcher. She graciously and efficiently responded to all my requests for information, meticulously working to dig out obscure files and reports. Reflecting on my experience with Schroeder, I believe that her actions stemmed in part from her confidence in the importance and quality of the projects created and built by the CCDC. If this was the case, I agree with Schroeder's assessment, and my experience with Schroeder led to my complete rethinking of race and racism in my case studies. With Schroeder's professionalism in mind, I began to consider that the wide range of people connected to policy formation, such as city staff members and members of commissions, include many individuals who see themselves operating in a way that they consider free of racial prejudice. If that is the case and if policymakers intend to make race-neutral policies, why do policies have racial consequences? That is the question I address in this book.

I spent more than a dozen years conducting this research, and many, many people provided assistance. Thanking those who have helped is always challenging because I am sure that, as a result of my faulty memory and incomplete records, I will miss naming friends and colleagues who have provided valuable assistance. In the early 1990s, I began working as assistant professor at the University of California at San Diego. Eager to learn about the Asian American political scene, I began attending events and met one of the key persons in city politics, Dorothy Hom. Energetic and full of warmth, she literally embraced me, always greeting me with a big hug and introducing me to everyone at community events. As a result, although I was a newcomer to the city, she made me feel welcome. She passed away in 1999, and the enormous and diverse gathering of people at her memorial service was a testament to the many lives she touched. Tom Hom, a successful business entrepreneur and former city council member and assemblyman, always agreed to talk and sit for interviews. Don Estes, who passed away in 2005, was the foremost expert on Japanese American history in San Diego, and he enthusiastically educated me about the region's history. Murray Lee, the main historian on Chinese Americans in the region, helped me through his research and extensive archives. Ralph Lewin, working in the San Diego office of the California Council for the Humanities at the time, invited me to present a talk on San Diego's historic Gaslamp District. This was one of the first opportunities I had to think deeply about development downtown and who was included in and excluded from the process. A number of other people provided help on the San Diego project, including Lilly Cheng, Alexander Chuang, Karen Huff Willis, and Elizabeth Yamada. Students at UCSD provided essential research assistance on this project, especially Hope Chau, Erika Gutierrez, and Liliana Rodriguez. Other students include Ben Bunyi, Judy Cho, Therese Cervas, Sandra Chong, Melany Dela Cruz, May Fu, Michelle Magalong, Jesse Mills, and Antonio Tiongson Jr. In the Los Angeles community, among those who provided important help or information are Judy Chu, Mike Eng, Kathay Feng, Daniel Ichinose, Stewart Kwoh, Paul Ong, Arturo Vargas, and Amadiz Velez.

I was looking for a new research project when I talked with Margaret Chin (then a graduate student at Columbia University and now a professor at Hunter College, not the city council candidate Margaret S. Chin) in New York City. She told me about the 1990 City Council redistricting in the city that divided Chinatown activists. That proved to be a perfect issue, complementing my work on the 1990 redistricting of state election districts in the San Gabriel

Valley of Los Angeles County. Arriving in New York as a stranger to the city, I was pleasantly surprised by all the help and information I received from such a wide range of people, including Sushan Chin, Fabiana Chiu, and Cynthia Lee at the Chinatown History Museum; and Devra Zetlan and the late Mary Ann Passadin in the New York Public Library. John Kuo Wei Tchen provided valuable help through his historical work, but he also arranged my stay as visiting scholar with the Asian Pacific American Studies Program and Institute at New York University. Margaret S. Chin, Rockwell "Rocky" Chin, Angelo Falcon, Margaret Fung, Andrew Hsiao, Peter Kwong, Gary Okihiro, Tito Sinha, William Sites, and Eric Tang were among the scholars and community activists who generously provided their time to help me learn about the city.

A number of people have provided comments by reading sections of this book or by responding to conference papers or presentations, including Bruce Cain, Sucheng Chan, Yen Espiritu, Joe R. Feagin, Colin Fisher, Herbert Gans, Alan Gartner, Ramon Gutierrez, Gregg Hennessey, Michael Jones-Correa, Moon-Kie Jung, Morgan Kousser, Jan Lin, George Lipsitz, John Logan, John Mollenkopf, Mike Murashige, Paul Ong, Edward J. W. Park, Laura Pulido, and Janelle Wong. My book is much improved by responding to their criticisms, and although I am sure that disagreements remain with my analysis and conclusion, I have enjoyed immensely the collegial discussions.

Kate Wahl, the acquisitions editor, Joa Suorez, assistant editor, and Carolyn Brown, production editor, at Stanford University Press, provided invaluable help throughout the publication process. Wendy Saito Lew, Albert Lew, Christopher Odoca, Melissa Hernandez, and Amber Thomas helped me with a number of tasks, especially computer issues. I am grateful for research support from the University of Southern California, the University of California at San Diego, Michael Schudson and the UCSD Civic Collaborative, and the Mott Foundation through Leadership Education for Asian Pacifics. I spent many, many hours working on this manuscript in the Pacific Beach and Chula Vista libraries in the San Diego area when I needed to leave my office and have a change of scenery. Thank goodness that our public libraries are still operating and now include free Wi-Fi.

I especially thank my family for the warm and caring support that they have always provided. My parents, George and Clara Saito; my spouse and her son, Sonia Ruan and Alexei; my sisters Wendy Saito Lew and Nadine Tateoka and their families, Albert and Sofie Lew, and Paul, Joseph, Elise, and Benjamin Tateoka; and my spouse's mother and her husband, Eliacer and Enrique Rieger.

The Politics of Exclusion

1 Introduction

The Racialized Outcomes of Race-Neutral Policies

SAN DIEGO CITY AGENCIES examined the Chinese Mission and the Douglas Hotel—the major community and cultural centers for Chinese Americans and African Americans in the pre–World War II era of segregation—in the center of the downtown area and concluded in the 1980s that they were not historically or architecturally significant and could be demolished. Community mobilization managed to save the Chinese Mission, turning it into a museum, but the Douglas Hotel was razed. In the 1990–1991 New York City Council redistricting, a district was created to enhance the political power of Asian Americans in the Chinatown area, which had one of the largest concentrations of Asian Americans in the city. The districting commissioners believed that the district provided the best opportunity to elect an Asian American in a city that at that time had never elected an Asian American to the council. White voters dominated elections in the district, however, and had never elected an Asian American. After the 2000–2001 redistricting of the California state assembly and state senate districts, a *Los Angeles Times* editorial declared that the districts protected incumbents and that "the plans shatter the concepts of community of interest and compactness of districts . . . and largely thwart the desires of Latinos and Asian Americans to win additional seats" (*Los Angeles Times* 2001: B14). The Mexican American Legal Defense and Educational Fund filed a lawsuit charging that the redistricting plan diluted Latino political power, but the lawsuit was dismissed in the federal district court, with the judges ruling that no harm had occurred to Latinos.

I examine how race shapes politics and public policy using these three case studies involving economic redevelopment and historic preservation in

1

San Diego and redistricting in New York City and the Los Angeles region, with Asian Americans playing a central role in each setting. Three cases, in three separate communities, with two in Southern California and one on the East Coast in Manhattan. On the surface, redistricting has nothing in common with economic redevelopment and historic preservation, and the landscape of the sprawling and ever-growing suburbs of Southern California is the opposite of the dense, vertical, and established Manhattan neighborhoods. Examining the public discussion of these issues, however, reveals a common debate on race, and because the assumptions and understandings of race are directly translated into public policy, I suggest that this debate is crucial to the formation and implementation of public policy in the United States today.

A key issue is a reliance by policymakers on the development of race-neutral procedures, or, in the case of redistricting, on deemphasizing race, which represents a fundamental shift in public policy from the explicitly race-based policies that previously generated and supported inequality in society. Race-based policies were exemplified by slavery and the genocide of Native Americans in the 1800s and by other policies in the first half of the 1900s, such as the forced repatriation of Mexican immigrants, the incarceration of Japanese Americans in internment camps during World War II, and segregation in employment, schools, neighborhoods, and public facilities.

One of the main themes of this book is how individuals and groups supporting race-neutral policies may in fact be contributing to policies that have racialized outcomes. I contend that people who consider themselves free of racial prejudice can play a part in supporting racial inequality in society. Previous forms of systemic racism—such as racially restrictive covenants in housing or segregated educational or transportation facilities—were put into place by people who were actively and deliberately working to create and enforce racial inequality. Instead of these explicitly race-based policies, I examine contemporary racialized policies enacted by people who sincerely believe that the policies they create and support are free of racial bias.

Gunnar Myrdal (1944), writing in the first half of the twentieth century, talked about the "American Dilemma" in regard to the racism experienced by African Americans and the yet-to-be-fulfilled-ideals of democracy. I focus on racial minorities and the American dilemma of the twenty-first century (E. Park and Park 1999). Employment, income, and educational indicators clearly show improving circumstances in important but, I would argue, narrowly defined areas, because such data do not reveal the ways that race continues to shape debate and policy, with unequal, racialized results in areas such as politics and economic development.

Analyzing the way policymakers view how race works in society is absolutely essential because such understandings serve to guide and legitimate policy formation. The case studies in this book demonstrate two opposing perspectives. On one side of the debate are those who support the effort to establish policies that strictly avoid race in their formation and implementation, leading to race-neutral policies. Two fundamental beliefs are incorporated into this perspective. The first belief is that the United States was founded on the principles of equality and democracy and that the history of the country is a movement toward realizing those ideals. As Alexis de Tocqueville (1969) concluded in his classic mid-nineteenth-century work on democracy in the United States, slavery was an aberration in a society striving for equality. Although racial discrimination was clearly a problem in the past, according to this view, discrimination has declined to the point where it has little effect on people's life chances and public policy in contemporary society.

The second belief is that racial minorities are experiencing integration into society, as demonstrated by rising educational levels, expanding occupational opportunities, and entrance into formerly all-white neighborhoods, and that considering race in public policy serves only to call attention to race and perpetuate its importance. Therefore developing race-neutral policies is the best way to eliminate the last traces of discrimination that remain. Supporting this perspective and discussing the history of race in the United States, historian Arthur Schlesinger Jr. contends that "a cult of ethnicity has arisen . . . to denounce the goal of assimilation, to challenge the concept of 'one people,' and to protect, promote, and perpetuate separate ethnic and racial communities" (Schlesinger 1998: 20). The result of a focus on race, according to Schlesinger (1998), interferes with integration because it "exaggerates differences, intensifies resentments and antagonisms, drives ever deeper the awful wedges between races and nationalities" (p. 106).

The other side of the debate, and my viewpoint in this book, suggests the explicit incorporation of race into public policies as a way to address past and present forms of racial inequality in society. This perspective contends that, although the country's early leaders expressed the ideals of equality and democracy, such ideals applied only to a narrow segment of society, and racial inequality was the norm, rather than the exception, and was encoded in the country's constitution, laws, and practices. As a result, these laws and practices have contributed to racial inequality since the founding of the United States, and race remains deeply embedded in our social, political, and economic institutions (Bonilla-Silva 2003; Haney Lopez 2003; Lipsitz 2006). As Joe Feagin explains, "U.S. institutions today reflect and imbed the white-over-black hierarchy initially created in the seventeenth century. . . . Systemic racism is not some unfortunate appendage to society that is now largely eliminated. Racial oppression persists as foundational and integral to society in the present day" (Feagin 2006: 8). To eliminate systemic racism in contemporary society, therefore, public policies must take race into account.

The analytical framework of this book is based on the perspective that recognizes continued inequality in society, and in the case studies I examined, two factors directly contributed to racialized outcomes. First, people working to enact and support race-neutral public policies may ignore the ways in which race is already present in the ideologies and practices of the larger society that shape the formation and implementation of policies. As a result, policies that appear race neutral may in fact be structured in ways that have racialized outcomes. This occurs because the policies do nothing to counter the ways in which race is already present, and thus the policies serve to reinforce racialized practices. Second, in the case of redistricting, policymakers viewed whites as a race-neutral group, despite evidence that whites actively worked to preserve their interests as a group through voting and redistricting. Failing to account for the racial actions of whites countered the attempts of redistricting to enhance the political effectiveness of racial minorities.[1]

Melvin Oliver and Thomas Shapiro explained the effects of systemic discrimination on capital accumulation: "To understand the sedimentation of racial inequality . . . is to acknowledge the way in which structural disadvantages have been layered one upon the other to produce black disadvantage and white privilege" (Oliver and Shapiro 1995: 51). Similarly, redistricting, economic redevelopment, and historic preservation demonstrate how a range of factors, both explicitly racial and seemingly race neutral, constitute the sedimentation of inequality in public policy. Economic redevelopment and the demolition of a building or neighborhood take place within a history of explicit racial inequality. This inequality manifested itself as racial exclusion, which created concentrations of racial minorities in residential and commercial areas, federal mortgage policies and practices of private financial institutions that opened up home ownership to new segments of the white population while denying the same to racial minorities, urban renewal efforts that disproportionately destroyed minority communities, policies of racial steering by real estate agents that support racial segregation, and historic preservation policies that ignore the social history of racial minorities. Redistricting and the creation of political districts occur within a history of literacy tests, poll taxes, grandfather clauses, white-only primaries, gerrymandering, racially polarized voting, and other race-based factors that have contributed to the disenfranchisement of racial minorities.

The extremely long and complex process of public policy formation and implementation involves many routine and institutionalized procedures as well as numerous individuals, community groups, and government committees and agencies. The established procedures and participants' assumptions about race—whether acknowledged or not—frame and influence the outcomes. As a result, race-neutral policies are only one part of a long chain of events that contribute to racialized consequences.

Race and Society: Assimilation Versus Systemic Racism

In the enduring debate in the United States about race and public policy, studies incorporating assimilation theory and the integration of racial minorities into society and studies on racial formation and the continued existence of systemic racism offer contrasting views of race and society. Assimilation theory provides the foundation for race-neutral policies, whereas racial formation theory frames the call to include race in policies to address racial inequality in society.

Social scientists developed assimilation theory in the early 1900s to explain the incorporation of new groups into a society undergoing massive transformation as a result of domestic and international migration, industrialization, and rapid urbanization (R. Park and Burgess 1967). Studies on assimilation examine the integration of immigrants and their descendants into society and conclude that integration is the inevitable route. In early versions of assimilation theory, Robert Park (1950) and Milton Gordon (1964) emphasized the gradual assimilation of all racial and ethnic groups into the American "mainstream," which Gordon (1964) suggested was defined by the customs and standards of European Americans. Assimilation occurred as newcomers learned how to adapt to American society and as discrimination gradually declined. Recognizing the historical importance of racial barriers, Gordon (1964: 78) noted that African Americans faced "unusually marked discrimination" compared to other groups in society, but he believed that the "emergence of the middle-class" was evidence that "the effect of discrimination will be seen to have been a delaying action only."[2]

Critics of assimilation theory note that adaptation is depicted as a linear and irreversible process, and the theory fails to take into account the contemporary development and reaffirmation of ethnic and racial identities (Espiritu 1992).[3] Critics also point out that assimilation theory was based on the experiences of European immigrants and was applied inappropriately to immigrants from Africa, Asia, and Latin America, who, these critics contend, face a fundamentally different experience in the United States because of their categorization as racial minorities. Where Gordon saw discrimination as "a delaying action," others saw race as a fundamental and established divide in society (Lipsitz 2006).

Richard Alba and Victor Nee (2003) offer a contemporary analysis and reformulation of assimilation theory. Alba and Nee (2003) critique the normative assumption and the implicit "hierarchy of racial and cultural acceptability" it contains: that all groups aspire to discard their old cultures and work to assimilate into the mainstream. Alba and Nee suggest that groups can retain an ethnic and/or racial identity, even though they attain high levels of integration into society along economic, education, and residential indicators.[4]

For Alba and Nee (2003), assimilation has occurred for the descendants of European and Asian immigrants whose ancestors came to the United States many generations ago. Four decades after Gordon's prediction that African Americans would achieve structural assimilation, Alba and Nee offer a more cautious assessment, although they recognize that African Americans have made great gains and that the possibility of future assimilation exists. Alba and Nee (2003) suggest that "there will be a black group for the foreseeable future, and membership in it will continue to be associated with disadvantages and discrimination" (p. 291).

Even with these words of caution, in general, from the perspective of assimilation, society operates in a fair, open, and meritocratic fashion, and the general trend in society is toward the incorporation of groups into the mainstream. Alba and Nee offer a hopeful view about the openness of society and, commenting on such groups as Japanese Americans during World War II, who faced extreme levels of intolerance, note the eventual assimilation of racial minority groups.

Liberal individualism, with its emphasis on the individual rather than on the group, offers an analytical focus distinct from assimilation, but the two views are related because they share assumptions regarding the reduced importance of race and the possibility of the integration of racial minorities into society. From the perspective of liberal individualism, the importance of race is understood in terms of individual rights, actions, and experiences. The impact of race on society and of racial discrimination is thus portrayed as the result of the actions of individuals and as an atypical occurrence in society (Thernstrom and Thernstrom 1997). According to this view, racial discrimination, although not completely eliminated, has declined to the point where it is no longer a major determinant of one's life chances and should be eliminated in the formation of public policy (D'Souza 1991; Steele 1990). Works on assimilation and liberal individualism conclude that the integration of racial minorities into society will occur without major changes in society to address discrimination.

In contrast to a focus on the individual and incorporation into society, with theories calling attention to systemic racism, racial discrimination remains a key factor in the organization of society for all racial groups. Whiteness studies, which examine the history of racial inequality in the United States, emerged in the 1990s, and key investigations (Jacobson 1998; Lipsitz 2006; Roediger 1994, 2007) looked at how racial hierarchy and racial privileges that favor whites and the systemic practices that support hierarchy and privilege became central features of U.S. society and remain so today. Directly contesting the principles of liberal individualism, Lipsitz (2006) explains that "conscious and deliberate actions have institutionalized group identity in the United States, not just through the dissemination of cultural stories, but also through the creation of social structures that generate economic advantages for European Americans through the possessive investment in whiteness" (p. 2). Federal legislation that advanced racial equality and changing racial attitudes among whites regarding race in the 1960s certainly marked important changes in society. According to research examining whiteness and structural inequality, however, race remains a major factor in society and is embedded in social, political, and economic institutions, thus contributing to systemic racism in society (Bonilla-Silva 2003; Feagin 2006; Feagin and Vera 1995).

In summary, research on assimilation measures the integration of racial minorities into American society through such indicators as income, intermarriage, and educational attainment and views racial inequality as a still troubling but disappearing factor in society. Research on whiteness and systemic racism, in contrast, emphasizes the continuing importance of racial discrimination based on deliberate and planned racial inequality. I certainly concur that such practices remain an important part of American society. However, in my examination of how public policies contribute to systemic racism, I am not directly addressing these forms of deliberate race-based discrimination. Instead, as revealed in my case studies, I investigate how public policy is racialized in the absence of racial prejudice and efforts to create racial inequality, an area ignored by assimilation theory and not a major focus of work on systemic racism. The focus of this book is the unintended racialized results of race-neutral public policy based on the assumptions of assimilation theory and liberal individualism. I document and analyze how the discussions and practices connected to policy formation and implementation contribute to the meaning and importance of race and, at times, result in racial hierarchy and privilege, with whites at the top and racial minorities in a subordinate position, as suggested by whiteness studies.

Understanding Public Policy Through Racial Formation

The three cases in this book illustrate the social construction of race and public policy in terms of the continuous struggle and negotiation over the meaning and consequences of racial categories, an essential aspect of what Michael Omi and Howard Winant (1994) called racial formation in the key explanatory work on the process. I draw on Omi and Winant's (1994) conceptual framework and on related works on race to highlight three areas regarding the social construction of race in contemporary society and how these processes contribute to the racialization of public policy.

First, the meaning and importance of racial categories in society are continually contested and redefined rather than fixed and static through time. As a result, understandings of race are fluid and are given significance because of their links to a variety of rights and privileges upon society. For example, local and federal policies directly conferred privileges upon whites and European immigrants regarding naturalization, voting, and the ability to own land while denying these privileges to Asian immigrants (Ngai 2004; E. Park and Park 2005). Through time and political struggle, each one of these privileges was eventually extended to Asian immigrants.

Second, racial formation emphasizes the importance of the way ideologies support public policies. As Stuart Hall (1995) explains, an ideology includes "images, concepts and premises which provide the frameworks through which we represent, interpret, understand and 'make sense' of some aspect of social existence" (p. 18). Thus a key aspect of racial formation is the struggle over competing ideologies and how particular ideologies become the established way of understanding race and the basis for shaping public policy (Vargas 2006). The history of urban areas in the United States shows how local governments have strategically manipulated and used such racial images as "slums" and "ghettos" to label communities in order to justify economic development plans that would eradicate neighborhoods and displace residents, and how these images and the consequences of race vary through time and place according to the purposes they serve (Gans 1995).

Third, racial formation occurs relationally, with racial minorities compared and ranked with one another as well as with whites (Almaguer 1994). Natalia Molina (2006), for example, documents how public officials in Los Angeles during the early 1900s viewed Mexican immigrants as assimilable, whereas Chinese and Japanese immigrants were deemed the opposite; the public officials used this judgment as a basis for incorporating Mexicans into public health programs while excluding Asians.[5]

The forces of racial segregation have worked to form communities in which racial minorities share the same neighborhoods, and as a result, residents analyze and construct the meaning of race and racial identities in relation to one another as well as to whites. Research that focuses on minority-white relations, ignoring minority-minority relations, excludes the reality of multiracial communities. In Monterey Park, California, for example, the first city in the continental United States with an Asian American majority population, some Asian Americans and Latinos sided with whites in the city's slow-growth movement in the 1980s. Other Asian Americans and Latinos, however, saw the movement as anti-immigrant and anti-Chinese, because development was primarily led by Chinese immigrants, and attempted to devise nondiscriminatory policies (Fong 1994; Horton 1995).

This understanding of the way racial minorities are compared to one another in the process of racial formation and the shared experiences arising from multiracial communities contribute to the possibility for racial minorities to interpret and explain their historical and contemporary experiences in ways that support an understanding of a common subordinate position as racialized minorities in a racial hierarchy (Pulido 1998, 2006). In this manner, coalitions form around policy issues through an explicit evocation and analysis of race and a recognition and interpretation of their linked racialized experiences, not through a deracialized strategy that erases race in favor of other factors, such as class, citizenship status, or place of birth (Jung 2003, 2006). In the case studies on redistricting in this book, Asian Americans, African Americans, and Latinos formed alliances based on their understanding of common interests.[6]

From Racial Inequality to the Civil Rights Movement and the Rise of White Ethnicity

The transformation of racial ideology and government policies in the post–World War II era, moving from state support of racial inequality to the era of civil rights legislation, framed the contemporary dialogue on race and the move to race-neutral public policies. Beginning in the 1970s, deindustrialization and the loss of jobs in the United States contributed to economic uncertainty, especially in the lives of people in the lower economic levels. The rise of white ethnicity in response to changing political and economic conditions and attacks on policies meant to address racial discrimination illustrate the malleable character of racial identities and how ideologies that serve to explain and legitimate such identities are directly linked to public policy.

The civil rights movement in the 1950s and 1960s and the black power movement in the 1960s initiated and reflected a transformation in race relations by challenging the legitimacy of racial inequality in society and government policies that contributed to racial discrimination (McAdam 1999; Morris 1984). Domestic pressures at home from the civil rights movement and concern over the American image internationally as the leader of the democratic world in the cold war contributed to the federal government's response (Dudziak 2000). Landmark federal legislation, including the 1964 Civil Rights Act, the 1965 Voting Rights Act, the 1965 Immigration Act, the 1968 Fair Housing Law, and government programs to address inequality, such as affirmative action and school busing to achieve integration, emerged during this time.[7]

The 1970s marked the beginning of major restructuring of the U.S. economy. Growing international competition and rising oil prices played a role in falling corporate profits. Corporations seeking to cut production costs contributed to the globalization of the production process and deindustrialization in the United States, as companies closed factories and shifted production to other countries, resulting in a massive loss of manufacturing jobs.[8] Economic restructuring led to a "hollowing of the middle," as corporations sent these jobs overseas, leading to a growing bifurcation in employment, with the expansion of low-technology, low-skill jobs with low wages and high-salary jobs requiring high levels of education and skills. From the end of World War II to the beginning of the 1970s, incomes grew across the board, but as a result of the restructuring of the economy, beginning in the mid-1970s, wages began to drop and the middle class began to shrink as income inequality rose (Harrison and Bluestone 1988; Levy 1998).

The Rise of White Ethnicity

As the United States emerged from the turmoil and massive social and economic changes of the 1960s and 1970s, one response among whites was the reemergence of white ethnicity. Countering the belief in the United States as a melting pot, Nathan Glazer and Daniel P. Moynihan (1970) called attention to the persistence of racial and ethnic identities in New York City in the 1960s.

Glazer and Moynihan (1970) suggested that cultural pluralism and the existence of distinct ethnic and racial groups in society, rather than assimilation, better described the racial situation in America.

White ethnicity among working-class and lower-middle-class Americans of Irish and southern and eastern European descent arose, in part, as a reaction to government programs—such as busing and affirmative action—that attempted to improve the condition of urban racial minorities while ignoring, white ethnics believed, the real needs of their communities (Novak 1996). According to this view, the politics of the 1960s differentiated between "'legitimate' minorities," such as African Americans, and the "'less favored' minorities," the white ethnics (Novak 1996: 356). White ethnics believed that they had to bear the inequitable burden imposed by race-based policies created and implemented by the economic and political elite. These burdens included competition exacerbated by affirmative action, with racial minorities competing for jobs in an economy transformed by deindustrialization; sending their children to schools affected by busing, which they believed created a threat to the safety and education of their children; and efforts to integrate neighborhoods, which threatened the racial "stability of their neighborhoods" (Rieder 1985: 57).

Matthew Frye Jacobson (2006: 19) explains that only after African Americans started to work for their rights "as a group" and with the achievements of the civil rights movement did the "dominant discourse of national civic life acknowledge the salience of group experience and standing." This "group-based mobilization" and record of legislative success provided a "model of action" for white ethnics (Jacobson 2006: 19). Questioning the melting pot model and embracing their white ethnicity, white ethnics stated that they supported the idea of civil rights and equality, but they also believed that they were being held responsible for problems caused by others, because their ancestors did not own slaves or enact the Jim Crow laws of the South. White ethnics explained that their ancestors had also suffered discrimination but had overcome these problems through their own efforts, not through government programs and subsidies (Glazer 1987; Greeley 1971; Waters 1990). From their perspective, taxes to fund programs for racial minorities hit their pocketbooks and racial integration negatively affected their housing values, placing an unfair burden on the working and middle classes (Edsall and Edsall 1992). Talking about the history of discrimination encountered by their ancestors allowed white ethnics to discuss race and oppose efforts to end racial inequality—such as school and neighborhood integration and affirmative action—in ways that they believed focused on fairness for all.

The rise of white ethnicity occurred during a fundamental shift in the national discussion on race from government-sponsored segregation to integration and equality. Understanding this change, embracing the group model of white ethnicity, allowed whites to adopt a new, supposedly antiracist rhetoric while defending their group rights. The end of colonialism and apartheid abroad and the changes brought about by the civil rights movement at home dramatically altered the national conversation on race (Edsall and Edsall 1992; Winant 2001). As Winant (2001) argues, "The upsurge of anti-racist activity . . . constitutes a fundamental and historical shift, a global rupture or 'break,' in the continuity of worldwide white supremacy" (p. 2). As a result, Omi and Winant (1994) explain that since the 1960s, "it has been impossible to argue *for* segregation or *against* racial equality" (p. 140, emphasis in the original).

Culture of Poverty

In the 1980s and 1990s, even with government programs to address inequality, racial differences in economic, social, and political life persisted, and in fact, some problems grew rapidly worse. Public attention focused on African Americans, and although occupational mobility and increasing incomes led to a growing middle class that benefited from the policies of the civil rights era, at the same time levels of poverty, unemployment, and crime increased among those in the lower economic levels (Wilson 1987). The views of social scientists and public opinion varied greatly regarding the causes of these problems and possible remedies. With overtly racist explanations based on biological inferiority no longer part of the mainstream racial dialogue, public discussion on economic and social differences among racial groups examined a range of possible causes. Consistent with the idea of liberal individualism, culture and personal responsibility provided one possible explanation.

The culture of poverty, a theory first developed in the 1950s and 1960s, provided an explanation of racial group differences that meshed with the beliefs of liberal individualism. Oscar Lewis (1966: xliv) developed his version of the theory in his study of Latinos in the United States and Latin America. Lewis explained how people developed a set of values, attitudes, and behaviors to adjust to a life as "poor" and "marginal" in society. One of the major consequences of the culture of poverty, according to Lewis (1966), is that it tends to perpetuate poverty from generation to generation. This occurs because those who have acquired such a culture lack the ability to pull themselves out of poverty and take advantage of opportunities that may arise.[9]

According to critics of this theory (Ryan 1971), the culture of poverty focused on the behavior of the poor and "blamed the victim" while ignoring structural factors, such as racial discrimination and disappearing jobs as a result of deindustrialization. Shifting the debate away from culture in a pivotal work on race, William J. Wilson (1980) contended that with the major changes of the 1960s, the state had gone through a fundamental change. Rather than establishing laws and institutions that generated and supported racial inequality, the state now worked to enforce racial equality. As a result of declining racial discrimination, race was no longer the major factor that determined one's life chances; rather, it was class level and access to resources. As Wilson (1980) explains, "Economic and political changes have made economic class position more important than race in determining black chances for occupational mobility" (p. 23).[10] Although theories that focus on culture and class give different explanations for continued problems, they accept the idea that racism in society has declined to the point where one's life chances are governed by factors other than race and allow for the support and enactment of race-neutral policies.

Whiteness Studies and the Critique of Liberal Individualism and the Claims of White Ethnicity

Research on whiteness offers a trenchant critique of the perspective of white ethnics that their history of discrimination is similar to that of racial minorities, that whites have not received government assistance to help them advance in society, and therefore that government policies that explicitly involve race should be replaced by race-neutral policies. For example, a critical area of economic difference pointed out in whiteness studies among racial groups is access to home ownership and choice of residential neighborhoods. Home ownership is one of the major ways that lower- and middle-class Americans accumulate capital and pass on wealth to their children. The history of home ownership, home mortgages, and residential segregation provides an example of white privilege that is often unrecognized by white ethnics.[11]

The Federal Housing Administration (FHA) and the Federal National Mortgage Association (Fannie Mae), established in the 1930s, transformed the home-buying process and opened up home ownership to a much broader segment of the public by insuring home mortgages and facilitating mortgages with smaller down payments, lower interest rates, and longer payment periods. With new construction stalled by the Depression and World War II, the housing boom after the war created new suburbs that rapidly filled with eager home buyers.

However, explicit racial federal guidelines for home mortgages and practices by financial institutions and home builders ensured that the new suburbs would be reserved for whites. In Long Island's famous Levittown, emblematic of the large-scale housing tracts rising in the nation, these exclusionary policies meant that as late as 1960, zero African Americans lived in the community of 82,000 (Jackson 1985: 241).

Billions of dollars of public funds from local, state, and federal levels of government spending went into the infrastructure necessary for suburbanization, such as the construction and maintenance of roads, highways, sewer and water systems, schools, and libraries. The policies and practices of segregation meant that racial minorities faced exclusion from the new suburbs and the opportunity to gain access to better housing, schools, and employment opportunities (Lipsitz 2006; Massey and Denton 1993).

Even after the passage of the federal Fair Housing Law and the Supreme Court decision in *Jones v. Mayer*, which ruled against racial discrimination in housing, both in 1968, limited access to housing for racial minorities continued. Studies repeatedly show that African Americans and Latinos with the same economic profile as whites have less access to home mortgages and receive loans with less favorable rates. A recent study by the National Fair Housing Alliance (NFHA 2006: 6, 9) on real estate practices found that whites received better service from real estate agents than African Americans and Latinos, including "financial incentives" to help purchase a home, and that racial steering occurred at the extraordinarily high rate of 87 percent when real estate agents showed houses to clients.

These practices of racial exclusion occurred over and over again in other areas of capital accumulation.[12] As Joe Feagin (2006) explains, the "federal government distributed hundreds of millions of acres of land, billions of dollars in mineral and oil rights, major airline routes, major radio and television frequencies . . . almost exclusively to white Americans" (p. 3). When white ethnics assert that they have not received government help, they ignore the history of massive subsidies they have disproportionately received in the purchase of homes and access to new suburban developments and other government programs.

Racial Images, Comparative Racialization, and Public Policy: The Model Minority and Affirmative Action

The national discussions on the model minority and affirmation action frame a range of policies on race and illustrate the debate between individual responsibility and the culture of poverty on the one hand and the effects of systemic racism on racial groups on the other. These discussions clearly show how racial formation occurs relationally, with Asian Americans directly compared with African Americans and Latinos. Although Asian Americans feature prominently in the discussions of each topic, the goal of these debates is more often about using images of Asian Americans as the model minority to preserve the status quo than about providing a rigorous analysis of race and addressing inequality in society. As Michael K. Brown and colleagues (2003) remark, "We found it quite striking that when Asian and Latinos enter the conservative consensus, it is usually to discount the impact of racism on the life-chances of blacks. Thus, Asians are presented as the 'model minority'" (p. x).

Model Minority

The radical change in the image of Asian immigrants and Asian Americans from the "yellow peril" to the "model minority" illustrates how racial images are altered to support particular racial ideologies and public policies. The characterization of Asians as "unassimilable aliens," "the yellow peril," and "coolie labor" by labor organizations and city officials in the western United States contributed to the passage of restrictive immigration laws in the late nineteenth and early twentieth centuries (Gotanda 2001; Saxton 1971). The emergence of the model minority label in the 1960s and 1970s, characterizing Asian immigrants and Asian Americans as high achievers in education and work as a result of cultural values, served to counter claims of institutional discrimination by members of the black power, Chicano power, and Asian American movements (S. Lee 1996; Suzuki 1977; Tuan 1998; Yoo 2003).

In 1966, amid the debates on the causes of racial inequality and how to address racial disparities, articles appeared in the *New York Times Magazine* and *U.S. News & World Report* celebrating the so-called educational and economic success of Japanese and Chinese Americans. These articles, and others that followed, laid the groundwork for transforming the image of Asian Americans. Stressing that Asian Americans had experienced extreme forms of racism, such as the incarceration of Japanese Americans during World War II, these articles talked about the achievements of this group through cultural attributes such as a reverence for education, hard work, and discipline and a supportive family and community.

A key goal of the model minority idea, however, was to contest government programs and to counter the claims of the black power and civil rights movements that institutional barriers were blocking the progress of racial minorities.

The articles in news magazines explicitly attacked African Americans and public programs through comparisons with the model minority, Asian Americans. The first sentence in a *U.S. News & World Report* article describes Chinese Americans as a "racial minority pulling itself up from hardship and discrimination to be become a model of self-respect and achievement" (*U.S. News & World Report* 1966: 73). The next sentence questions the need for government programs, declaring that "at a time when it is being proposed that hundreds of billions be spent to uplift Negroes and other minorities, the nation's 300,000 Chinese-Americans are moving ahead on their own—with no help from anyone else" (*U.S. News and World Report* 1966: 73).

Stressing individual effort and culture, *U.S. News & World Report* quoted a professor who had studied New York City's Chinatown and who emphasized the work ethic. The professor said, "They're willing to do something—they don't sit around moaning" (*U.S. News & World Report* 1966: 74, 76).[13] William Petersen suggested in a *New York Times Magazine* article that it may well be that Japanese Americans have experienced "the most discrimination and the worst injustice" of "persons alive today" but that they have managed to advance "by their own almost totally unaided effort" (Petersen 1966: 20, 21). As Thernstrom and Thernstrom (1997) would later write in their comparison of Asian Americans and African Americans, "Asian organizations . . . took a strongly integrationist and assimilationist stance" and "few group leaders . . . indulged in racist antiwhite rhetoric of the kind that is too often heard today within the African-American community" (p. 536).

As the Asian American model minority image gained increasing strength, a number of critiques of the image emerged and scrutinized the ideological work done by the image to attack the claims of racism by African Americans and Latinos. The news articles suggest that African Americans have focused their energy on condemning society instead of on improving their own situation and addressing the culture of poverty that has impeded their economic progress. This view, of course, ignores the educational and neighborhood-building programs established by African Americans (Morris 1984). The model minority image, however, serves the ideological purpose of placing blame on African Americans and reinforcing a culture of poverty argument rather than seriously examining the effects of racial discrimination in society. By emphasizing Asian American "success," the image ignores the actual situation of the population—for example, the large segments of the Asian American population living in poverty and experiencing low levels of educational attainment (Ong and Hee

1994). Thus the model minority image serves more as a critique of African Americans and support for the status quo than providing an understanding of the situation of Asian Americans.[14]

Affirmative Action

Just as Jewish Americans faced restrictions as their numbers grew at Ivy League institutions in the early 1900s, in the mid-1980s Asian Americans charged that elite colleges in the United States had restricted the number of Asian Americans through quotas, adding an ironic twist to the idea of meritocracy, the model minority image, and the celebrated educational success of Asian Americans (Karabel 2005). Evaluations of admission policies and practices produced varied conclusions, but after reviews by state agencies, the chancellor of the University of California, Berkeley, offered an apology in 1989 for "disadvantaging Asians." As a result of a federal investigation, the graduate mathematics program at the University of California, Los Angeles, accepted a number of Asian American students who previously had been denied admission (Takagi 1998: 9).

In an analysis of the admissions controversy, Dana Takagi explained that the debate involving America's elite colleges and universities created a way to change the discussion from discrimination in admissions to affirmative action. Takagi (1998) stated that the "discourse about Asian admissions facilitated a subtle but decisive shift in public and intellectual discourse about affirmative action" (p. 10). It also allowed African Americans and whites to become the focus of the discussion, with Asian Americans relegated to the margins but brought forward to discredit affirmative action when depicted as victims of quotas that helped African Americans and Latinos. Missing from the debate were the benefits that underrepresented Asian American groups at these educational institutions, such as Filipinos and Southeast Asians, may have gained from affirmative action and retention programs. The debate by affirmative action opponents also steered clear of admission policies that benefited legacy admissions and athletes, who at the Ivy League institutions tend to be white.

Then-president Bill Clinton declared on July 19, 1995, that affirmative action was "good for America," that the nation should "mend it, not end it," and that "we're still closing the gap between our founder's ideals and our realities" (Richter 1995: A1). Coincidentally, on the next day, the regents of the University of California voted 14 to 10 to abolish affirmative action in the admission of students and, in a separate vote, also ended such policies in the hiring of employees and in the contracting process. Then-governor Pete Wilson, as an ex-officio member of the Board of Regents, voted with the majority and asked, "Are we going to treat all Californians equally and fairly? . . . It takes all the state taxes paid by three working Californians to provide the public subsidy for a single undergraduate. . . . The people who work hard to pay those taxes and who play by the rules deserve a guarantee that their children will get an equal opportunity to compete for admission" (Wallace and Lesher 1995: A1). In contrast, Jack W. Peltason, president of the University of California system and also an ex-officio member of the Board of Regents, spoke in strong support of affirmative action, arguing, "We are a public institution in the most demographically diverse state in the union. . . . Our affirmative action and other diversity programs, more than any other single factor, have helped us prepare California for its future. . . . To abandon them now would be a grave mistake" (Wallace and Lesher 1995: A1).

As the University of California regents voted to do away with affirmative action, to "guarantee . . . an equal opportunity to compete for admission," special preferences remained, but for the rich and powerful. Public officials and donors used their influence to help the children of the wealthy and politically powerful gain admission to UCLA and UC Berkeley, the two University of California schools with the most competitive admissions process, according to the *Los Angeles Times*. The *Los Angeles Times* investigation also showed that regents who voted to end affirmative action, including Ward Connerly, had used their influence to gain special attention for applicants (Gladstone and Frammolino 1996: A1).

The *Los Angeles Times* reported that from 1980 to the mid-1990s, records showed that "more than 200 students were admitted after initially being rejected" at UCLA (Frammolino et al. 1996: A1) and that from 1993 to the mid-1990s, "19 students who would not otherwise have been admitted" gained entrance to UC Berkeley (Gladstone and Frammolino 1996: A1). In 1998 the regents acted on the issue but stopped short of banning such practices, preserving this advantage for the privileged few and giving campuses the leeway to consider the political and financial benefits of admitting particular applicants.[15]

In 1996, the year after the University of California Board of Regents did away with affirmative action, Californians voted to extend the actions of the regents to cover the entire state. Passed with 54 percent of the vote, Proposition 209 ended affirmative action in "public employment, public education, or public contracting" (Chavez 1998: 271). By ending affirmative action, coupled with the earlier ban by the regents, the vote marked the beginning of the "colorblind" era in California's public institutions. Proposition 209 generated efforts to end affirmative action across the country, and by 2006, Washington, Florida, and Michigan had passed similar regulations. The California vote, however, reflected the wishes of whites, who voted 63 percent in favor, versus the wishes of African Americans, Asian Americans, and Latinos, who voted against the proposition, at 74, 61, and 76 percent, respectively. Because whites represented 74 percent of the voters in the election, their preferences carried the proposition (*Los Angeles Times* 1996).

Rather than a vote for fairness, individualism, and a color-blind society, however, research shows that for some whites awareness of group identity and interests contributes to "opposition to affirmative action" that is motivated by the "desire to protect fellow whites" (Lowery et al. 2007: 1). Support of white group interests, however, may not be viewed as a way to gain advantages for whites at the expense of minorities or as prejudice toward minorities. As research by Brian Lowery and colleagues (2006) suggests, whites do not necessarily connect white privilege with disadvantages for racial minorities. Because of this disconnect, whites can oppose affirmative action and support race-neutral policies while supporting established but unrecognized "privileges that dominant-group members have grown to see as their due" (Lowery et al. 2006: 972). Support for race-neutral policies and taken-for-granted privileges, therefore, is not meant to harm racial minorities, but the result is the failure of whites to acknowledge the protection of white group rights, support of the status quo and of leaving systemic inequality untouched, and an attack on policies meant to address racial discrimination.

Community Activism and Policy Formation Versus the "Sleeping Giant"

One theme of this book is to examine how race-neutral policies lead to racialized results. The second theme is to examine community activism among Asian Americans, Latinos, and African Americans as a way to document and analyze how understandings of race are publicly expressed, contested, and incorporated into public policy. Central to this book is the understanding by community activists that public policies—such as redistricting, economic redevelopment, and historic preservation—have directly affected their everyday lives and are part of a long history in which local, state, and federal levels of government have exerted tremendous control over access to space and the activities allowed within its boundaries (Cuff 2000; Dreier et al. 2001; Feagin 1998; Fulton 2001; Gilmore 2002; Gottlieb et al. 2005; Logan and Molotch 1987).

Asian immigrants and Asian Americans have played a key role in the policy-formation debate and their experiences demonstrate the ways in which government policies and regulations control entrance to the United States, land use, and access to business and residential areas, creating a racial hierarchy through public policy. Historians Roger Daniels and Sucheng Chan (2003) point out that Asian Americans have actively worked to create their place in America, in contrast to portrayals of Asian Americans as passive objects of discriminatory acts. These opposing views are part of the ideological struggle over images that are used in the process of defining racial groups and how these definitions support views of the United States as either an open and fair society or a society in which discrimination and racial hierarchy exist. Supporting the notion of the uninvolved immigrant, for example, articles in the media (Ivins 2006; Tumulty 2001) write about Mexican Americans as a "sleeping giant," with vast potential for political power once their voting power matches their numbers.[16]

The sleeping giant image is an inaccurate and partial view of politics because it explains the supposedly low level of activity among minorities through the inaction of minorities. This explanation ignores the long history of whites enacting restrictions to counter the numerous attempts of minorities to become involved in politics and the disenfranchisement faced by people of color through such tactics as poll taxes, grandfather clauses, "white-only primaries," and intimidation and violence. Long after such procedures were abolished or reduced, other practices, such as gerrymandering in redistricting and restrictive voter registration procedures, continued to weaken the political strength of minorities and hinder involvement in electoral politics (Grofman and Davidson 1992; Hardy-Fanta 1993; Lien 1997, 2001).

Understanding the long and active political history of people of color requires an expanded framework that recognizes a wide range of activities in addition to electoral politics (Nakanishi 1985–1986; Nakanishi and Lai 2003). Charles McClain's (1994) study of Chinese immigrants in the nineteenth century, for example, demonstrates that Chinese actively resisted and contested policies of exclusion enacted by the San Francisco Board of Supervisors through the judicial system, demonstrating their knowledge of U.S. institutions and active engagement in civil society. More broadly, the history of Asian immigrants and Asian Americans shows that they have actively contested discriminatory policies and negotiated the terms of their participation in American society on issues such as naturalization, residential segregation, employment discrimination, and immigration policy.

The establishment of the Japanese-Mexican Labor Association in Oxnard, California, in 1903 and of the United Farm Workers Union by Filipino and Mexican laborers in 1966 (Almaguer 1994; Ichioka 1988) and the civil rights movement, black power movement, and Chicano movement in the 1960s through the 1970s (Chavez 2002; Mariscal 2005; Munoz 2007) demonstrate the long history of activism and struggle by people of color. Through their efforts, they have gained rights for themselves and also forced change in the country's institutions to the benefit of everyone. For example, the lawsuits based on the Voting Rights Act filed by African Americans and Latinos to challenge redistricting plans and voter registration procedures in the South and Southwest have increased political access for all (Davidson 1984). As Gary Okihiro (1994) explains, "Racial minorities, in their struggles for inclusion and equality, helped to preserve and advance the very privileges that were denied to them, and thereby democratized the nation for the benefit of all Americans" (p. 151).

San Diego, New York City, and the Los Angeles Region

The cases in San Diego, Los Angeles, and New York City reflect current debates about race and public policy and varying interpretations of the social changes of the past half-century. As Howard Winant (2001) explains, before World War II, racial inequality and racial privilege reigned. However, efforts to end colonial rule and apartheid around the world and to address civil rights in the United States challenged the legitimacy of regimes based on racial inequality. Although these decades clearly brought dramatic changes to U.S. society—such as federal legislation addressing racial inequality in housing, employment, and electoral politics—the actual impact of these changes on deeply embedded societal inequality is highly contested, with some arguing that the United States has entered a color-blind era and others contending that systemic racism continues.

As William J. Wilson (1980) points out, since the middle of the twentieth century, the state has experienced a dramatic change, moving from the creation and enforcement of racial inequality in society to supporting racial equality. Although there are important arguments that counter Wilson's claim of state-sponsored efforts to dismantle systemic discrimination (Feagin 2006; Winant 2001), the point here is that there is a difference between state-sponsored inequality and supporting what are believed to be color-blind or race-neutral policies, which can produce, as I argue, racialized results. I suggest that my case studies illustrate how policies that on the surface appear to be race neutral or that deemphasize race can have a negative impact on racial minority groups because the policies are racialized in their implementation and outcomes.

The very structure of institutional processes such as redistricting, economic redevelopment, and historic preservation and the dialogue on race that they produce can generate and support or contest and dismantle racial hierarchy and privilege. Understanding that these procedures are not simply neutral instruments through which interests are contested and expressed (Crenshaw et al. 1995), groups struggle over the form and implementation of these policies and the resources that the policies control.

San Diego

In the first case study, involving economic redevelopment and historic preservation, San Diego city agencies in the 1980s launched a massive investment of public funds to economically revitalize the declining downtown area. The city examined the Chinese Mission and the Douglas Hotel, structures built in the 1920s, and concluded that neither building was historically or architecturally significant. The Chinese Mission was the center of religious and social life for Chinese Americans in the pre–World War II era, and a wave of protest and lobbying by Chinese Americans saved the building from destruction. Likewise, the Douglas Hotel served as the foremost center of entertainment and lodging in the downtown area for African Americans from the 1920s to the 1940s, but it was demolished in 1985 with little protest by any individual or group.

Motivated by the loss of the Douglas Hotel, African American community activists established the Gaslamp Black Historical Society (GBHS) in 1999. In 2001 the GBHS determined that the Clermont/Coast Hotel was the first in the region reserved exclusively for African Americans in the era of segregation, and the hotel became the first structure related to African American history added to the city's list of historical sites.

The histories of the three structures illustrate how the implementation of race-neutral historic preservation and economic redevelopment policies by city officials would have led to the destruction of all three structures if community activists had not intervened in the process. Nationally, development efforts have gone through two major changes in the effort to go from racially explicit to race-neutral policies, and they illustrate the ways that community members have challenged and changed government-imposed racial images and policies to save important structures and neighborhoods from destruction. After World War II, the trend toward suburbanization contributed to the economic decline of urban areas (Jackson 1985). Cities worked with the federal government to re-build their downtown areas from the 1950s through the 1970s using the urban renewal program. These projects, however, were marked by the large-scale destruction of entire neighborhoods, especially those inhabited by people of color. Contributing to the destruction of structures is the growth machine strategy of economic redevelopment. Controlled by local political and economic elites, this strategy emphasizes development to revive declining downtown areas and generate profit for major developers and property owners and tax revenue for local governments, often through the replacement of old buildings with new buildings (Feagin 1988; Logan and Molotch 1987; Molotch 1976).

The first struggle over racial images occurred when city officials depicted neighborhoods inhabited by racial minorities as dysfunctional and crime-ridden slums to justify the destruction of these areas through urban renewal. To save their communities, activists had to work to change these negative descriptions from ghettos to healthy communities with strong networks and social institutions worth protecting. Historic preservation became the second site of activism as residents worked to change development policies from the indiscriminate destruction of buildings to the selective preservation of buildings and neighborhoods.

Redevelopment threatens all historic structures, regardless of their relation to any racial group, but racial minorities are at a disadvantage for two reasons. First, traditionally, historic preservation favors buildings that are aesthetically exceptional, designed by famous architects, or connected to events of national importance—criteria that often do not apply to buildings connected to racial minority communities. Second, the shift in historic preservation policies brought about by the National Historic Preservation Act of 1966 resulted in the inclusion of social history representing important aspects of the everyday lives of residents and local events. This opened up the possibility of preserving structures related to racial minorities but also the major challenge of convincing city officials of the importance of the social history of minorities.

The San Diego case illustrates the process of racialization in which city officials and developers do not explicitly target the history and buildings connected to African American and Chinese American communities, but because the importance of these histories is not acknowledged in the way that the social history of white residents is documented and recognized, communities of color disproportionately experience the destructive effects of redevelopment (Hayden 1997).

Redistricting in the United States

Casting a ballot is the quintessential symbol of democracy in the United States, and as Abigail Thernstrom (1987) contends, in terms of empowering racial minorities, government actions should be limited to ensuring access to voting. J. Morgan Kousser (1999) argues, however, that Thernstrom's call for limited government intervention ignores the historical and contemporary practices that have produced institutional barriers that continue to hamper the political participation of racial minorities. This debate is based on two opposing conceptions of society, with Thernstrom (1987, 1995) arguing that political institutions are basically equitable and unbiased. Kousser (1999) contends, however, that redistricting, which is the redrawing of political district boundaries, coupled with Supreme Court rulings on the application of the Voting Rights Act on redistricting, has often served to empower whites and disenfranchise racial minorities.

Redistricting directly affects the political power of racial groups, for example, by consolidating a group within a district and concentrating voting strength or by fragmenting a group into two or more districts and possibly diluting the group's political impact. Thernstrom's argument that government involvement should be limited to ensuring access to voting ignores the history of the way that groups in power have used redistricting to preserve their power and weaken the electoral strength of opponents. Emerging from the civil rights struggle, the 1965 Voting Rights Act requires the recognition and protection of the political rights of racial minorities. Redistricting requires that political districts should recognize communities of interest composed of individuals with shared social, economic, and/or political concerns and keep those communities intact within districts. For racial minorities organizing on the basis of race and claiming that they constitute a community of interest, they must publicly explain the factors that unite them as a group along racial lines. These public declarations provide an important opportunity to examine the relationship between race and electoral policies.

The Los Angeles region and New York City now have majority-minority populations. Because African Americans, Latinos, and Asian Americans generally live in multiracial neighborhoods, creating political districts must take into account relations among groups and the potential for conflict or common interests. Even as the number of whites declines in these areas, however, their voting power often plays a deciding role in local elections, and therefore their relations with racial minorities are a key part of the redistricting process.

In the case studies involving redistricting in New York City's Chinatown and the Los Angeles region, Asian Americans and Latinos discuss why race remains politically significant and should be considered in the redistricting process. In contrast, court decisions related to redistricting and commission members involved in creating districts support the argument that race should no longer be a key issue to consider when creating district boundaries. I argue in support of Kousser's (1999) contention that this move toward race-neutral redistricting by the courts and commissions works to disenfranchise racial minorities while protecting white voters.

New York City

In the second case study, centered on redistricting in New York City, I examine the creation of a city council district explicitly crafted in 1990–1991 around Manhattan's Chinatown to enhance the political power of Asian Americans. This was a key historical moment for redistricting. The number of council districts had just increased from thirty-five to fifty-one to enhance the political representation of minorities, and the 1990 *Garza v. Los Angeles County Board of Supervisors* federal court decision emphasized the rights of minorities in redistricting. This was a unique opportunity because this set of favorable conditions would soon disappear in 1993, when a Supreme Court redistricting decision reduced the importance of race.

Community participants in redistricting decided that uniting Chinatown in one district was the main goal, ending the fragmentation and dilution of political power that had occurred in previous redistricting plans. The 1990 census data determined that Chinatown's population was too small to create a council district based only on that neighborhood and that additional areas had to be added to develop a council district that met the population requirement. Chinatown activists offered two opposing plans, based on different criteria, for what areas should be added. Asian Americans for Equality (AAFE), a well-established Chinatown social service provider, created a plan to link Chinatown with areas inhabited primarily by whites to the west and south, such as SoHo, Tribeca, and Battery Park City. AAFE based this plan on election data that showed that liberal white voters in those areas supported Asian American candidates. A coalition of residents formed an organization, Lower East Siders for a Multi-Racial District, and proposed a plan that would connect Chinatown with the Lower East Side to the east and create a majority Latino, Asian American, and African American district. This district was based on the interests of low-income and working-class residents and the history of multiracial activism in the area that its supporters believed represented a tightly knit political community of interest.

The Districting Commission, in charge of creating the new districts, met one of the major goals of both plans by uniting Chinatown in one district. The commission decided to follow AAFE's plan and joined Chinatown with the white neighborhoods to the west, guided by the belief that whites would be more likely to vote for an Asian American candidate than Latinos would, and keeping Latinos and Asian Americans in separate districts offered the best opportunity for each group to elect officials of its own choosing (Gartner 1993). Whites, compared to Latinos in this analysis, become a race-neutral group that would recognize the legitimacy and need for minority representation and would vote for an Asian American candidate. This assumption ignores the long history of whites' working to protect their interests in the city. In the new district, although Asian Americans slightly outnumber whites, whites dominate elections with 61.5 percent of the registered voters and have consistently elected whites to represent the district; no Asian American has held the council seat.

In addition to the way the Districting Commission interpreted community input and created the boundaries of the districts, other important factors shaped the redistricting process in major ways and served as barriers to the enfranchisement of Asian Americans. One of the most important was the 1989 city charter reform process in which the number of city council districts rose from thirty-five to fifty-one. Increasing the number of districts reduces the population requirements of each district and provides an opportunity for creating districts that would enhance the voting strength of racial minorities. Asian American and Puerto Rican community organizations advocated for sixty districts, but the Charter Commission believed that fifty-one was a good compromise between increasing the number of districts to protect the voting rights of minorities and keeping the number to a manageable size in terms of the cost of running the council and providing an opportunity for the meaningful participation of council members (NYC-CRC 1990).

For Asian Americans in Chinatown, fifty-one districts rather than sixty and the large undercount of Chinatown residents by the 1990 census added up to additional white voters who were added to the district and created a situation in which white voters controlled elections in that district. The Chinatown district reflects the decisions of the members of the Census Bureau, the Charter Commission, and the Districting Commission and their understanding of race and how this understanding served to privilege whites over minorities in politics.

The Los Angeles Region

In my third case, I examine the 2000 redistricting of state electoral districts in the Los Angeles region. The rapidly growing Latino population was one of the major issues to consider in redistricting. A clear possibility for interracial conflict existed because Latinos often shared neighborhoods with Asian Americans and African Americans and creating districts that considered the interests of all groups would be extremely difficult.

Despite the potential for conflict, redistricting generated an unprecedented statewide working alliance among Latino, Asian American, and African American redistricting groups. A number of factors led to the alliance. First, U.S. Supreme Court decisions, particularly *Shaw v. Reno* (1993), limited the use of race in redistricting. This increased the possibility that areas with high concentrations of racial minorities could be fragmented into a number of districts, diluting their political power. Second, the California legislature controls redistricting and has a long history of gerrymandering and dividing racial minority communities. Ultimately, the organizations representing African Americans, Asian Americans, and Latinos understood that if they presented a plan that all three groups supported at public hearings held by the state legislature's redistricting committee, they would have a much better chance of influencing the process in ways that would benefit their communities.

Concern about the state legislators working to protect their own election futures rather than the political rights of racial minorities proved accurate when the redistricting plans were made public. The new plan was dubbed an "incumbent protection plan" by political pundits (*California Journal* 2002). In 2001, the Mexican American Legal Defense and Educational Fund (MALDEF) filed a lawsuit, *Cano v. Davis*, charging that the redistricting plan diluted Latino political power. In contrast to the interracial alliance among the community redistricting groups, the lawsuit created a racial divide because the plan was supported by the majority of Latino state legislators. Unlike past battles involving whites against racial minorities, the lawsuit pitted progressive Latinos in MALDEF against progressive Latinos in the state legislature.

The lawsuit revealed how the varied perspectives of the participants were heavily influenced by the different interests of each group and the constituencies they served. MALDEF, as a civil rights organization, was concerned about the optimal districts for Latino voters, balanced by their working alliance with African American and Asian American redistricting allies, and the effects of racially polarized voting. In contrast, Latino elected officials declared that MALDEF's lawsuit was based on an outdated model of racial voting rendered obsolete by Latinos winning races with white votes and white officials serving Latinos with distinction (Escutia and Romero 2001: B13). Siding with the legislators, the federal district court justices dismissed the lawsuit, rejecting the charges of vote dilution and racially polarized voting.

The U.S. Supreme Court decisions in the 1990s on redistricting and the judges' decision in *Cano v. Davis* reflected Thernstrom's sentiments about the basic impartiality of the political process and the decline in racially polarized voting. I argue, however, that both the court decisions and the redistricting process limit the impact of challenges to institutional barriers by racial minorities.

In short, redistricting, economic redevelopment, and historic preservation illustrate how race-neutral policies ignore the ways in which racial obstacles continue to operate, even while individuals and groups make the impressive gains in society that Alba and Nee (2003) document. The three case studies illustrate how racial formation is directly linked to struggles over the benefits and costs associated with public policy and the ways in which multiple processes work together to create advantages and disadvantages and hierarchy and privilege along racial lines in society.

California and New York

The political institutions of the San Diego, New York City, and Los Angeles regions have been shaped by different historical forces, such as the importance of the Progressive movement in the West versus political parties and machines in the East. What struck me as I documented and analyzed each case study, however, was the continuing importance of race and the varied ways that government officials crafted race-neutral policies, or viewed whites as a race-neutral group, with racialized results.

In demographic terms the three regions are similar because each is much more racially diverse and has a higher proportion of immigrants than the nation as a whole.[17] California and New York serve as ports of entry and major destination points for immigrants. The two states rank number 1 and number 2 in the nation, respectively, and the cities of Los Angeles, New York, and San Francisco are the top three metropolitan regions in terms of the number of foreign-born residents (Sabagh and Bozorgmehr 2003). Although the United

States as a whole in 2005 had approximately 33 percent people of color, California had about 56 percent and New York had 39 percent (see Table 1). The specific ethnic makeups of California and New York differ, producing different issues. Both regions have significant Latino populations, for example, but in Lower Manhattan, Puerto Ricans are the major group, whereas in California, Mexican Americans are the major group. Puerto Ricans, as citizens of the United States, do not share the issues of immigration and naturalization that Mexican and Asian immigrants face.

Compared to New York, California has had more explicit political movements against immigrants and people of color (Sabagh and Bozorgmehr 2003). The 1994 anti-immigrant Proposition 187, which was meant to end social services to undocumented immigrants, and Proposition 209, which was approved in 1996 and eliminated affirmative action in public institutions, exemplify this tendency. This could be explained, in part, because the number of undocumented immigrants is much higher in California. Although estimates indicate that California and New York rank number 1 and 2, respectively, in terms of the number of undocumented immigrants, California had nearly four times as many as New York when Propositions 187 and 209 went on the ballot (NYC Department of Planning 1993). California's undocumented immigrants are more easily stigmatized as the "other" because the majority of them

Table 1 Racial composition, 2005 (New York City, 2000)

	Percentage of population				
Area	*African American*	*Asian American*	*Latino*	*Native Hawaiian and American Indian*	*Whites*
United States	12.8	4.3	14.4	1.2	66.9
California	6.7	12.2	35.2	1.6	43.8
Los Angeles County	9.7	13.1	46.8	1.4	29.5
San Diego County	5.6	10.2	29.5	1.6	52.3
New York State	17.4	6.7	16.1	0.6	60.9
New York City	26.6	9.8	27.0	0.6	35.0

SOURCES: Data for 2005: U.S. Census Bureau, "State and County Quick Facts," http:// quickfacts.census.gov/qfd/states/ (accessed October 31, 2007). Data for New York City, 2000: U.S. Census Bureau, Table DP-1, "Profile of Demographic Characteristics: 2000," http:// censtats.census.gov/pub/Profiles.shtml (accessed September 13, 2008).

are from Latin America. In contrast, no one region dominates as the origin of the flow of New York's undocumented immigrants, with significant numbers coming from Europe, the Caribbean, and Latin America. In addition, California's whites, with their last migrant journey linked to the Midwest rather than Europe, are generally further removed from the immigrant generation (Sabagh and Bozorgmehr 2003).[18]

Politically, contexts differ, with California politics shaped by the Progressive movement of the early 20th century, which aimed to create an efficient, professional government, removed from the corruption of party organizations, machine politics, and other special interests. The Progressive movement attempted to make government more responsive and democratic, using such methods as the recall and the initiative. At the same time, however, led in part by affluent whites worried about the growing power of immigrants and racial minorities, changes by the Progressive movement also worked to decrease the political influence of these groups, such as at-large rather than district elections (Pincetl 1999; Sonenshein 1993). The ballot initiative also created the possibility for Propositions 187 and 209, which passed because they were supported by white voters, although a majority of African Americans, Asian Americans, and Latinos voted against the two propositions (*Los Angeles Times* 1994, 1996).

The history of East Coast politics is marked to a much greater degree than the West Coast by political machines and party organizations. In terms of the importance of these organizations for incorporating Asian Americans and Latinos, however, neither has had a significant impact. Steven Erie (1988) explains that the use of political machines and Democratic Party organizations to incorporate and empower new immigrants has been overstated. Control of these organizations was used to consolidate the power of particular groups, such as the Irish, rather than to incorporate new immigrant groups that followed. Similarly, the political parties of New York City have not served as a vehicle to incorporate racial minorities (Jones-Correa 1998; Mollenkopf 1990; Wong 2006).

In summary, William J. Wilson is partly correct, I believe, in his assertion that government policies have undergone a fundamental change from explicitly supporting racial inequality to moving toward racial equality. Richard Alba and Victor Nee accurately point out that Asian Americans have made tremendous economic and political gains. What I suggest, however, is that claims that the United States is moving toward a color-blind society disregard the important ways in which race continues to shape life in the United States. I emphasize the debates and policies regarding redistricting and economic redevelopment that carefully consider race to protect the rights of racial minorities or involve actions that are considered race neutral. I argue that the implementation of race-neutral policies has important racial consequences that are often unrecognized by decision makers on city commissions, city councils, and the courts. As a result, although New York City and the state of California have different political contexts, the case studies suggest similar outcomes of racialized policies. These cases illustrate the American dilemma of the twenty-first century: addressing the racialized results and inequality produced by so-called race-neutral policies. In this book I examine the efforts of community members to identify, understand, and contest those layers of exclusion that constitute the sedimentation of inequality. These contemporary efforts build on the long and varied history of political activism by racial minorities.

2 Economic Redevelopment, Historic Preservation, and the Chinese Mission of San Diego

MARKING THE CULMINATION of a decade of work by the San Diego Chinese American community, the Chinese Mission building, originally constructed in 1927, was officially dedicated on January 13, 1996, as a Chinese American museum and cultural center. The effort to relocate and preserve part of San Diego's history and insert a Chinese American physical and cultural presence into the core of the massive economic redevelopment of the city's historic downtown area saved the building from demolition in the 1980s to make way for a proposed high-rise luxury residential complex.

The Chinese Mission account illustrates that, although one of the major themes of race relations in the United States is one of exclusion, control, and containment, the story is more complex and contains movements aimed at both the segregation and the integration of Asian immigrants and Asian Americans into society. Chinatowns, or the spatial clustering of commercial and residential usages by people of Chinese ancestry, are partly the result of racial ideology translated into institutional practices and physical place (Anderson 1987). Chinatowns reflect official and informal policies of segregation, understandings of Chinese immigrants of local threats to their safety and the attempt to protect themselves against anti-Asian violence, and the development of services for the immigrant community (Kwong 1996; Kwong and Miscevic 2005).

Using the Chinese Mission, I examine the negotiations between city officials and local residents over competing images of race and history and how the outcomes of these negotiations were used to support and legitimate economic redevelopment and historic preservation policies. Contemporary debates on redevelopment are part of the shift from the mid-twentieth-century urban renewal policies that explicitly sought to clear low-income and working-class communities of color from downtown areas and destroyed entire neighborhoods, to the preservation movement of the 1970s, which worked to prevent the displacement of long-term residents and save historic structures. A second debate centers on what is considered historic and worthy of preservation versus what is simply blighted and should be demolished. Critical to each debate is the discussion of race and labels—such as slum and blight—applied to communities and structures to legitimate development plans.

My main point is that city officials strive to create redevelopment and preservation guidelines that are race neutral. However, a narrow focus by city officials on the policies they create ignores how the implementation of these policies is framed and influenced by a long history of explicitly and implicitly racialized regulations and practices that remain in place. As a result, recently enacted race-neutral policies do not counter existing racialized procedures and have a disproportionately negative effect on racial minority groups compared to whites. I suggest that the discussions and practices linked to redevelopment and preservation contribute to the social construction of race in terms of meaning, images, and labels that explain and legitimate policies that can result in racial hierarchy and privilege, with whites at the top and racial minorities in a subordinate position (Lipsitz 2006). Racial exclusion, however, is not inevitable, as demonstrated by the successful campaign by the Chinese American community to contest racial images and intervene in the fate of the Chinese Mission and create the downtown Asian Pacific Thematic Historic District.

Race and Economic Redevelopment in the United States

Urban renewal and economic redevelopment illustrate the change from explicit racial inequality to race-neutral public policies. Urban centers across the country experienced decline in the post–World War II era as suburbanization accelerated and residents, businesses, and manufacturers increasingly favored suburbia over the aging downtowns (Jackson 1985). Through urban renewal and the construction of the interstate highway system, cities partnered with the federal government to revitalize their urban cores from the 1950s through the 1970s. Established by the Housing Act of 1949, the major goals of urban renewal were to revive urban economies and improve housing for the poor by eradicating substandard structures in business and residential areas and building new, modern structures. The Interstate and Defense Highway Act of 1956 provided funding to build new freeways connecting urban areas.

The history of these projects, however, was marked by the destruction of low- and moderate-income communities, especially those inhabited by African Americans, Latinos, and Asian Americans (Anderson 1964; Gans 1962; Mohl 1993). Rather than improving the housing situation for low-income and working-class residents, urban renewal and highway construction made the situation much worse for the displaced residents. This occurred because fewer units of housing were built than destroyed and because the new housing built by city officials primarily served middle-class and affluent residents. As a result, a class and racial transformation occurred as higher-income and primarily white residents replaced racial minorities (Frieden and Sagalyn 1991).

Urban renewal and infrastructure projects were racialized because of their impact on communities of color and the way that local governments strategically developed and used images of racial minority communities as "blighted" and "slums" to justify displacing residents and businesses through urban redevelopment projects (Wong 1995). The targeting of minority communities could be clear and purposeful, as when "officials from several cities told highway lobbyist Alf Johnson that the urban interstates would give them a good opportunity to get rid of local 'niggertowns'" (Frieden and Sagalyn 1991: 28); as a result, urban renewal and highway projects earned the title "Negro Removal" (Anderson 1964).

In Los Angeles the Community Redevelopment Agency (CRA) was dubbed the "Chicano Removal Agency" (Villa 2000: 145), and the razing of the Mexican American neighborhood at Chavez Ravine, just north of downtown, exemplified one of urban renewal's major contradictions in the destruction of neighborhoods. The city judged that the area was blighted, but the inhabitants considered it a well-established community with long-term residents and strong social networks and institutions (Hines 1982). "Asian removal" was also a common theme in city-assisted projects in Los Angeles, with the displacement of the original Chinatown by Union Station in the early 1930s and the destruction of major segments of Little Tokyo by the construction of the police department headquarters, the Parker Center in the 1950s, and the New Otani Hotel in the 1970s (Ling 2001; Little Tokyo Anti-Eviction Task Force 1976).

Concern about the massive displacement of residents and small businesses, loss of housing for low-income residents, and urban renewal's limited success as an economic stimulus for cities despite its enormous fiscal and social costs led to the end of urban renewal and its replacement by the Community Redevelopment Act of 1974. This act also aimed to improve housing and the economies of urban areas but attempted to end the worst practices of urban renewal by incorporating greater involvement of community residents in the planning process for projects; in addition, rather than the large-scale demolition of entire neighborhoods, the act emphasized the conservation and rehabilitation of existing structures (Frieden and Sagalyn 1991).

One of the worst abuses of urban renewal was the clearance of entire communities covering many acres. This wholesale destruction was curbed beginning in the 1970s, but contemporary urban redevelopment projects continue to have a disproportionate impact on racial minorities because of the legacy of explicitly racist policies. Policies that enforced segregated housing and limited access to federally insured home mortgages to whites subsidized and aided the movement of whites to the suburbs while concentrating minorities in the urban core. As a result, urban redevelopment projects today are more likely to displace racial minorities.

Shifts have also occurred in historic preservation as a result of early criteria that tended to favor the history of whites, with a focus on structures that reflect historical events of national significance, major buildings of aesthetic importance, or the work of prominent architects (Hayden 1997). The expansion of criteria to include the social history of structures and the importance of properties with local significance by the National Historic Preservation Act of 1966 added to the national focus of the 1935 Historic Sites Act (Lea 2003). These changes have been used to preserve sites related to the important events and trends reflected in the everyday lives of immigrants, the working class, and racial minorities (Dubrow and Graves 2002; Hayden 1997; Upton 1986). Examples include the World War II internment camps in which Japanese Americans were incarcerated, Angel Island Immigration Station in the San Francisco Bay, which was the major port of entry for Asian immigrants in the first half of the twentieth century, and the eighteenth-century African Burial Ground in New York City (Lee 2003).

If economic redevelopment and historic preservation practices have undergone fundamental changes and if government policies strive to be race neutral or are intended to promote racial equality, as William J. Wilson (1980) claims, then why would I argue that development and historic preservation policies are in fact racialized and contribute to racial inequality? I suggest that two factors play significant roles in the racialization of public policies. First, the growth machine strategy of urban economic redevelopment is controlled by local political and economic elites and is aimed at generating profit for major developers, business interests, and property owners and tax revenue for local governments (Logan and Molotch 1987; Molotch 1976). Promoting new development and luring tourists, conventioneers, and suburban shoppers back to downtown are the primary objectives. As Alexander Reichl (1997, 1999) documents in his study of the redevelopment of Times Square in New York City, the goal of preserving the area's historic theaters helped unify the development interests and garner public support for a massive redevelopment project that included enormous public subsidies. Commercial development, including office towers, dwarfed historic preservation in the new Times Square, but preserving the theaters made the project attractive to politicians, the public, developers, and members of cultural institutions. Historic preservation, rather than an important goal in itself, becomes another tool in the development of "theme parks" or "tourist bubbles" that are geared toward spending and consumption (Gottdiener 1997; Judd 1999). As a result, historic structures may be razed unless they contribute to the interests of the growth machine.

The growth machine and redevelopment threaten all historic structures, regardless of their connection to any particular racial group, as city officials and developers plan to increase profit through new construction. In the mid-1900s in the United States, city officials believed that replacing old buildings with new buildings was the way to economically revive declining downtown areas. Historic preservationists led the effort to convince city planners that historic buildings could play a key role in revitalizing the urban core. As urbanist Jane Jacobs (1961) argued in her defense of the preservation of older neighborhoods, a vibrant and appealing city needs "a most intricate and close-grained diversity of uses that give each other constant mutual support, both economically and socially" (p. 14). The Faneuil Hall complex in Boston and Pike Place Market in Seattle illustrate the "shift in public opinion away from tear-it-down renewal and toward the care of popular landmarks" in the 1970s and the recognition that historic structures contribute to the economic strength of a project by creating a unique atmosphere that distinguishes urban shopping centers from suburban malls (Frieden and Sagalyn 1991: 117).

Second, race enters the picture, I contend, because the history of racial minorities is less likely to be recognized as a contributor to historic centers. The San Diego case studies highlight two key issues among the challenges faced by racial minorities to include their structures in the historic preservation movement. First, as with many structures involving racial minorities, the San Diego structures were not the work of famous architects, nor were they aesthetically or architecturally exceptional. Therefore activists had to establish the importance of the structures in terms of their social history. Second, activists confronted a ghettoization of history in which events and history in ethnic communities were seen as isolated and insular and not important to others outside those communities. As a result, activists needed to explain how important local and national issues such as immigration, segregation, exclusion, and popular culture were reflected in these structures (Dubrow and Graves 2002; Hayden 1997).

The San Diego case illustrates the process of racialization in which city officials and developers do not explicitly target for destruction the history and buildings connected to African American and Chinese American communities. The critical point is that because the importance of these histories is not acknowledged in the way that the social history of white residents is documented and recognized, communities of color disproportionately experience the negative effects of redevelopment (Hayden 1997). Thus, although the clear intent of urban renewal's "Negro Removal" is missing, with seemingly race-neutral policies the results are similar.

As a result of the institutional processes that overlook or disregard the social and historical importance of structures connected to racial minorities, these communities must mobilize to enter into the redevelopment and historic preservation process. Replacing the Chinese Mission and the Douglas Hotel with upscale residential or commercial projects illustrates the conflict between the growth machine strategy in urban development and the preservation of structures and re-creation of neighborhoods that are connected to history, community, and place for racial minorities (Kropp 2001).

Historic preservation may be a luxury that cities cannot afford since, as some urban analysts suggest, the policy options of city officials are highly constrained by market forces because city officials compete with one another to attract highly mobile capital in an era characterized by the international flow of capital and goods (Peterson 1981). Even with competition among cities that are dominated by development interests and pro-business environments to attract investment capital, Logan and Swanstrom (1990) argue that local political and economic conditions create a variety of policy options for city officials. San Diego, with its history of environmental and controlled-growth initiatives, is a prime example of the way development is affected by local concerns (Calavita 1992; Davis et al. 2003). Clearly, San Diego pro-growth forces have prevailed, as witnessed by the transformation of the natural habitat of Mission Valley and its San Diego River into the present-day Hotel Circle, located within city limits and just north of downtown, and the continued encroachment of housing into the region's open space, but each step in development was met with vigorous opposition (Davis 2003). Preserving, demolishing, or reestablishing urban ethnic communities is another area in which local officials exert tremendous influence, and as events surrounding the Chinese Mission demonstrate, community activists can shape local decisions regarding historic preservation and the investment of public and private funds.

The Rise of San Diego's Growth Machine

The major downtown landowners, concerned with the area's decline and the long-term value of their property, formed San Diegans Inc. in 1959 to support major new construction that would enhance the importance of the central city (Hof 1990). As with similar groups that formed in other cities, such as New York City's Downtown Lower Manhattan Association and Atlanta's Central Atlanta Improvement Association, these groups provided an organization that could utilize the resources of the downtown elite to fund planning studies and advocate for development that would protect and enhance their assets (Fitch 1993; Stone 1989). San Diegans Inc. formed a crucial part of the city's growth machine, facilitating an informal but sustained relationship among local politicians and large corporate actors who guided downtown's long-term economic development. These groups had the political expertise and resources to counter the voting public. For example, when San Diego residents voted against issuing bonds to finance the construction of the Community Concourse in 1962, "composed of a convention hall, a city hall and a performing arts center," San Diegans Inc. provided a $1.6 million grant so that construction could begin (Hof 1990: 5). Completed in 1964, the Community Concourse was part of a larger city effort to construct new government buildings in downtown to act "as the catalyst to millions of dollars worth of downtown construction projects" from private investors (Hof 1990: 5).

The 1965 development plan for the downtown area (San Diego City 1965), with San Diego Inc. playing a major role in its formation, focused on the goal of reversing decentralization and restoring the area to its pre–World War II position as "the City's dominant center of administration, of finance, of specialized retail sales, and of cultural and entertainment activities" and "the focus of metropolitan passenger transportation" (p. 6). Problems that needed to be addressed, according to the 1965 plan, included a "decline in retailing," "office space shortage," "lack of close-in housing," and "inadequate hotel and convention facilities" (San Diego City 1965: 19–20).

The city council's commitment to use federal funds and heavily invest in the urban core and revitalize business, entertainment, and tourist activities reached a new level with the approval of the Horton Plaza Redevelopment Plan in 1972, which aimed to develop large-scale commercial and office projects. With a previous emphasis on development guided by private investment and free market principles, unrestrained by outside intrusion represented by federal government oversight, this plan represented a fundamental shift in policy "in a city that had earlier considered federally assisted urban renewal politically unacceptable" (Gordon 1985: 146). This was a major change for a city that "had no experience with retail development projects" and "had undertaken publicly assisted redevelopment only twice: for a small housing project for the elderly and a community college" (Gordon 1985: 6).

The San Diego strategy paralleled the national trend of restructuring downtown areas from declining manufacturing and retail districts into "modern" corporate centers of upscale office space, commercial establishments, residences, hotels, and tourism-convention facilities (Feagin 1998; Hill 1983). Responding to the area's business community and a proposal submitted by San Diegans Inc., the mayor and city council established the Centre City Development Corporation (CCDC) in 1975 as "a public nonprofit corporation charged with handling all redevelopment efforts in downtown San Diego. Its seven-member board of directors is made up of business and real estate professionals" (Trimble 1984b: 8–9). Gerald M. Trimble, executive vice president of the CCDC in 1984, summarized the opinion of city officials of downtown San Diego in the mid-twentieth century. Trimble (1984b) stated, "If ever an urban core cried for change, it was downtown San Diego in the late 1960s and early 1970s. . . . Its tax base was deteriorated, its adult entertainment uses proliferated, most of its residents occupied single rooms in old hotels, its street people abounded, and its overall appearance south of Broadway was one of acute physical decline" (p. 4).[1]

Using federal funds for redevelopment and with the creation of the CCDC, development in San Diego resembled trends across the country. Newly created public-private organizations operated with limited public input to support the interests of the growth machine and major downtown property interests (Stone 1989). The California Community Redevelopment Act of 1945 authorized the establishment of redevelopment agencies, and San Diego created one in 1958 with the city council members serving as the board of directors. The CCDC prepared redevelopment plans and made recommendations to the city's redevelopment agency. Because the redevelopment agency has the power of eminent domain and the ability to assemble parcels of land for major projects, the partnership between the redevelopment agency and the CCDC was a key factor in downtown building efforts. The CCDC's first major task was Horton Plaza, a major regional shopping mall that opened in 1985. According to an MIT study, Horton Plaza "was national news. This retail and entertainment complex . . . blends elements of festival markets, regional shopping malls, and mixed-use developments in a unique design that prompted the *Wall Street Journal* to describe it as a forerunner of the next generation of shopping centers" (Gordon 1985: vii).

The first designs for Horton Plaza resembled a traditional covered mall found in the suburbs, but to take advantage of San Diego's temperate climate, the plans radically changed to an open-air structure that would create a festive atmosphere and pare down costs by eliminating some of the walls and the roof structure and by reducing air-conditioning expenses. As Frieden and Sagalyn (1991: 192) describe the dramatic change in architectural design, the developer Ernest Hahn

> recalled waking up at two in the morning and thinking, "we're going to take the damn roof off of this thing, and we're going to make it look like part of the city, and we're going to make it exciting." . . . He called Jerde [the project architect] in the middle of the night and said, "take the damn roof off of it." . . . Jerde yelled in excitement . . . and his imagination and his talent took off.

In a 1998 interview, Jon Jerde described his thoughts on how the unique design of Horton Plaza contributed to its success as a shopping center.

> The main purpose was for it to be a place to go to be a human—out in the sun, walking around, visiting other people, seeing spaces in ways that you would never normally see spaces. . . . It worked: The normal, really great shopping center, at a great location—say at the crux of two big freeways—would absolutely guarantee 9 million people a year. . . . Horton Plaza got 35 million people a year—in a burned-out downtown. So, the point was if you designed the human experience, it would serve the final purpose—to sell stuff—better than anything you could think of. (Silver 1998: M3)

The Horton Plaza project area and the Community Concourse construction several blocks to the north formed the hub for three major redevelopment projects that San Diego established in the 1970s and 1980s. Property owners in the historic core (just east and extending south of the Horton Plaza project) formed the Gaslamp Quarter Association in the early 1970s and in 1974 petitioned the city council to support the "preservation of the Gaslamp Quarter as a living, exciting office and visitor oriented commercial area reflecting the history and architectural heritage of San Diego at the turn of the century" (Stepner 1977: 26).

Michael Stepner, a San Diego city planner at the time, described this form of "adaptive use" as "the economic and functional utilization of an old building for a new, contemporary purpose that relates to the modern city while retaining the fabric of the city's unique past history and culture" (Stepner 1977: 26). With 35.6 percent of its buildings constructed between 1870 and 1899, 34.2 percent between 1900 and 1919, and 16.2 percent between 1920 and 1934, the Gaslamp Quarter contained an impressive number of historic structures in its 16½-block, 38-acre area (San Diego Planning Department 1982: 1, 13). The city responded with a preliminary redevelopment plan in 1976, and in 1982 the city council approved the Gaslamp Quarter Redevelopment Project to promote "retail, entertainment, business, cultural, social and other commercial functions" (Redevelopment Agency of the City of San Diego 1992: 1) (see Map 1).

The neat, rectangular boundaries of the Gaslamp District, however, excluded nearby historic buildings that did not fall within the designated area. Paul Alley (1988), an architectural historian for the National Park Service, examined the plans and stated that they demonstrated how historic preservation was used to promote the goals of redevelopment, resulting in an artificial "theme park" disconnected from history. Alley (1988: 1–2) wrote that

> the designated district was limited to a neat linear configuration that did not include additional portions of historic blocks and "streetscapes" that existed in adjacent areas, because these adjacent areas were targeted for new development. This selective and very controlled designation was the first manifestation of a heavily "interventive" and manipulative approach to the treatment of the district—an approach that is essentially more development than preservation. . . . What is being undertaken and proposed for the Gaslamp Quarter is most similar to the creation of a commercial theme park, neatly bounded by, and an integral part of, the massive redevelopment of downtown San Diego. While the park does incorporate selected historic buildings *in situ*, this original area of downtown is being completely reworked, and its ability to convey its authentic historical sense of time and place seriously diminished.

The developer of Horton Plaza and city officials believed that housing, transportation, hotels, and a convention center were essential to create a clientele

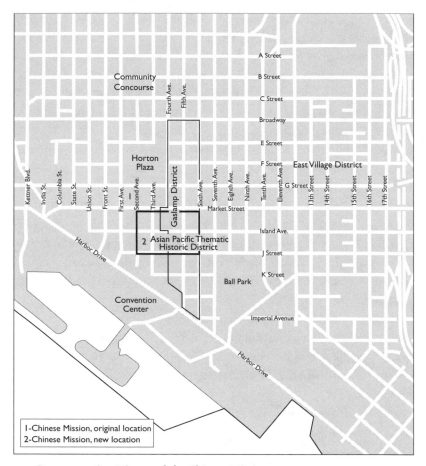

Map 1 Downtown San Diego and the Chinese Mission

SOURCE: San Diego City Centre Development Corporation. Additional information added to map by Wendy Saito Lew.

for Horton Plaza and to increase the commercial and business activities of the core, echoing the 1965 redevelopment plan (Gordon 1985). In 1976 the city approved the Columbia Redevelopment Project, located to the west of Horton Plaza, as a "commercial/tourist area"; and the Marina Development Project, beginning south of Horton Plaza and extending to the west, was conceived to "create a new residential community" (Redevelopment Agency of the City of San Diego 1992: 1, 3, 5).

Established in 1976 to build the transportation component of the city's plans for downtown and the region, the Metropolitan Transit Development

Board created the San Diego Trolley, a light rail system that in 2006 included 54 miles of track and served more than "33 million passengers" from July 2005 to June 2006 (Ristine 2006: B1). To emphasize the role of downtown as a transportation hub, tourism site, and renewed destination for retail sales and to recognize the growing purchasing power of the nearby residents of Mexico, the first trolley line opened in 1981 and connected downtown to the Mexican border at Tijuana, 16 miles away (Gordon 1985; Holle 2002). Today, the trolley routes through the downtown area and passes right in front of the Convention Center and the surrounding cluster of luxury hotels, adding to the appeal of the city for conventions. As Sal Giametta, a vice president of the San Diego Convention and Visitor's Bureau, explained, "The big plus is the ease of getting around and about. . . . Literally being able to step outside your hotel or walk a block . . . and finding a trolley station" (Ristine 2006: B1).

To become a serious competitor for the nation's convention business and attract larger events than the aging Community Concourse could accommodate, the San Diego Convention Center opened in 1989 on the southern border of the Gaslamp District; it nearly doubled in size when a new addition opened in 2001 (see Map 1). The convention center was built with the collaboration of San Diego's Port District, which had the land and access to funding for the project, allowing city officials to proceed with the convention center despite repeated rejections by the city's voters, as with the construction of the Community Concourse (Sanders 1992).

The convention center followed San Diego officials' preference for "clean growth" and nonpolluting industries, such as tourism, academic institutions, and high technology, rather than heavy industry, framed by the ongoing "geraniums" versus "smokestacks" debate on the city's development in the twentieth century (Davis 2003; Sanders 1992). The emphasis on business travelers and tourists took advantage of San Diego's natural resources, such as temperate weather and beaches, reinforced by investment in such attractions as the Hotel del Coronado, the largest hotel on the West Coast at the time of its opening in 1888; the 1915–1916 Panama-California Exposition and the creation of what became known as Balboa Park; the development of the San Diego Zoo in the 1920s and 1930s; and the opening of Sea World in 1964.

The corporate center strategy, guided by the growth machine, has transformed the Gaslamp District into the premier entertainment destination for the region. Signs of downtown's economic boom and continued strength as a tourism site include luxury condominiums under construction at a rapid pace, new convention center hotels, the Midway Aircraft Carrier Museum, which opened in 2004 (Powell 2004), and a new downtown ballpark completed in 2004 (Engle 2004). Taking advantage of the booming housing market in San Diego, the top floors of the luxury hotel built next to the ballpark contained thirty-six condominiums, which sold for $1.2 to $9 million (Engle 2004). Showing the continued strength of the growth machine, more than $2.5 million was spent supporting the successful 1998 ballot proposition on the downtown ballpark; the opposition was basically an "all-volunteer" operation that raised $25,000 (Braun 1998: A1).

Asian Americans in San Diego and the Chinese Mission Church

Historian Arthur McEvoy (1977) suggests that the small number of Chinese in San Diego and the lack of direct economic competition with whites muted the anti-Chinese activity in the city during the 1870s and 1880s compared to other parts of the West, where Chinese were beaten, driven out of towns, or killed. The early history of San Diego's Chinese and Japanese in fishing and agriculture indicates that Asians fared well when they entered occupations not yet claimed by whites; however, when whites began desiring such jobs, limitations or exclusion followed.

Early reports of San Diego history suggest that Chinese, probably fishermen, lived by the bay during the 1850s, similar to the development of Chinese fishing industries in the northern part of the state in San Francisco in the early 1850s and in Monterey Bay in the early 1860s. Chinese developed commercial fishing in San Diego and exported dried fish to other parts of the state and to China. By 1870, they supplied all the fresh fish in the city. San Diego's Chinese fishing industry covered the area from Monterey to the north to Cabo San Lucas, Mexico, in the south and reached its peak in the mid-1880s. Thereafter, enforcement of fishing laws regarding the use of the fine-meshed nets used by the Chinese and the Scott Act of 1888, which prohibited the reentry of Chinese laborers into the United States, effectively ended the Chinese fishing industry (Liu 1977). The *San Diego Union* newspaper reflected the shift in views regarding the Chinese fishermen as European immigrants entered the fishing industry, writing in 1884 that "the Chinese fishermen ... are about the most industrious set of individuals to be found anywhere," but in 1887 the newspaper supported the enforcement of fishing regulations that "would soon drive the heathen from the bay" (McEvoy 1977: 16–17).

The discovery of gold and labor recruiters brought additional Chinese to San Diego in the 1860s and 1870s, and the growth of the downtown Chinese settlement led to attempts in 1876 to burn it down. Threatened violence against the Chinese was put down in 1877 when the sheriff put together the Committee of Public Safety and issued weapons to its members (Griego 1979). As elsewhere in the western United States, Chinese workers were a prominent part of the labor pool for railroad construction in San Diego, and in the 1880s and 1890s Chinese laborers were heavily recruited, bringing a new wave of migrants to the region. As their numbers grew, so did efforts by whites to control the employment of Chinese, and in 1885 the Anti-Chinese Club was organized to "protest the hiring of Chinese as long as a white man was out of work"; the group convinced the San Diego Water Company to replace its Chinese workers with whites (MacPhail 1977: 10).

The forces of segregation and business opportunities near the port led to the development of Chinatown within the downtown vice district known as the Stingaree. Although illegal, gambling and prostitution were tolerated in defined areas such as the Stingaree until citizen groups formed in the early 1900s to pressure city officials to end these practices. As a result, in preparation for the 1915 Panama-California Exposition, when the "eyes of the world would be on San Diego," San Diego officials followed the efforts of other California cities in the early 1900s and attempted to close the bordellos (MacPhail 1977: 15).

The Health Department destroyed 120 buildings that violated public health codes in the vice district. City reports described the poor conditions found in the condemned living spaces and suggested that Chinese were able to thrive in places that whites could not tolerate, implying biological differences between Chinese and whites rather than the Chinese coping with poor housing conditions resulting from racial exclusion and low incomes. "Many inside rooms in Chinatown were like ratholes, without light or ventilation. . . . Any normal person entering a room with such a high percentage of impure air would strangle and stagger out in a hurry. Yet these orientals lived to a ripe old age" (MacPhail 1974: 14). After the razing of the buildings, the city health inspector, Walter Bellon, proclaimed, "The waterfront had been cleaned up, the Stingaree had been wiped out, Chinatown had almost disappeared" (MacPhail 1977: 27).

In terms of other Asians and Pacific Islanders in San Diego, Richard Henry Dana Jr. (1990: 204), in his account of his sea journey in the 1830s, noted "quite a colony" of Hawaiians in the town, working as crewmen on the sailing vessels. Japanese came to San Diego in the mid-1880s as laborers, established farms in the early 1900s, and made Chula Vista, a city south of San Diego, into the "Celery Capital of the World" (Estes 1978: 3). In the 1930s, however, Chula Vista was considered by Japanese around the state as the "heart of the anti-Japanese movement" because a number of Japanese were arrested "for violations of California's Alien Land Laws" (Estes 1978: 23). Conflict slowly decreased after Japanese and white farmers formed the San Diego Celery Growers Association. Japanese men were an important part of the tuna fishing industry, working as boat crew members and introducing the bamboo pole, refrigerated boats, and Japanese lures; Japanese women worked in the fish canneries (Estes 1978). In a 1935 court case, Japanese won the right to obtain fishing licenses from the California Fish and Game Commission, which had denied licenses to "aliens ineligible for citizenship" (Estes 1978: 24).

Both the Chinese and Japanese established business centers downtown, including stores, restaurants, and laundries. With their residential options limited by the efforts of whites to keep nonwhites out of their neighborhoods, Chinese and Japanese residential communities were also concentrated downtown, as were African American and Mexican American neighborhoods (Harris 1974). The first Filipino residents were college students who arrived in 1903. Their numbers increased to include farm workers and other laborers, and their businesses were also concentrated downtown (APTHD 1995). Increased residential options for minorities following World War II and the forces of suburbanization that led to the decline of the urban core contributed to the gradual disappearance of the urban ethnic enclaves. The exception was the Japanese American community, which was eliminated when the U.S. government removed and incarcerated Japanese Americans during World War II (Hasegawa 1998).

With the movement of Chinese into California, Christian churches in the state established Sunday schools to teach Chinese immigrants English and religion as part of the effort to "Americanize" immigrants and integrate them into society. In San Diego, the Presbyterian and Baptist churches started Sunday schools for Chinese children in the 1870s (MacPhail 1977). First established in a rented home in the downtown region in 1885, the Chinese Mission repeatedly changed locations until the present building, including an eighteen-room dormitory in back, was constructed in 1927. Located on First Avenue, between Market and G Streets, its construction was funded by donations from Chinese American and white residents. In addition to language and religious instruction, the Chinese Mission became the main social center for the Chinese American community. In 1959, with the growth of the Chinese American population and its movement to residential areas throughout the city, the church was sold and the final worship service was held January 31, 1960. A new church was built at 1750 47th Street (MacPhail 1977).

Redevelopment and the Chinese Mission

The city council's commitment to invest heavily in the urban core and revitalize business, entertainment, and tourist activities began with the approval of the Horton Plaza Redevelopment Plan in 1972, aimed at developing large-scale commercial and office projects. Although these projects were proposed in the early 1970s with the intention of generating economic development downtown, what remained unclear was the exact form that such development would take and which areas would be included. Los Angeles, for example, abandoned its historic core and shifted new development to the west, whereas other cities, such as San Francisco, worked to incorporate new high-rises into their historic fabric (Davis 1990).

Property owners concerned with historic preservation and economic development in San Diego's aging downtown, such as Tom Hom, formed the Gaslamp Quarter Association in the mid-1970s. Hom, a former city council member who held office during the mid-1960s, possessed substantial knowledge of economic redevelopment policies and city politics. Hom served as the Gaslamp Quarter Association president for four years and assisted the effort to establish the Gaslamp Quarter Redevelopment Project, adopted by the city in 1982 (Chau and Gutierrez 2001). The opening of Horton Plaza and its commercial success marked the turnaround of the downtown area as new hotels, apartment buildings, condominiums, and office buildings were constructed. New businesses transformed the Gaslamp Quarter as restaurants, bars, art galleries, and other businesses moved into the historic buildings. Although many buildings were renovated, others were threatened with destruction as developers sought to maximize their profits.

Prompted by the requests of members of the Chinese American community, the CCDC decided to conduct research and evaluate the historical significance of buildings associated with the Chinese community (Vo 2004). On March 7, 1986, the CCDC commissioned a study by Ray Brandes, a professor at the University of San Diego and an authority on the city's history (Trimble 1986). The report, *Research and Analysis of Buildings Within the Marina Redevelopment Project Area Known to Be Connected with Local Chinese History* (Brandes 1986b), was submitted just one month later in April 1986. In the report, Brandes "evaluated and rated structures with respect to the criteria which he considers most important in determining which structures would be most important to retain" (Trimble 1986: 1).

Brandes found few buildings worth saving and gave little support to the idea of a Chinese or Asian historic district. He wrote that the results "make for a disappointing picture. . . . In general, time has taken its toll. Too few buildings remained after the city 'cleanup of 1912' and the effect of the destruction of residences and living quarters since that time has also taken away the few grocery stores or merchandise buildings which were Chinese-Japanese" (Brandes 1986b: i). In a letter to the CCDC containing his ratings, Brandes (1986a) wrote that the Chinese Consolidated Benevolent Association, Ying-On, Quin, and Quong buildings received high to medium scores (50, 48, 33, and 28, respectively, on a 50-point scale), suggesting that preservation would be worth considering.

Brandes (1986a) gave the Chinese Mission a score of 18 out of 50, concluding that "the Mission was closed some years ago and when no longer used was sold, and rehabbed. The current condition is not good; it does not fit within that architectural category of an Oriental structure, and the building is not in proximity to the Chinese District" (n.p.).[2] The Chinese Mission sat boarded up and empty, and its owner, Charles Tyson, planned to demolish the building and construct a high-rise residential project on the property, a use encouraged by new city plans. With approximately twenty-eight blocks in the downtown residential area of the Marina redevelopment area, the Chinese Mission sat on part of one of only two blocks that were zoned for buildings of up to 300 feet, the maximum height limit allowed for the district (CCDC 1988). Tyson's attorney (Lia 1987) stressed this point in her letter arguing against the historic designation of the building, stating, "The building's location . . . slated for the highest density development allowed, also militates against designation" (p. 10).

Marie Burke Lia was the CCDC special counsel dealing with historic preservation (Trimble 1986). She supported the findings of the Brandes report on the condition and historic value of the buildings and advised against establishing a historic district. Lia stated, "I believe the non-contributing [non-historic] buildings would outweigh the contributing buildings," and based on the San Diego Historical Site Board criteria, she suggested that "probably only the Benevolent and the Ying On buildings would qualify, but since both are already protected by the Historical Site Board listing and . . . procedures, there appears to be no practical reason to pursue a local historical district" (Lia 1986: 3).

The CCDC operated largely out of the public eye as it carried out the objectives of the growth machine, but it was responsive to effective lobbying. Chinese Americans, as well as the larger Asian American community, were virtually nonexistent in electoral politics. Only one Asian American, Tom Hom, had been elected to the city council in the history of the city as of 2007, and it was local non–Asian American Republicans who supported his campaign (Chau and Gutierrez 2001). Chinese Americans, however, mobilized to save the Chinese Mission. Although a small group, numbering only 19,686 out of a population of about 2.5 million in San Diego County in 1990 (APALC 2005: 5), they did have the resources to lobby the CCDC.

Establishing the Chinese Historical Society and Community Mobilization

Sally Wong and Dorothy Hom (spouse of Tom Hom), motivated by their interest in studying and preserving the Gaslamp and historic Chinatown areas, worked to create the Chinese Historical Society, which was chartered in 1986 and which would serve as the key organizational and fiscal vehicle in the preservation effort. The Homs, of Chinese ancestry, spearheaded the drive to save the Chinese Mission, which grew into an effort to establish an Asian Pacific American historic district in the Gaslamp area. With their knowledge of city politics, redevelopment policy, and prominence in the general city and Chinese American business communities, the Homs were extremely effective advocates and organizers.

Sally Wong, the Chinese Social Service Center director, noted in the mid-1980s that "we have a Chinese school; we have social services; we have a Chinese church; we have a Chinese supermarket; we don't have a Chinese museum" (Lee 2007: 13). Wong contacted Dorothy Hom and expressed her desire: "We don't have a museum; I would like to start one" (Lee 2007: 13). At a meeting with many of the local Chinese American community leaders, the attendees expressed unanimous support for a museum. The idea was expanded to become a historical society, and Wong became the first president and Dorothy Hom became the vice-president (Lee 2007). Recognizing the long history of Chinese immigration and settlement across the border in northern Mexico, the name of the group became the Chinese Historical Society of Greater San Diego and Baja California. The organization became the center of the effort to garner community support and to demonstrate to city officials that the effort to save the Chinese Mission had strong backing among Chinese Americans; it also set about gathering funds to renovate the Chinese Mission and turn it into a museum and center for historical research.

The effort to save the Chinese Mission began, according to Tom Hom, when Dorothy Hom learned from someone at the Historical Site Board that the mission was going to be demolished. She went to City Hall to see what could be done to save it (Chau and Gutierrez 2001). Dorothy Hom explained, "Tom and I worked so hard with the Gaslamp, and here we were losing our own heritage. . . . So I got really involved" (J. Clifford 1990: D2).

Tom Hom was born in San Diego in 1927, on the corner of Third Avenue and J Street, and grew up speaking Chinese until he began elementary school in the old Chinatown. His father owned a produce business that grew into one of the largest in the city, farming land in San Diego and Mexico. Tom Hom remembered driving through town in the produce truck delivering vegetables, talking with his father and getting his first civics lesson and the first thought that he might enter politics. Tom Hom told the story of the conversation and his father's words, "'That's City Hall there. Here in America, the kind of laws that people have come right out of there.' And my dad always felt that he was outside looking in. And maybe then, I kind of felt I'd like to be inside looking out" (Chau and Gutierrez 2001: 9). Discussing an episode of racial discrimination, Hom described his family's attempt to buy a house in 1947 and how their efforts were thwarted by restrictive covenants. "We couldn't buy the first house we wanted . . . because it had its racial covenants on its grant deed saying that anyone who was not Caucasian could not buy the house. That was my first encounter, perhaps, when I realized that they had these barriers because of racial differences" (Dea 1985: 4). As a testament to the racial changes in society, Hom would later go on to get his real estate license and become a major developer in the region. In 1985, talking about his roots in the area, Hom mentioned that his grandfather entered California in about 1890 and then returned to China and that his father came in 1914 at the age of 16; counting Tom Hom's children and grandchildren, "there are five generations that have been in California" (Dea 1985: 15).

In the spring of 1993, Tom Hom gave a talk on the history of Chinese Americans in the United States at an event celebrating the Centro Cultural de la Raza, located in San Diego's Balboa Park. Hom described the famous photograph taken to commemorate the completion of the transcontinental railroad in 1869 at Promontory Point, Utah. Hom pointed out that the photograph, crowded with workers and officials, did not contain a single Chinese person, despite the fact that they made up the majority of the workforce building the rails from west to east. Hom raised an important issue: When history is documented, who is included and who is excluded? As Tom and Dorothy Hom's work regarding historic preservation in downtown San Diego demonstrated, the same question applied.

Negotiating the value of the Chinese Mission echoed past urban renewal battles when city officials across the United States labeled minority communities as blighted to legitimate their destruction. In San Diego the selective enforcement of health and safety codes when much of Chinatown was destroyed in preparation for the 1915 Panama-California Exposition was part of a national pattern of negative images attached to Chinese. John Tchen's (1999) study of nineteenth-century New York City noted that to whites, "Chinese and their habitat embodied filth, disease, sexual mixing, and all that was repulsive to the Victorian middle-class sensibility" (p. 263). Speculation on the consumption of rats and dogs by the Chinese filled the city's media (Tchen 1999). Similarly, Nayan Shah's (2001: 1) study of San Francisco showed that public health reports described Chinatown as a "cess pool" and, as Shah summarized the reports, depicted Chinatown as "the preeminent site of urban sickness, vice, crime, poverty, and depravity" in the city during the nineteenth century. Charles McClain (1994) noted that San Francisco city officials attempted to close laundries owned by Chinese and displace Chinese residents from the downtown area during this period.

Although tourism by adults eager to catch a glimpse of the "criminal" and "exotic" world of Chinatowns existed in the late nineteenth and early twentieth centuries, a major transformation of the public image of Chinatowns was necessary before they could become the "safe" family tourist attractions that they are today. Shah (2001) and Ivan Light (Light 1974; Light and Wong 1975) explain that Chinese Americans had to change the image of Chinatowns from bachelor societies engaged in gambling, drug use, and prostitution to a more wholesome image as communities of families. Adding to these efforts, non-Chinese property owners also worked to improve the image of Chinatowns to increase the value of their downtown holdings. Carl Grodach's (2002) analysis showed that Harry Chandler, the owner of the *Los Angeles Times*, used the newspaper to promote the attractions of Chinatown. As a major landowner of downtown property, Chandler was interested in promoting tourism and development to improve land values, and creating "ethnic" areas was a key part of his effort. Previously, Chandler had worked with Christine Sterling to save Avila Adobe, which was the last standing structure at the site of the founding of Los Angeles. The two successfully gained support from city officials and local businesspeople to preserve Avila Adobe and to create a Mexican marketplace in the alley by the adobe to attract tourists, which opened in 1930 and is now known as Olvera Street (Estrada 2006; Kropp 2001).

When the city demolished Chinatown in 1933 to build Union Station to consolidate the train terminals, Christine Sterling and Harry Chandler worked together again to increase tourism in the downtown area. They created "China City," located north of Olvera Street and south of the new Chinatown created by the displaced residents and merchants of the original Chinatown, using Hollywood sets from movies such as *The Good Earth*. Christine Sterling explained her reasons for establishing China City.

> Since the Days of Marco Polo . . . the world has heard of the wonders and beauty of Cathay, its old civilization and its contributions of culture to the Western world. With this background, the Chinese came into California in the gold rush of '49, and became a part of our Pacific Coast tradition. They helped to build the Central Pacific, our first railroad; and the merchants and mandarins brought from China, rare works of Chinese art and literature and so—because all of this must not be lost or forgotten in the progress of modern times—China City was created. (Louie 2001: 38)

Although Sterling may have focused on historical preservation in the case of Avila Adobe, celebrating the importance of the city's Mexican past with Olvera Street, and on commemorating the history of the Chinese in the Americas with China City, Chandler understood the importance of tourism to increase the value of his downtown property.

In the 1990s the Chinese Historical Society of Southern California interviewed more than eighty people who had some connection with China City. Although an early version of a tourist theme park rather than an actual historic community, it did have some value to the Chinese American community. Many of those interviewed said that it provided an opportunity for entrepreneurs to set up a business in the block-long attraction, and it was an important spot for social interaction among the new Chinatown residents (Louie 2001). Fires in 1939 and 1949 destroyed many of the structures, and China City was not rebuilt, possibly because, with an increasing number of shops and restaurants, the new Chinatown was becoming more attractive to tourists and could serve as a replacement for China City (Pitt and Pitt 1997; Smith 2000).

By the end of the 1930s, the work of Chinese Americans and business interests had proved successful, and as Shah (2001: 225) notes, Chinatown had become a "sanitized tourist destination for middle-class white families." Chinatowns are now recognized as tourist attractions, a significant achievement given the vile images once associated with these communities, but historic preservation represents another battle over racial images.

The Chinese Mission: From Blighted to Historic

The struggle to preserve the Chinese Mission illustrates one of the fundamental issues in the historic preservation of buildings: the determination of what is historically significant and the propensity for city commissions to overlook the history of people of color. A 1986 evaluation of "Los Angeles's designated cultural-historic landmarks," for example, determined that only 2.3 percent referred to African Americans, Asian Americans, Latinos, or Native Americans, despite the long histories of these groups in the city (Dubrow 1986). Brandes conducted his study of Chinese buildings in 1986, and the Douglas Hotel was torn down in 1985. Examining the San Diego Historical Resources Board's list of historical landmarks as of 1986 provides an indicator of what was considered historically important at that time (HRB 2006). The list had 369 sites and structures. In terms of historical connection with racial minority communities, two deal with Mexican American history, one with Filipino American history, and eight with Chinese American history. No site or structure dealing with African Americans made the list. Eleven out of 369, or 3 percent, is better than the Los Angeles list, but still a small number, especially taking into account that five of the Chinese American sites and the one Filipino American site made the list primarily because they were part of the ninety buildings grouped together and listed in the Gaslamp Quarter Historic District.

The small percentage of structures related to the history of minorities on the Los Angeles and San Diego lists of historic landmarks and the complete absence of structures relating to African Americans until 2001 in San Diego, I believe, demonstrate the tendency of routine, institutional processes to recognize structures that reflect the history of white communities rather than those of racial minorities.[3] Because the Chinese Mission was not the work of a famous architect and because it was a modest structure in appearance and size, Chinese Americans had to establish its importance in terms of its social history in relation to their community as well as to San Diego in general. The Brandes report's comment that the Chinese Mission did not match the architecture of an "Oriental structure" neglects the social history of the structure.

A strong protest arose among Chinese Americans and city historic preservation groups in response to the Brandes report, and a number of letters were sent to the CCDC. Gil Ontai was the only Asian American on the CCDC board, and he proved to be central to the effort, advising the Asian American community about issues of preservation and later advocating strongly for the establishment of a CCDC Asian Pacific Thematic Historic District Advisory Committee (Vo 2004). In response, the CCDC held a meeting on June 16, 1986, to receive public input on the Brandes report. About fifty Chinese Americans attended and voiced their strong disagreement with the report's assessment of the buildings and the area's potential as a historic district. As Dorothy Hom pointed out, "That area really does represent our roots in America" (Krey 1986: A1). An important step was taken at the meeting when a community advisory committee was established to assist the CCDC with the "research and evaluation effort" of the buildings (Trimble 1987: 2).

In the weeks after the meeting, members of the Chinese American community continued to attend CCDC meetings, send letters to the CCDC regarding the Brandes report, and inform the CCDC that Chinese American community groups intended to build new facilities in the area. Frank Wong, president of the Chinese Consolidated Benevolent Association (CCBA), submitted a letter at the June 27, 1986, CCDC board meeting.

> It is our intent to develop senior citizen housing unit(s) along with ancillary supporting functions for senior citizens. Also within this complex, we will include construction of some commercial activities and preserving the existing cultural/historical buildings that reflected the heritage of the community. Our formal appearance today is to let the Board know of our intent and to ask the CCDC to "reserve" the area for the local community rather than to have outside developers take over the area without regard to the community. (Wong 1986a: 1)

Along with the letter, the CCBA submitted petitions to the CCDC on June 27, 1986, and July 7, 1986, with 524 signatures, requesting that the city preserve and restore the buildings, including the Chinese Mission. As the petitions stated, "Redevelopment by the City should not allow a developer to destroy these historically significant structures where the people of Chinese background lived, worked, and worshipped" (Wong 1986b).

Wong (1986b) discussed the long history of Chinese and other Asian groups in the downtown area, the need to preserve the buildings in recognition of that history, and the negative effects of redevelopment. "We are deeply concerned that developers are interested only in the financial aspect of the development of the area without due regard to the local community" (Wong 1986b: 1). David

Seid, president of the House of China, pointed out that the study was conducted in a short period of time and that there appeared to be a "lack of contact with community organizations and members for information" (Seid 1986: 2–3). He noted that "only *one* Chinese is listed as being interviewed." Furthermore, as Seid (1986) states, "a very serious flaw" with the criteria used by Brandes for evaluating the building was "not considering the human loves, joys, tragedies of the people who lived in the buildings" (p. 3).

On July 11, 1986, Tom Hom wrote a letter criticizing the Brandes report for its lack of input from the Chinese American community.

> I find that Dr. Brandes' report does not substantiate nearly enough as to how he had concluded that a number of the Chinese buildings are not significant enough to be classified of higher historical value. In judging historical significance he should have done more research with the Chinese community, people who were there fifty to seventy-five years ago in order to gain additional background, as to significance. From all indications, he did not do that. . . . I feel because of the time constraints CCDC gave him to get the report in, he was not able to do as complete a report that he is normally noted for doing. (Hom 1986: 1)

Reflecting a similar view, Ron Buckley, secretary to the Historical Site Board, wrote in a July 11, 1986, letter to the CCDC that he believed "that the historical significance, architectural integrity and the categories regarding Chinese community concern over demolition and the degree to which the original exterior remains intact are undervalued" for the Chinese Mission and two of the other low-rated buildings (Buckley 1986: 1–2).

At the August 21, 1986, advisory committee meeting, the CCDC agreed to commission an architectural and engineering study by the firm of Milford Wayne Donaldson to assess the general state of the buildings (Trimble 1987). Released in November 1986, the report, *Historic Chinese Community Buildings: Survey Analysis* (Donaldson 1986), contrasted sharply with the Brandes report. The Donaldson report stated that "it is important to realize the collective historic value of these nine structures, particularly for the Chinese community. Most of the buildings are in good structural condition. It is our opinion that rehabilitation can be accomplished without major cost" (Donaldson 1986: 35). In terms of the feasibility for rehabilitation, the report rated the Chinese Mission "Good," stating that the "building retains much of its original exterior historic fabric" (Donaldson 1986: 9, 35).

As the effort to save the Chinese Mission and create an Asian Pacific American historic district moved through the review process with the CCDC, the Historical Site Board, and the city council, the owner of the Mission, Charles Tyson, fought against its preservation because he hoped to develop high-rise housing on the site. Tyson explained:

> While I respect and understand the sentimental attachment members of the Chinese Community Church have for their former home, the property today bears no resemblance to what it was twenty-eight years ago when they vacated it. Nothing is left that is reminiscent of their use. The building is a vandalized shell, the condition of which fails to do justice to the integrity of the congregation's history. I understand and admire the importance of local history to the San Diego Chinese community, but I respectfully submit that San Diego's Chinese history is not honored by the property today. (Tyson 1987: 2)

In a discussion two months later on whether or not the building should be on the local and national register of historic places, Tyson argued that "this is not even the original (Chinese Community Church Building). It was built in the 1920s. I find it difficult to understand the passions that seem to go beyond common sense here" (Sullivan 1987a: A1). In an earlier May 20, 1987, letter to the Historical Site Board, Marie Burke Lia, now representing Tyson, wrote "to express the strong objections of the owners of . . . the former Chinese Mission building, to its designation as part of the proposed Chinese/Asian Thematic Historic District" (Lia 1987: 1). In response, Ron Buckley, secretary of the City of San Diego Historical Site Board, stated, "For them (Tyson and Lia) to say it's not significant is to deny its history" (Sullivan 1987a: A1).[4]

At the August 7, 1987, CCDC meeting, Tom Hom, speaking as the representative of the Chinese Community Church, stated their preference for incorporating the Chinese Mission Church, or its façade, into Tyson's proposed residential project. Plans developed by architect Milford Wayne Donaldson showed how this could be accomplished, and Hom stated in approval that "it gives a real uniqueness and I see no reason why it can't be done" (Showley 1987: B3). Kristen Aliotti, a member of the San Diego Save Our Heritage Organization, also supported the idea, stating that "preservation is economically viable to a community" and that "Mr. Donaldson's drawings incorporating the Mission give the project a more public feeling and would attract more people" (CCDC 1987a: 4). Dorothy Hom also spoke in favor of keeping the Chinese Mission in place and suggested that the CCDC board "direct the architect to find a way to incorporate the building" (CCDC 1987a: 4). Tyson rejected this idea as unfeasible because of the added costs and design problems. Gerald M. Trimble, CCDC chief executive, voicing his judgment on the topic, suggested that "the appearance of it might be crazy" (Showley 1987: B3). Although Tyson had applied for a demolition permit in February 1987, he offered to delay demolition so that a different site for the Chinese Mission could be found (CCDC 1987a: 3).

Supporters of the Chinese Mission drew on a range of images involving Chinese Americans that justified the mission's preservation, focusing on history but also on the economic importance of Chinatowns in major cities across the country and the growing economies of Asia. This linked preservation with the city's goal of reversing downtown's decline and turning it into a modern corporate center that could attract business travelers, tourists, affluent local residents, and local and international investment capital. "Los Angeles, San Francisco, Chicago and New York all have a China Town," said Winnie Chu of the CCBA. "We think here (lower Third Avenue) is our China Town" (Krey 1986: A1). Harold Jow, a former pastor in the Chinese American community, stated that "the Chinese people have contributed a lot to the growth of the West, the railroad, mining and agriculture. . . . We hope that one day that history will be written" (Furey 1987: B3). Jow "emphasized . . . the economic importance of San Diego increasing its ties with Pacific Rim countries, 'I think it's imperative, if this city is going to become an international city, that we do our best to retain whatever is left of the cultural heritage of the Chinese people'" (Furey 1987: B3).

Preservation in general is difficult, but the task of convincing city officials of the importance of structures related to the history of racial minorities is even more demanding. Tom Hom remarked on the difficulty of getting across the importance of the Chinese Mission to non-Chinese: "Sometimes I think the agency [the CCDC] loses sight of the fact that this structure is not just for the Chinese community but for all of San Diego. . . . It's going to be a museum to share the heritage of a people that were here in the early stages of the city's history" (Sullivan 1989: B7).

A historic district and the preservation of buildings contributed directly to CCDC efforts to revitalize downtown San Diego, providing another reason for the success of the Chinese American community efforts. As the Asian Pacific Thematic Historic District (APTHD) Master Plan would later state:

San Diego is the only large metropolitan area in the western United States that does not have a thriving Historic Asian district. . . . By recognizing the historically

significant buildings and heritage of this district, they contribute . . . to a continued redevelopment of the downtown area. . . . This in turn will lead to opportunities for a destination for visitors and tourists seeking the rich architectural
and cultural heritage of San Diego's past. . . . This Master Plan recognizes the
proximity of San Diego as a Pacific Rim city and the opportunity to revitalize the
historic Asian Pacific District as a visitor and business destination with cultural
ties to other Pacific Rim nations and cities. (APTHD 1995: 3–4)

Resonating with the ideas of Jane Jacobs about the contribution of older
buildings to the social and economic vitality of a neighborhood, Michael
Stepner, the acting planning director for San Diego, stressed the importance
of saving the common buildings of everyday life to preserve the history and
uniqueness of the area.

Preservation of special communities provides cities with variety, context, history, and roots. Preservation does not always mean preserving monumental
architecture. The Chinese/Asian District would provide the City of San Diego
with a contextual base of a series of "ethnic communities" which made up what
our city is today, and an architectural base of small wooden buildings which
are important to our understanding to how our urban center began. (Stepner
1987: n.p.)

The campaign by Chinese Americans and historic preservation groups to
counter the negative Brandes report and to educate the members of the city
commissions and council about the significance of the buildings related to the
city's Chinese American history, the value of preserving these structures, and
the use of redevelopment funds to support these efforts eventually succeeded.
As Dorothy Hom stated, "When preservation is brought to their attention, the
people on the City Council are very enthusiastic. . . . But they're so busy wor-
rying about everything else before them that unless someone brings (preservation) to their attention, it goes by the wayside" (Sutro 1991: E1).

The San Diego City Council voted to establish a Chinese/Asian thematic
district on October 13, 1987. The council also designated for the local historic
register twenty buildings associated with the Asian American community, but
a decision on the status of the Chinese Mission was continued to the November 10, 1987, meeting. At that meeting, the council did not designate the Chinese Mission to the local or national historic registers, denied the "issuance
of demolition permits for the Chinese Mission . . . for a reasonable period of

time," and referred the matter "back to the Corporation to explore alternatives for reconstructing the buildings elsewhere within the Chinese/Asian Thematic District" (Trimble 1987). Four months later, the council approved a resolution, dated March 22, 1988, designating the Chinese Mission to the local historic register with the understanding that the mission would be moved to the Chinese/Asian thematic historic district (City Council Resolution R-270599, 1988: 2). Recognizing the overlapping settlement of Asian American communities historically in the downtown area and reflecting the panethnic goals of the Asian American community, the name was later changed to the Asian Pacific Thematic Historic District.

Agreeing to move the building to another location was a key compromise that saved the Chinese Mission, although it was a difficult one for those interested in preservation to accept. The CCDC issued a "Request for Proposals for the Relocation/Reconstruction and Reuse of the Chinese Mission Building" on December 2, 1987, noting that Tyson was "willing to pay for dismantling, storage, and donation of the Mission building" (CCDC 1987b: 1). Hom explained why he had favored keeping the building in place: "If you move London Bridge to a big lake in Arizona, it's not London Bridge anymore. If you move the mission building elsewhere, the echoes of history don't ring as true." Hom stated, however, that "if there's no other alternative we'll have to go along with it" (Sullivan 1987a: A1). In contrast, the chair of the CCDC, John Davies, suggested that "the preservation purists don't like to move historical buildings, but I think it would be an improvement moving it closer to the other sites" (Sullivan 1987b: C1). A proposal was submitted by Tom Hom on behalf of the Chinese Historical Society with the goal of moving the mission to the historic district and transforming it into a museum and cultural center (Hom 1988).[5]

The Chinese Historical Society chose the northeast corner of Third Avenue and J Street as the site for the Chinese Mission (see Map 1). The location was within the boundaries of the old Chinatown and near existing and planned Chinese structures; coincidentally, Tom Hom had been born on that block. The city agreed to acquire the property and lease it to the Chinese Historical Society for $1.00 per year for 55 years. The CCDC estimated that it would spend "$325,000 for land acquisition, $50,000 for administration and relocation, and $61,000 for off-site public improvements" (Hamilton 1989: 1). Wayne Donaldson had examined the original building plans and found an addendum indicating that it "had been structurally reinforced when it was constructed in 1927. Field testing of portions of the walls and inspection by several structural engineers confirmed that the building could be safely moved rather than dismantled" (Hamilton 1988).

The Chinese Mission was moved on August 17, 1988, and placed temporarily at 428 Third Avenue. The *San Diego Daily Transcript* (1988: n.p.) remarked, "Newsworthy about the move was how smooth it went. Not a brick came loose from the 1927-built structure." Charles Tyson, working with Dorothy and Tom Hom, donated the $40,000 needed to move the structure (Hom Zemen and Lee 2000: 1). To formalize the fundraising, moving, and restoration efforts of the Chinese Mission, Alexander Chuang organized the Historical Museum Planning and Management Committee in 1992, and approximately $460,000 was raised (Chuang et al. 2006; Lee et al. 2000). The mission was moved to its permanent location on March 7, 1995 (Figure 1).

The official dedication ceremony was held on January 13, 1996, on a clear, sunny day, with then-mayor Susan Golding and representatives from Taiwan participating in the day's events (Lee et al. 2000). A large crowd gathered for the

Figure 1 Exterior of the Chinese Mission at the northwest corner of Third Avenue and J Street, 2008. Photograph by author.

festivities, filling the chairs set up in the street in front of the mission and with many standing around the chairs. Watching the proceedings, I stood next to a woman who rested her hands on a stroller containing her 3-year-old daughter. As it turns out, the woman was Phyllis Hom, one of the six children of Dorothy and Tom Hom, and she mentioned that her parents first met in the Chinese Mission. Dorothy was from Hawaii, and when she met Tom, she was in the city attending San Diego State University (Saito 2004). For Dorothy and Tom Hom, the Chinese Mission represented a connection to the city's history, the Chinese American community, and their own personal histories, showing the many layers of memory connected to significant structures and varied reasons for people's involvement in historical preservation.

Asian Pacific Thematic Historic District Advisory Committee

The significance of the effort to save the Chinese Mission went beyond the preservation of the structure because the struggle broadened to establish an institutional voice for the Asian American community in downtown development through a CCDC committee. Following the prompting of members of the Asian American community, the CCDC proposed in 1991 that the Asian Pacific Thematic Historic District Advisory Committee review projects within the boundaries of the historic district. This suggestion, however, was met with resistance from other downtown groups and within the CCDC. The members of the Gaslamp Quarter Planning Board voted against the plan, believing that a new committee would be redundant and would unnecessarily complicate the review process for new projects.[6] The CCDC executive director believed that little interest in the committee existed among Asian Americans and that the committee would create extra work for the CCDC with little benefit (Vo 2004). Concerned that the proposal for an advisory committee would not be implemented, Asian Americans attended a CCDC board meeting and supported the formation of the committee. Asian Americans later sent a letter reaffirming the importance of a committee.

> The community proposes to have a meaningful participation in what happens to the future of our property, our cultural activities, our organized senior citizens events, our jobs, our cultural landmarks, our residences, our businesses, and our community appearance, which should be Asian in character. (Vo 2004: 182)

The group of Asian Americans pushing for the establishment of the advisory committee broadened the effort by gaining the support of other groups in the city, including the mayor's Asian Advisory Board and the Asian Business Association. Acknowledging widespread support in the Asian American community for the issue, the CCDC established the committee in 1991. As stated by the CCDC (n.d.), the advisory committee provides input to the CCDC staff and board members on issues involving "planning goals, land uses, rehabilitation of historic structures, compatibility of the design of new development, and working with exiting owners, tenants and community to promote and enhance the District." The committee would also work to "sensitize the public, city staff, and legislators to the benefits of conserving and enhancing the rich heritage of the multi-cultural Asian community" (CCDC n.d.). The advisory committee members intended to inform the general public and city staff about the history of the Asian American community by going beyond the economic concerns of the growth machine and stressing the importance of historical preservation "and considering social, economic, and cultural aspects of the development" (Vo 2004: 183). Although the committee had only an advisory capacity, its involvement could alter CCDC decisions on projects, as illustrated by the case of the Lincoln Hotel.

Built in 1913, the Lincoln Hotel was linked to early Asian American history and was located on Fifth Avenue, two blocks east of the Chinese Mission in the Asian Pacific Thematic Historic District and in one of the busiest sections of the Gaslamp District. The CCDC bought the four-story building in 1990 and released a request for proposals for projects for the structure in 1991, with an emphasis on low-income housing. The Vista Hills Community Treatment Foundation, a non–Asian American organization, was selected by the CCDC board over the San Diego Chinese Center, and the issue then went to the city council for approval. The Asian American community mobilized, and as Linda T. Vo explains, they filled the council chambers with "approximately thirty elderly Chinese who still lived in the downtown area" (Vo 2004: 179). One of the San Diego Chinese Center members stated, "The city council was on their best behavior when they had all these senior citizens show up" (Vo 2004: 179). As Vo (2004) noted, the city council voted against the CCDC recommendation for the Vista Hills project, the first time ever that a CCDC recommendation did not win approval. After a new request for proposals, the San Diego Filipino-American Humanitarian Foundation was selected in 1994, and the group used the upper floors for low-income housing, the ground level space for commercial activity, and the basement for a library, marking the return of another Asian American group to the downtown core (Vo 2004).

By working together as Asian Americans and increasing their political resources, the various Asian ethnic groups in San Diego gained the attention of the CCDC and the city council members through the establishment of the advisory committee and were able to educate the city officials about the interests of the community collectively. At the same time, Asian Americans could inform city staff about the distinct interests and needs of particular Asian groups. Linda T. Vo pointed out that during the debate over the Lincoln Hotel, the executive director of the CCDC expressed the belief that one Asian American center could service all the different Asian ethnic groups. Vo explained that the director "declared that the Chinese Mission would be the cultural center of the district and questioned the viability and feasibility of designating and building centers for the Japanese American and Filipino communities" (Vo 2004: 193). The successful panethnic efforts to establish the advisory committee and gain control of the Lincoln Hotel helped to transform the Asian American community into a growing political force in the city. Vo reports that a former chair of the advisory committee stressed the importance of these achievements, stating that "since then we've had successes after successes. . . . I can't emphasize how important for it to happen more often, for us to really pull together and lobby more and have strategic planning for it" (Vo 2004: 189).

In 1994 the CCDC put out a "Request for Qualifications for Consultant Services to Prepare a Master Plan for the Chinese/Asian Thematic Historic District." The master plan would have three components involving research on the history of the district, suggestions on the development of the area and its buildings, and a program to implement the recommendations. The San Diego architecture and planning firm of Fehlman LaBarre was chosen, and the project team included Tom Hom as the Chinese American community advisor, Don Estes (a professor at San Diego City College and the foremost authority on the history of Japanese Americans in the city) as the Japanese American community historian, and the landscape architect firm WYA, with Joseph Yamada, who along with his spouse, Elizabeth Yamada, had a long history of involvement in the Asian American community. In 1995, Fehlman LaBarre produced the 98-page "Asian Pacific Thematic Historic District Master Plan." With its maps of the districts and histories and photographs of the twenty structures designated as historically significant, the master plan is a useful document of the area's history as well as a sign of commitment from the city to support the concept of a historic district.

The advisory committee's reviews and recommendations have had an impact on the final form of other projects, as demonstrated by two Intracorp structures. Unlike the bitter battle involving the Lincoln Hotel and the withdrawal of the city's support for the Vista Hills Community Treatment Foundation project, however, a cooperative relationship developed between Intracorp and the advisory committee. Intracorp's first project called for condominiums on the corner of Third Avenue and Market Street, just two blocks north of the Chinese Mission. In recognition of its site along an entrance corridor to the historic district, the developer agreed in 1999 to donate $10,000 to paint a mural along its Third Avenue wall with an Asian motif (Cate 1999).

Intracorp planned another condominium project, Pacific Terrace, that came before the advisory committee in 2000. The project would be located directly across the street from the Chinese Mission, and in plans presented to the advisory committee the entrance to the underground parking garage would face the Chinese Mission on Third Avenue. The driveway on Third Avenue presented a potential problem because that street was often closed by the city for Asian American street festivals. For example, the San Diego Chinese Center, an organization that provides social services, moved its annual Chinese New Year festival in 1998 to Third Avenue (SDCC 1998). The festival was a well-established event, celebrating its sixteenth year in 1998, and drew large crowds on both days of its weekend run. Members of the advisory committee expressed their concern that if the parking entrance remained in its proposed location, the street could not be closed and that would put an end to community celebrations on Third Avenue. The project representatives agreed to consider moving the entrance to the garage from the west side to the east side of the building on Fourth Avenue, but because of the slope of the land, this would add to the cost of the structure and reduce the number of parking spaces. Despite these problems, the developer recognized the importance of Third Avenue for community events, because the block contained the Chinese Mission, the San Diego Chinese Center, and CCBA senior citizen housing and was in the center of the Asian Pacific Thematic Historic District, and agreed to move the entrance.

During the discussion of the Pacific Terrace project at the advisory committee meeting, Alexander Chuang, executive director of the Chinese San Diego Historical Society and Museum, grew intrigued by the prospect of purchasing ground floor space and expanding the museum. Chuang brought up the idea with the project representatives and asked, "'Is the retail area up for sale?' They indicated to me that they preferred to lease, but they would consider selling the retail space located on the first floor at the corner of 3rd Ave. and 'J' St." (Chuang 2004: 1). Chuang later contacted the developer, who said that he would be willing to sell; Chuang brought it before the Museum Board, and the proposition "overwhelmingly passed." They purchased the space, Chuang donated his time to serve as the general contractor to transform the empty shell into a museum annex, and Joseph Wong donated his services as the project architect (Chuang 2004). Chuang also led the successful two-year drive to raise the $900,000 needed to acquire the 2,450-square-foot space and build the interior. The official opening of the museum annex occurred on October 2, 2004.

The Chinese Museum members have worked to expand their activities in the area. The museum extension offers additional exhibition and meeting space. A yearly Chinese New Year festival attracts large crowds; streets around the museum are blocked off for the weekend fair. Tours of the area's Asian American history are offered and attempts to start a farmers' market and Asian bazaar have drawn more people to the museum and neighborhood.

Conclusion: From Blighted to Historic

At the time of the debate over the fate of the Chinese Mission in the 1980s, downtown economic redevelopment was at an early stage and the economic return was uncertain as city officials attempted to reverse the effects of suburbanization and the reluctance of businesses and residents to locate in the urban core. Two decades later, major achievements generated by redevelopment include the preservation of many of the older buildings in San Diego's Gaslamp District, new office buildings, and a revitalized urban core that serves as the region's dominant entertainment site for residents, tourists, and conventioneers.

In addition to economic success, however, the San Diego negotiations over the Chinese Mission illustrate a number of points about the ways in which economic redevelopment and historic preservation were contested and racialized. First, San Diego's redevelopment was guided by a growth machine strategy, and historic preservation was more likely to occur when it fitted the needs of the growth machine. Clearly, redevelopment occurred under severe fiscal constraints; however, the re-creation of the downtown area as a center of business, commercial, and leisure activity and increasing property values often worked more toward the creation of a theme park than historic preservation, as noted in the letter written by architectural historian Paul Alley (1988) on San Diego's downtown plans.

Second, when historic preservation did occur, city officials were more likely to save "monumental" buildings, such as the major structures of the old business district that became the Gaslamp Quarter, rather than the structures representing the social history of racial minorities. The CCDC reviewed the Chinese Mission in terms of its historical and architectural significance to San Diego in general and the Chinese American community in particular and concluded that the building was not worth saving.

Third, the effort by Chinese Americans to save the Chinese Mission is part of the long-standing struggle to define ethnic communities and to move away from images of Chinese American neighborhoods nationally as centers of crime, poverty, and depravity to the view that they are attractive business and cultural centers and that Chinatown's family businesses exemplify the American phenomenon of entrepreneurial success. The first major effort to eradicate San Diego's Chinatown occurred when city officials attempted to "clean up" the town in preparation for the 1915 Panama-California Exposition. At that time, most of Chinatown was targeted by city health officials and destroyed, along with other officially labeled "problems," such as prostitution and gambling. Other Chinatowns, such as the ones in San Francisco and New York, proved more effective at combating the "cesspool" label and rumors of serving dogs and cats in restaurants. By the late 1930s and 1940s, Chinatowns had a new image as family tourist attractions with affordable restaurants serving tasty fare. Communities of color across the nation, however, had to battle a new threat of displacement by urban renewal in the 1950s through the 1970s that once again labeled their neighborhoods as crime-ridden and dysfunctional slums.

In the contemporary struggle to preserve their buildings and history, the strategy for the supporters of the Chinese Mission was to put forward their interests by explicitly stating how their goals supported the city's overall economic redevelopment goals. Aware of the city elite's support for development—and its power, displayed, for example, by the construction of the convention center, despite repeated rejection by voters—members of the San Diego Chinese American community did not attempt to change the overall goals of the growth machine. Instead, by pointing out the ways in which Chinatowns contribute to tourism in major cities across the United States, how an Asian Pacific Thematic Historic District would increase the attractiveness of San Diego for overseas Asian investors, and the city's commitment to saving historic structures as part of the downtown development plans, Chinese Americans used the city's goals of redevelopment, tourism, and preservation to gain support for their goals.

In the 1980s the Brandes report stated that the Chinese Mission's architecture was not an "Oriental structure," and Tyson described the building as a "vandalized shell." By emphasizing attributes of the physical structure, Brandes and Tyson ignored its historical importance. The work of Chinese American activists to replace the label of "blighted" with "historic" echoed the earlier battles of urban renewal and demonstrated the continued importance of images in the process of racial formation to define and legitimate public policy. The team of Dorothy and Tom Hom provided knowledge of the political and redevelopment process, and the Chinese Historical Society provided the organizational base, so that the Chinese American community could effectively mobilize and use their considerable financial and organizational resources to challenge the negative label and replace it with one that justified preservation.

As the APTHD Master Plan recognized, San Diego was the only major city in the "western United States that [did] not have a thriving Historic Asian District" (APTHD 1995). Therefore, as a result of the lobbying efforts of Chinese Americans in contemporary San Diego, a "Chinatown" was appreciated as a positive element that would contribute to the ambience of the area, unlike the period of the Panama-California Exposition, when "Chinatown" was synonymous with "slum." As a result of community activism, city officials recognized the Chinese Mission as a historic building representing the early immigration and settlement history of the city and as an important part of past and present Chinatown rather than as a "vandalized shell" suitable for destruction.

3 African Americans and Historic Preservation in San Diego

The Douglas Hotel and the Clermont/Coast Hotel

EMBEDDED IN THE SIDEWALK at the San Diego downtown corner of Second Avenue and Market Street, on a block bordering the southern side of Horton Plaza, is a commemorative 24-inch-by-18-inch brass plaque. The plaque reads:

> Former Site, Douglas Hotel, 1924. Known as the "Harlem of the West," the hotel included the Creole Palace nightclub where black stage and screen stars of the 1930's and 1940's performed. The Douglas Hotel was the only major downtown hotel to provide accommodations to black visitors in San Diego during the era of segregation.

The plaque is the only reminder of the most important entertainment venue and the main place of lodging for African Americans in downtown San Diego during that era. Celebrities such as Billie Holiday, Duke Ellington, and the Mills Brothers stayed and played there (Austin 1994). Today, most pedestrians walk by or over the plaque without ever noticing its existence, unaware of the city's history represented by the Douglas Hotel, which was torn down in 1985 to make way for a mixed-use residential and commercial development.

The demolition of the Douglas Hotel led to the establishment of the Gaslamp Black Historical Society (GBHS) in 1999. The GBHS directed the effort to preserve the Clermont/Coast Hotel. Those in favor of demolishing the Clermont/Coast Hotel, including its owners, focused on the building's physical condition, labeling it a "wretched building" and an "eyesore." As with the Douglas Hotel and the Chinese Mission, studies commissioned by the city declared that the Clermont/Coast Hotel was neither historically nor architecturally significant, once again demonstrating how official historic evaluations fail to recognize the social history of a structure connected to racial minorities.

The growth machine led by the city's corporate and political elite favored new construction and threatened to wipe out older buildings in the pursuit of profits for developers and property owners and increased tax revenue for the city. With popular sentiment in favor of demolition, city studies declaring the hotel's insignificance, and the possibility of constructing a parking structure on the site to serve the newly built ballpark, the routine processes of redevelopment and evaluation for historical significance that typically favored structures connected to whites over those linked to racial minorities would have led to the hotel's destruction. In fact, at the time, the city's list of historical landmarks contained no site or structure related to African Americans.

Echoing past battles involving urban renewal that wiped out entire communities, the struggle centered on transforming the label of "wretched building," which justified demolition, to "historically significant," which would support preservation. In contrast to the effort to save the Chinese Mission and the model minority image of Asian Americans, however, African Americans face stereotypes that link negative images of crime and poverty to their contemporary communities. As one leader of a local neighborhood group that favored demolition of the Clermont/Coast Hotel cautioned, the city needed to be careful about establishing "affordable housing" and creating a "ghetto." Although this individual did not mention race, clearly race is implied in those terms (Gans 1995; Wilson 1987), and such stereotypes add to the challenge of convincing city officials of the importance of the social history of African Americans as a contributor to downtown development.

Research by members of the GBHS established that the Clermont/Coast Hotel was significant because it was one of the first hotels that catered exclusively to African Americans in the era of segregation, and the GBHS rallied community support to save the structure. By combining research that documented the hotel's significance in representing legal segregation in the pre–civil rights period with the argument that cities across the country have highlighted African American cultural attractions to boost tourism, the GBHS proved successful when the city declared the hotel a historical landmark in 2001.

African Americans in San Diego

People of African ancestry have a long history in the San Diego region, and a small number first entered the San Diego area in the early Spanish and Mexican periods (Madyun and Malone 1981). A census conducted by the United States military in 1847 during its occupation of San Diego during the Mexican-American War listed only 3 "Negroes," along with 483 "Converted Indians," 1,550 "Wild Indians," 3 "Sandwich Islanders," and 248 whites (Harris 1974: 2); however, the census figures were approximations, because of variations in racial classification across the nation. Individuals of African ancestry who might be considered African American in the southern United States as a result of the "one drop rule" could be categorized as "Mexican" or "Californio" in California and listed as "white" on the census (Madyun and Malone 1981). Overall numbers of people of African ancestry were low in California but even lower in San Diego because of the lack of direct rail service from the east and difficult land routes into San Diego and because San Diego had less economic development and fewer jobs compared to other California cities (Carlton 1975).

African Americans in the San Diego region in the mid-1800s primarily settled in the rural areas, which offered better economic opportunities than the city itself. The region's minor gold rush began in 1869 when Fred Coleman, an African American, discovered gold in Julian, a city in the low mountains to the east of San Diego; African Americans also established farms in the area (Madyun and Malone 1981). An African American couple, Margaret and Albert Robinson, established the Hotel Robinson in 1887. The hotel is still in existence today as the Julian Hotel, and it is the "oldest continuously operated hotel in Southern California" (Parker 1980: 1).

As the African American population slowly grew in San Diego, churches were established to serve the community, notably the Second Baptist Church, founded in 1886, and the Bethel African Methodist Episcopal Church, founded in 1888. Also, in 1892 Isaac Atkinson started the area's first newspaper owned by an African American, the *Colonizer* (Madyun and Malone 1981). In 1900, the census listed 313 African Americans, but it was not until after World War II and the expansion of the economy as a result of military spending and the growth of the defense industries that the African American population grew at a rapid rate. In 1940, the census counted 4,143 African Americans, which grew to 14,904 in 1950 and to 34,435 in 1960 (Harris 1974: 8). Restrictive covenants and the practices of real estate agents confined African Americans to the downtown area and the southeastern region of the city (Harris 1974), with a downtown concentration of seventeen businesses owned by African Americans from 1880 to 1930 (Madyun and Malone 1981).

The Douglas Hotel and Downtown Redevelopment

African American businessman George Ramsey and his partner, Robert Rowe,[1] built the Douglas Hotel in 1924 (Figure 2). According to local historian Micheal Austin, the hotel provided the "only place of quality lodging and entertainment for Black visitors to the city of San Diego during a period of intense segregation in the United States" (Austin 1994: 1).[2] A decade after the hotel's 1985 destruction, an article in the *Voice and Viewpoint*, San Diego's major African American community newspaper, described conditions in the United States at the time of the construction of the hotel and the racism of whites in that era. According to the article, whites lynched twenty-nine African Americans across the nation in 1923, and "leeches from that parasite became infectious in San Diego's White population with posted signs reading, We Do Not Cater to Negro Patronage, and For Whites Only" (Picou 1996: C9). Given this context of extreme discrimination, the article described the importance of the hotel, stating:

> Segregation had created an insufferable and bleak situation for African Americans. And their most common problem[s]: Where could a[n] African American get something to eat? What hotel would accommodate him? Where would someone go for entertainment? When the Douglas Hotel opened in 1924, the African American finally found that everything he needed, was in one place. Located at 206 Market Street, the hotel maintained a restaurant, card room, barbershop, dry cleaners, bell boys and billiard rooms. The adjoining room was the Creole Palace nightclub, well known for its jazz/ blues, boogie-woogie, Charleston music and dancing. (Picou 1996: C9)

Another newspaper article said, "'There wasn't another place like it. People came from L.A. just to visit the Creole Palace,' said Fro Brigham, a longtime jazz musician and bandleader who booked acts for the club in the late 1940s and 1950s" (Pattee 1988: D1).

The hotel also served as an important place of employment. As Austin noted, "There was a lot of tourism in San Diego during that period, and there were plenty of jobs, mostly service-oriented, for black people." Austin explained that "the most prized work was at the Douglas because it paid relatively high wages and its success ensured job security." "People valued their jobs there," Austin said. "They worked very hard to make it a nice place" (Green 1991: C1).

Micheal Austin suggested that the hotel provided "a sort of refuge for people" in an era of racial exclusion (Green 1991: C1), a belief echoed by African

Figure 2 Exterior of the Douglas Hotel facing Market Street, undated. Copyright San Diego Historical Society, Sensor 7-139. Reprinted by permission.

Americans who shared their memories in *San Diego Union-Tribune* articles. They described the hotel as a welcome safe haven and an entertainment mecca. Bea Wilson stated that "the hotel was a comfortable place, with no fear of being bothered day or night. People felt right at home there. I remember Earl and Louise of the Chapman Family, that lived over on Webster Avenue. They waited on tables, cooked good food, and practically ran the place. . . . Walking into the Douglas, gave the African American a sense of having a place that they could call their own" (Green 1991: C1).

The Creole Palace nightclub had a 25 cent cover charge, but on Thursdays, the usual day off for the city's maids, the nightclub had a "Kitchens Mechanics' Night" and maids could enter free (Picou 1996: C9). The hotel thrived into the 1940s, and the large military presence, with growing numbers of African Americans in the armed forces, helped the Creole Palace prosper (Figure 3). As Austin (1994) described it, "The men, many of them sailors and soldiers, would save their month's pay for a night at the Douglas" (p. 5). Even this place of "refuge," however, had its limitations. On Friday and Saturday nights, whites would populate the club, and with the increased cover charge and higher drink prices on those nights, few African Americans could afford to enter (Austin 1994; Krueger 1991; Picou 1996).

The expanding postwar economy, changing patterns of segregation, and suburbanization drew African Americans to new residential, shopping, and commercial opportunities beyond the downtown area, however. Austin (1994) explained that "by the late 1950s the glory days were gone" (p. 7). Similarly, the *Voice and Viewpoint* wrote, "By the end of the '50s, the Douglas Hotel had become a flophouse, with rented out rooms" (Picou 1996: C9). George Ramsey died in 1963 at the age of 72, and the *San Diego Union-Tribune* wrote that he was known as the "mayor of San Diego's Harlem" (Carrico and Jordan 2004: V-45). The *Voice and Viewpoint* (Picou 1996: C9) wrote that he and Mabel Rowe "passed away penniless" but that "no one will forget the luxury and party times that they both provided for people of color, and service men that had

Figure 3 Creole Palace performers at the Douglas Hotel facing Market Street, c. 1934. Copyright San Diego Historical Society, #20009. Reprinted by permission.

fought in two world wars, and famous musicians, that had no place to eat and sleep between Tijuana and Los Angeles."

Located directly across the street from Horton Plaza's southern edge and just west of the Gaslamp District, the Douglas Hotel was in a prime location for the city's redevelopment efforts (see Map 2). The city's long-range planning goals envisioned this area, known as the Marina Development Project, as a site for new residential construction. Keyser Marston Associates Inc. prepared an

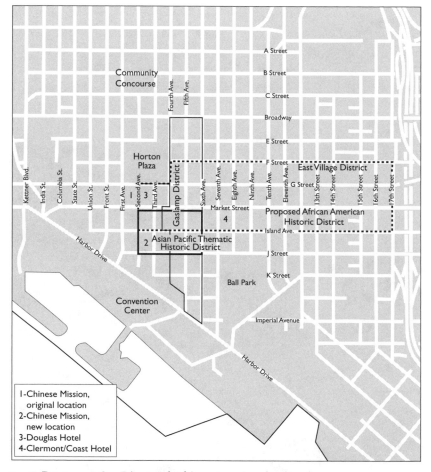

Map 2 Downtown San Diego and African American landmarks

SOURCE: San Diego City Centre Development Corporation. Additional information added to map by Wendy Saito Lew.

analysis of the site occupied by the Douglas Hotel for the CCDC and noted that the rectangular block measured 200 by 296 feet and that "the site is improved with an old hotel and two small old commercial buildings. Two-thirds of the site is being used for surface parking" (Keyser Marston Associates Inc. 1984: 5). The CCDC proposed a four-story project for the Douglas Hotel site that would cover the entire block, with street-level commercial space, underground parking, and 192 apartment units in the floors above, compared to the two-story Douglas Hotel with ground-floor commercial space and forty rooms on the second floor (Trimble 1984a: 2).

Building new housing to create a critical mass of downtown residents was a key goal that was explicitly stated in the 1965 development plan, the Horton Plaza Redevelopment Plan, and the Marina Development Plan. Building rental units, in addition to building for-sale residential projects, was crucial because it provided a way for people to try out living in the rapidly changing downtown scene at a time when few affluent residents lived downtown. According to CCDC officials, "Affordable rental housing is a key to the success of downtown, allowing more people to experiment with living there without having to make the hefty financial commitment of buying a condominium" (Spivak 1985: C1).

A 1984 San Diego City study of the area documented the rapid growth of new residential properties, with 1,047 units constructed since 1980, and the demographic change that resulted, with a larger percentage of whites moving into the new for-sale housing compared to the older rental housing stock. Since 1980, according to the report, about 164 low-income hotel units had disappeared, leaving the Douglas Hotel, with its forty residents, as the only residential structure from the city's pre–World War II era remaining in the Marina district.

The 1980 census reported a combined minority population of 23.8 percent, compared to 76.2 percent white in the city (San Diego City 1984: H.2:1). The 1984 report found a high overall percentage of low-income people of color in the Douglas Hotel, with 29 percent of the residents African American, 13 percent Latino, and 53 percent white. The residents of the three new "assisted elderly projects" also contained a high number of people of color compared to the city as a whole, with 6 percent African American, 15 percent Asian American, 13 percent Latino, and 65 percent white (San Diego City 1984: H.2:1). Although the report noted that racial data were not available for the new condominium projects, condominium sales managers estimated that 10–12 percent of the buyers were people of color, showing a dramatic change in the demographic makeup of the new residents in market-rate housing (San Diego City 1984: H.2:2).

According to the report, in addition to a racial shift, demolition of the old housing stock and construction of new condominiums also resulted in a dramatic increase in household income, with a projected 1986 $6,000 per household income for the elderly assisted housing and a range of $84,500 to $150,000 for the new condominiums. Three major condominium projects were under construction in 1984, with prices ranging from $82,000 to $1.4 million (Keyser Marston Associates 1984: 4). As a project in a redevelopment area and under the terms of the federal grant that provided some of the funds, the forty units lost from the Douglas Hotel had to be replaced with forty units of affordable housing in the new apartment complex.[3]

Historic Preservation and the Douglas Hotel

The standard city procedures for redevelopment and historic preservation led to the demolition of the Douglas Hotel, as they had with earlier urban renewal projects. The disregard for the history of people of color is reflected in the San Diego and Los Angeles lists of significant historic sites. Evaluating the physical condition of the Douglas Hotel and other structures on the block, the CCDC in 1984 stated that "the block is extremely blighted" (CCDC 1984: 2). In terms of the Douglas Hotel's historical value, the 1984 CCDC environmental impact report noted that "the Douglas Hotel is not listed on any city, state or national historical list or register. In addition, it was not identified in the 'Report on Significant Structures in the Centre City Redevelopment Projects' compiled by CCDC and approved by the City Historic Sites Board" (Redevelopment Agency of the City of San Diego 1984: 8). Although the structure was not considered significant architecturally, the report did recognize its possible value in terms of the city's social history, acknowledging that "although the Douglas Hotel has not been identified as a unique ethnic cultural resource, its previous use as a nightclub and hotel catering to black patrons in the 1930s and 1940s may be of historical interest." However, rather than saving the building from destruction, the report suggested that "the Redevelopment Agency proposes establishment of a photographic/commemorative display on the early days of the Douglas Hotel within the proposed development" (Redevelopment Agency of the City of San Diego 1984: 19).

Although there was interest among city residents to preserve the Douglas Hotel, ultimately no major lobbying effort occurred, in contrast to the Chinese Mission case. As the *Voice and Viewpoint* confirmed, "Most African Americans wanted to try and raise money to restore and preserve the Douglas Hotel, but that never happened" (Picou 1996: C9). A 1979 article in the *Voice and Viewpoint* had the title "Drive Starts to Save Douglas Hotel." The article explained that "James Pusey, 42, a retired Navyman and graduate student in history at the University of San Diego said if there is a campaign to restore the Old Globe Theater and the Aerospace Museum, why can't there be a drive to preserve and restore the Hotel Douglas?" (*Voice and Viewpoint* 1979: A5). Interviewed in 2001, Pusey recalled that his efforts did not go beyond his class research. He explained, "I wasn't really involved in an effort to save the Douglas, it was more a class project to do research" (Chau 2001). Pusey remembered that his class professor, Ray Brandes, "was really concerned with making a monument" to commemorate the building (Chau 2001). Ironically, despite his appreciation of the building's history, one of the few comments that Brandes put in his CCDC "Report on Market Street Square Archaeological Monitoring" during the demolition process was not one of appreciation of the building's history and regret that it could not be saved but one that affirmed its removal. He wrote, "A universal, and unsolicited opinion voiced by passersby at the area was 'It was good to see the old building gone, it was an eyesore'" (Brandes 1985–1986: 4).

Leon Williams, the first African American on the city council, served from 1969 to 1982 and was a strong supporter of downtown economic redevelopment because, as he put it, a city "needs a heart and economic investment downtown." He worked to save much of the historic core, including the Spreckels Theater, which he characterized as the "flagship theater of San Diego," Balboa Theater, and Pantoja Park. In terms of the Douglas Hotel, Williams stated that it "didn't occur to me to preserve the Douglas Hotel as a historic site. When I was on the council, I didn't think of ethnic history." Williams's time on the council finished before the hotel was demolished in 1985, and he noted that while he served, no individual or group brought up the issue. He said that he "did not remember any discussion of it at the council level. I would have been sensitive to it if any group initiated a discussion. If someone had raised it, I would have been willing to consider it" (Saito 2003b). Williams was a pioneer and tireless voice for historic preservation, but his efforts focused on the traditional centers of cultural life, such as the Spreckels Theater, rather than on buildings representing the social history of other segments of the community, such as early centers of African American business and entertainment.

African Americans held conflicting opinions about the Douglas Hotel's historical significance, as did whites, and this may have contributed to the lack of action to save the hotel. In contrast to the Chinese Mission as a place that represented conventional values, such as religion, building community, and learning English, and that fostered the process of integration into American society, the Douglas Hotel had a much more controversial history. Its existence was a stark reminder of racial discrimination, exclusion, and segregation in society. Although exclusively all-white hotels from that era also existed and were part of the redevelopment of downtown, this aspect of their history did not generate the same concerns as did racial discrimination against African Americans because white racial privilege often goes unrecognized. Also, even though the Douglas Hotel's importance as an African American–owned business and place of entertainment was clear, others noted its location in the Stingaree District, San Diego's former center of illegal behavior, such as "prostitution, gambling and other illicit activities, said Jaspar Davis, a retired San Diego policeman who was the second black on the force" (Parker 1984: J1). There is disagreement on whether or not prostitution actually occurred in the hotel. When Robert Rowe passed away several months after the hotel opened, Mabel Rowe, his widow, took over his work responsibilities, lived in the hotel, and as a madam, ran her prostitution business at a nearby hotel (Parker 1984; Picou 1996).

Considering the importance of churches as sites of political mobilization for African American communities (Morris 1984), the stigma of the Douglas Hotel as a "place of sin" did not encourage activism. As Reverend George Walker Smith, an African American and one of the city's major community leaders, explained, "I don't know why people place so much emphasis on the Douglas Hotel. There are other historic things that happened down there" (Mills and Bunyi 2000: 12). Reverend Smith, the son of an Alabama sharecropper, came to San Diego in 1956 to become a pastor after graduating from the Pittsburgh Theological Seminary. Soon after, Reverend Smith established the Catfish Club, a lunch forum that became an important place for major figures in politics, business, and cultural affairs to appear as guest speakers to discuss issues of the day. The *San Diego Union-Tribune* described the Catfish Club as the city's "best-known multiethnic forum" and noted that Reverend Smith "broke the color line in local politics" in 1963 in his successful run for the Board of Education (Morgan 2000: A3).

Honoring Martin Luther King Jr.

The failed campaign to rename Market Street, which runs along the northern side of the block where the Douglas Hotel once stood, to honor Martin Luther King Jr. was one of the major issues of the mid-1980s in the downtown area that

Reverend Smith believed took precedence over the preservation of the Douglas Hotel. Reverend Smith worked with a group for several years in an effort to have a major street in San Diego renamed to honor the slain civil rights leader. Boosted by a visit in 1985 to San Diego by Coretta Scott King, who came to the city to discuss celebrations in honor of her deceased spouse, the group had convinced the city council to vote in 1986 to change the name of Market Street to Martin Luther King Way (Glanton and Smolens 1986; Griffin and Nelson 2000). Reverend Robert Ard, the Black Leadership Council president, explained his support for renaming Market Street: "We believe it's time for this city to join those other cities who have already recognized the contributions of Dr. King to the world. . . . We're a little late, but it's time to rectify that" (Glanton and Smolens 1986: B1).

The decision met with resistance from members of the business community, who expressed concern over the cost of renaming a major thoroughfare. Verna Quinn, vice chair of a community development group, stated that it was a matter of economics: "The issue wasn't whether we should have a street named after him, but the expense to local businesses and the confusion to residents. . . . It's not just a matter of changing street signs. It is an enormous expense for people who have to change telephone listings, business papers and other things" (Glanton and Smolens 1986: B1). Instead of renaming an existing street, Quinn suggested that a new street offered the opportunity to honor King without the problems of renaming an existing street. The controversy led to a proposition the following year, and voters favored Market Street over King Way.

In his interpretation of these events, Reverend Smith believed that race, not economics, drove the effort to overturn the council decision to rename the street. He declared, "I know bigotry. . . . This was a hurt to the Black community" (Mills and Bunyi 2000: 6). A 1989 effort to rename the San Diego Convention Center after King also failed, but in 1991 the city council voted to name a promenade to commemorate King. The CCDC built a narrow park and walkway called King Promenade along the southern part of the Marina District, just across from the convention center (Griffin and Nelson 2000). The King Promenade is tucked away from major pedestrian thoroughfares, and as with the plaque to honor the Douglas Hotel, most who pass it are unaware of its existence. As Fahari Jeffers, one of the supporters of the effort to rename Market Street and the convention center explained, "Because of the grandeur of Market Street, it seemed appropriate to pay homage to a grand human being with grand ideas. He was not just a black civil rights leader, but was a human rights leader for everyone. . . . The promenade is beautiful, and the intentions of building it are honorable, but unfortunately, it falls short of the mark" (Griffin and Nelson 2000: E1).

Carrol Waymon, a sociology professor at San Diego Mesa College, has been an outspoken critic of race relations in the city. In 1968, serving as chair of the city's Citizen's Interracial Committee, he called the city the "Mississippi of the West" because of the disparities in income between African Americans and whites, high levels of housing segregation, inequality in the public schools, and employment discrimination (Waugh 1968: 5). In July 1992, several months after the April 29, 1992, "not guilty" verdict of the Los Angeles police officers who were video-taped beating motorist Rodney King, which triggered the city's civil unrest and reminded the nation of the persistence of racial problems in the West, Waymon talked about racial discrimination in San Diego. Speaking about the slow rate of progress, Waymon said, "I used to call San Diego the Mississippi of the West, but I don't use that name any more. Mississippi is ahead of San Diego in many respects—including the employment of blacks and their involvement in govern-ment" (Lau 1992: B1). Noting the problems that African Americans continue to face in the city, Waymon stated, "Just look around and see where the blacks live. . . . Look at the incidents of cross-burnings. . . . The conditions that made for the explosions in Los Angeles are right here at our doorstep" (Lau 1992: B1).

Given the lack of support by San Diego's mainstream institutions for Afri-can American issues, the African American community needed to lead the effort for historic preservation of African American structures. African Americans in San Diego achieved a fair record of electoral success, a much stronger history of political power than Asian Americans. Since the election of Leon Williams in 1969, African Americans have elected a steady stream of representatives to the San Diego City Council, a much more successful record than the lone election of Tom Hom in the 1960s for Asian Americans. San Diego uses a district rather than an at-large election system, with the city divided up into eight districts. At about the time that the city demolished the Douglas Hotel, the 1990 African American population in the county was 159,306, compared to 19,686 for Chi-nese Americans (APALC 2005: 5), and African American community activism was focused on economic development, public education, political empower-ment, and employment issues in southeast San Diego, the contemporary center of the African American population.

Focused on southeast San Diego, African Americans did not use their polit-ical capital on downtown historic preservation in the 1980s, according to Larry

Malone, who was the community program director for the San Diego Historical Society when the Douglas Hotel was slated for demolition. He explained, "No one was really advocating at that time and historical preservation was just taking off. No individual or groups organized. We lost a jewel" (Saito 2003a).

Karen Huff and the Gaslamp Black Historical Society

As with Malone, San Diego resident Karen Huff believed that the failure to save the Douglas Hotel resulted from a lack of knowledge about local history. Huff explained that "San Diego itself didn't know much about historic preservation until the 1970s, and clearly by the 1980s there was not any movement in the black community in preserving historic sites. . . . There was no organization" (Bradley 2001). This changed, however, when Karen Huff helped establish the Gaslamp Black Historical Society in 1999 to prevent the further loss of downtown's African American history.

The GBHS's brochure states that the organization's "mission is to preserve, protect, interpret, and restore the historic Harlem of the West" (Gaslamp Black Historical Society, n.d. (a), n.p.). Huff explained her motivation for creating the organization: "The Douglas Hotel was black-owned and it was a beautiful structure where all the top jazz acts played. Once I heard that it was being torn down, I couldn't believe it. . . . I promised myself that I would become involved in the community to prevent the loss of other black historical sites in San Diego County" (Bunch 1994: 3). Huff co-authored a February 2000 proposal submitted to the CCDC requesting that the city recognize the importance of downtown's African American history, stating:

> (a) the City of San Diego, and the Centre City Development Corporation should recognize the contributions of Blacks to the development of the Gaslamp/ Stingaree districts, (b) [create] a CCDC committee working in conjunction with the Gaslamp Black Historical Society's preservation and restoration efforts, (c) assist with, and allow for, the creation of a museum in the spirit of the Harlem of the West. (Huff et al. 2000: 2)

The proposal repeatedly stated that the city should follow the precedent established by the creation of the Asian Pacific Thematic Historic District and similarly recognize African American history: "The Gaslamp Black Historical Society is seeking similar acceptance and accommodations from CCDC on behalf of the Black community" (Huff et al. 2000: 7). As a critical first step, the proposal requested that the CCDC fund a study of the history of African Americans in the area, just as the CCDC had done for Asian Americans in 1994. A study would provide important historical information and would serve to show the city's recognition of the importance of this history. The proposal stated that "in order to prevent further destruction . . . CCDC must immediately provide for a historical study of the Harlem of the West district. Similar to the series of studies conducted by CCDC to identify historic properties within the China Town area. CCDC, and the City of San Diego must admit and recognize the contributions of Blacks to the developments of the Gaslamp/Stingaree districts, similar to its recognition of the contributions of Asians and Pacific Islanders" (Huff et al. 2000: 10).

The proposal also stressed the economic benefits of such a district, noting that in the past, "urban renewal [was used] for tearing down and erasing its Black culture sites" but that currently "worlds of changes have swept across this nation in recent years whereby the advantages of recognizing the contributions of Blacks to the development of American cities have proven to be an economic boom, enhancing the flavor of a particular historic area" (Huff et al. 2000: 8). Huff and colleagues pointed out that "Memphis, Tennessee . . . with its focus and redevelopment of Beale Street as the Blues-Mecca is attracting valuable tax dollars to the city" and that "other cities like Atlanta, Chicago, Detroit, and even Boise, Idaho are reclaiming and restoring their Black Cultural Sites" (Huff et al. 2000: 8–9).

African Americans in the United States: Cultural Tourism and Economic Redevelopment

The Huff et al. (2000) document reflects a growing trend in cities that have recognized the economic importance of cultural tourism. Large multiracial and international cities such as New York and San Francisco have marketed their ethnic communities as well as their well-established traditional cultural offerings, such as art museums, live theater, and music performances. In her analysis of tourism and Harlem, Lily M. Hoffman (2003: 291) points out that the state of New York went from its "anti-urban" "'I love NY' campaign in 1977," which featured "parks and waterfalls," to the celebration of Harlem in guides and websites since 2000. The Harlem renaissance established the community as the nation's center of African American cultural life in the early twentieth century, forever giving it "mythic stature as the cradle of black culture," and performance landmarks such as the Apollo Theater remain intact (Taylor 2002: x). Acknowledging Harlem's significance, San Diego's Douglas Hotel was locally known as "the Harlem of the West" during its heyday.[4]

Although cultural tourism and historic preservation are gaining in importance today, Clarence Stone's (1989) study of politics in Atlanta suggests two reasons that community residents did not mobilize to save historic structures in the past. First, Stone (1989) describes how white business and political leaders joined with African American leaders—especially after African Americans became the majority population, according to the 1970 census—to form a coalition that steered city politics. Stone (1989) points out that African American leaders supported economic development policies pushed by Atlanta's growth machine because their support and involvement in the alliance directly resulted in tangible gains in the form of employment and contract opportunities for African Americans.

Second, resonating with Reverend George Walker Smith's disregard for the history of San Diego's Douglas Hotel, Andrew Young, an African American who was Atlanta's mayor during the 1980s, was concerned about how development expressed the present and future of the city, not the past, which Young thought of as part of the South's Jim Crow era. As Stone explained, Young suggested that "preservationists should 'find a way to make decisions in such a way that if a developer wanted to come in and do something that might be expressive of the new wealth we have in Atlanta right now, that we can create a history of the golden age of integration and development, rather than preserving the old days of segregation and poverty'" (Stone 1989: 130).

Historic preservation was not a primary goal of Atlanta's political elite, but nonetheless in 1980 a national historic site was established around Auburn Avenue in the city. The site recognized the African American community that developed in the area in the early 1900s as well as the birthplace of Martin Luther King Jr. and the Ebenezer Baptist Church, where King served as co-pastor with his father in the last years of the junior King's life (NPS 2003). In its heyday as the center of the area's African American residential and business community, *Fortune* magazine labeled Auburn Avenue "the richest Negro street in the world" (Fausset 2006: A18). The area today also contains the Martin Luther King Jr. Center for Nonviolent Social Change and the King tomb.

Unlike San Diego's downtown historic African American area, which has long been abandoned since African Americans moved to southeast San Diego, the area around Auburn Avenue in Atlanta contains a significant African American population. Most of the buildings in the area remain in private hands, and residents and business owners have been divided on redevelopment issues. As Stone (1989) notes, fear of displacement as a result of gentrification was a major

concern for residents and small businesses in the area. Other than the construction and renovation of buildings connected with Martin Luther King Jr., the area
has seen the deterioration of many of its older structures, and new construction
and rehabilitation of buildings is struggling to offset decline in the area.

In contrast to Atlanta's early reluctance to invest in historic preservation
on Auburn Avenue, Birmingham mayors in the 1970s and 1980s embraced the
struggles of the civil rights movement and worked to create the Civil Rights
Cultural District, which includes both historic landmarks, such as Kelly Ingram
Park and the Sixteenth Street Baptist Church, and new institutions. In 1963,
demonstrators used Kelly Ingram Park and the surrounding streets to stage ral-
lies, and scenes of firefighters turning their hoses on demonstrators and of police using their dogs to attack protestors symbolized the virulent racism of the
city. Members of the Ku Klux Klan bombed the Sixteenth Street Baptist Church
in 1963, killing four young girls. Using public funds and private donations, the
city established the Birmingham Civil Rights Institute in 1992. A former United
Nations ambassador and a supporter of civil rights, Andrew Young, although
he did not push for historic preservation as mayor of Atlanta, served as the
keynote speaker at the 1992 dedication (BCRI 2006).[5]

L. Douglas Wilder, former Virginia governor, is working on developing the
National Slavery Museum in Fredericksburg, Virginia. The grandson of slaves,
Wilder began thinking about creating a slavery museum on a 1992 trip to
Africa and a visit to Goree Island, the launching place for many of the slave
ships bound for the Americas (Dunham 2006: 58). About $50 million of the
needed $200 million had been raised by 2006, and Wilder recognizes that for
many individuals and corporations, the issue is a difficult one to support or
connect their name to because it examines a negative rather than a positive aspect of U.S. history. Wilder explains that when possible donors are approached,
"they say: 'it's too sensitive. You're just trying to pull scabs off of old wounds'"
(Dunham 2006: 58). Wilder remembers that his father did not want to discuss
slavery with him. "My father didn't want to talk about it, even though his parents were slaves. My mother had to force him to talk about it. . . . And he would
bite down on his pipe, clench it, and almost snap it in two. And he would tell a
little, and I would ask for more, and he would say: 'I got to go now'" (Dunham
2006: 58). Wilder's plans correspond to the recognition of a growing interest in
tourism connected to history, or heritage tourism, and the increasing amounts
spent by African Americans. As a result, states such as Virginia and Missouri
have specifically targeted African American tourists (Gehlert 2006).[6]

San Diego's Ballpark and the Clermont/Coast Hotel

Concern over new development and historic preservation in Atlanta is echoed in Karen Huff's promise to herself to work against the destruction of San Diego's African American historical sites. In a press conference held by the GBHS on February 28, 2000, Huff explained that the rapid development occurring in downtown San Diego was destroying evidence of the early African American community that was centered in the area north of the ballpark that was then under construction. Huff pointed out that "redevelopment projects, including the ballpark, have eliminated traces of a once-thriving black settlement" (*San Diego Union-Tribune* 2000: B3). Wilma Dockett-McLeod, the GBHS's executive director, explained that the organization was not against the ballpark but hoped that consideration would be given to the area's history: "We do not want to stop the ballpark project; we want to stop the omission" of history (*San Diego Union-Tribune* 2000: B3).

Larry Lucchino, the president of the Padres baseball team, expressed his interest in discussing preservation with the group and developing a project on the history of African Americans. Lucchino stated, "One of the important aspects of this ballpark . . . is that we want to capture the history and heritage of San Diego." Huff was pleased with Lucchino's statement: "It's very positive, and I didn't expect it, to tell you the truth. That lets me know that they're taking it seriously" (*San Diego Union-Tribune* 2000: B3).

Four years later, an exhibit in the ballpark was unveiled, containing items from 1870 to 1910 unearthed in the African American neighborhood during the construction of the ballpark. "Spoons and kettles, jars, brown whiskey bottles, translucent green wine bottles and hair combs" as well as photographs and portions of newspaper articles fill the display cases (Graham 2004: n.p.). Huff noted that it was the "first archaeological display of black history in San Diego" (Graham 2004: n.p.). The Padres had employed archeologists during the construction of the ballpark, and the display cost the team about $50,000. The display is housed in the Western Metals building, an old industrial structure incorporated into the new ballpark. According to Dick Freeman, president of the Padres, "Western Metal has evolved into our showcase of the history of San Diego" (Graham 2004: n.p.).

Members of the GBHS continued to press the city to consider establishing an African American historic district, repeating their argument that the city had already recognized Asian Americans and adding that the establishment of Little Italy just north of downtown recognized Italian Americans.

Acknowledging the cluster of downtown businesses owned by African Americans and catering to an African American clientele in the first half of the twentieth century, Jerry Schaefer, an archeologist working on the ballpark, stated, "Clearly, there is a geographically defined (black) community that existed partly during the Victorian period" (Powell 2000: A1). Angeles Leira, a San Diego city planner, said that the Historical Resources Board would be open to examining a request by the GBHS for a historic district: "It's really exciting to be able to memorialize the way an area has been settled with different waves of immigration. . . . That's truly the story of the United States, and it's a way to develop a truer image of San Diego" (Powell 2000: A1).

The next major battle waged by the GBHS involved the Clermont/Coast Hotel, located at 501 Seventh Avenue, two blocks due north of the new ballpark (see Map 2). Built in 1887 as a lodging house, a century later the hotel served as an aging halfway house that locals expected to be demolished to make way for a parking structure for the new ballpark. In contrast to the absence of any major attempt to support the preservation of the Douglas Hotel, the GBHS intervened in the Historical Resources Board's evaluation of the historical significance of the Clermont/Coast Hotel and successfully lobbied to have the structure added to the list of local historical landmarks in 2001, the first building identified as a local historical landmark associated with African American history. The three-story hotel, with its fifty rooms, currently serves as a residential hotel to low-income renters.

The Historical Resources Board examined the building for historical and/ or architectural significance in 2000, as required by the Centre City Planned District Ordinance for any building listed in a historic site inventory before a permit is issued for alteration or demolition. The CCDC wished to issue a request for proposals for the redevelopment of the site and requested that the Historical Resources Board evaluate the Clermont/Coast Hotel (HRB 2000). The CCDC commissioned Scott Moomjian to conduct a study of the hotel, and Moomjian released his report in July 2000. Moomjian reported that the hotel's name changed repeatedly; first it was called the Occidental, and later, after other names, became known as the Clermont and then the Coast in the 1960s. The 1988 Centre City Historic Survey of the Clermont/Coast Hotel gave the building a "Tentative Rank: 3" (Brandes et al. 1988: 5). Moomjian (2000) referred to the 1988 report and stated that "prior historical research has determined that the Coast Hotel is both historically and architecturally insignificant" (p. 1), explaining that the ranking of 3 "meant that it was not eligible for the local register" (p. 6). Conducting his own research on the hotel, Moomjian (2000) concluded that the hotel was neither historically nor architecturally significant. Moomjian (2000) explained that his research found that "no historical evidence was identified which would support a determination that the Coast Hotel exemplifies or reflects elements of San Diego's, Centre City's, or the 7th Avenue area's historical, archaeological, cultural, social, economic, political, aesthetic, engineering, landscaping or architectural development" (p. 12), and he concluded that "no historically significant events or individuals were ever associated with the Coast Hotel" (p. 15).

The Historical Resources Board considered the designation of the Clermont/Coast Hotel as a historical resource at its July 27, 2000, meeting. The board decided to request that Moomjian conduct further research and respond to questions raised by board members concerning the architectural and social significance of the building, particularly because of its location in an area associated with early African American businesses. Moomjian's second report noted that the GBHS had prepared a "Black Cultural Sites List" and for the Clermont/Coast Hotel, stated that "though never black owned, hotel catered to blacks during era of segregation 1920's–1960's. Hotel's occupants continued to be primarily black until the mid-1980's" (Moomjian 2001: 14).

The studies on the Clermont/Coast Hotel involved researchers who conducted the earlier studies of the Chinese Mission, the Asian Pacific Thematic Historic District, and the archeological survey of the Douglas Hotel. Ray Brandes conducted the 1988 CCDC historic survey, and he was also the person who gave low marks to the Chinese Mission and the idea of a historic district. The 1988 CCDC report, as well as the two Moomjian studies, were affiliated with the law office of Marie Burke Lia. Lia had worked with Brandes on his study of the Chinese Mission and had represented the owner of the mission, Charles Tyson, in his quest to demolish the mission. Lia worked with Moomjian in his study of the Clermont/Coast Hotel and wrote a letter on August 28, 2000, to Karen Huff asking for the GBHS report under preparation on the hotel. Lia wrote that "by referring to this report and other documented sources, we will be able to provide a full, comprehensive history of this resource for designation consideration at the Historical Resources Board's October meeting" (Lia 2000). In a September 6, 2000, letter replying to Lia and Moomjian, Huff declined to supply the report, stating that based on the 2000 Moomjian report, the "interests" of the GBHS were in "direct opposition" to those of Lia and Moomjian and that "preserving the aforementioned structure does not appear to be one of your goals" (Huff 2000).

Although the Clermont/Coast Hotel was associated with African Americans during the period of segregation, that in itself was not important enough for a historic designation according to Moomjian's second report, released February 2001, which confirmed the findings of the first report. The second report (Moomjian 2001) stated that additional research "failed to identify any evidence which would establish that the Coast Hotel was ever important to the San Diego African-American community" (p. 14) and concluded that "no historical evidence was identified which would support a determination that the Coast Hotel is either historically or architecturally significant" (p. 16).

The following month, the Historical Resources Board issued their report, finding that because the building had experienced extensive alterations, it was not architecturally significant. In terms of its historical and social significance, the report acknowledged that similar hotels in the city once served African Americans and that a number of African American–owned businesses and properties previously existed in the area, but no substantial evidence existed that demonstrated the importance of the Clermont/Coast Hotel to the African American community. The report stated that the hotel did not meet the criteria for historical designation, explaining that "although staff recognizes from the record and additional studies that hotels of this type did play a significant role in providing housing for African-Americans and there is information available to point to a number of African-American owned properties in the general area, there is no clear or specific evidence on the record of the role of this particular hotel in serving the African-American community" (HRB 2001: 3).

Karen Huff, representing the GBHS, researched and wrote the August 2001 report, "Hotel for Colored People (A Supplemental Assessment to the Clermont/Coast Hotel)" (Huff 2001a), that acted as the catalyst for the reversal of the Historical Resources Board's assessment of the hotel. Before the report, the GBHS had not expressed a keen interest in the hotel, noting in their list of black cultural sites (Gaslight Black Historical Society, n.d. [b]) that the Coast Hotel was "never black owned," but the GBHS did point out that the "hotel catered to blacks during era of segregation 1920's–1960's. Hotel's occupants continued to be primarily black until the mid-1980's."

An early February 2001 letter from Karen L. Huff to Beverly Schroeder, a CCDC senior planner, revealed the mixed assessment of the hotel by the GBHS. In the letter, Huff explained that because GBHS board members were organizing the first "Harlem of the West Fest," a musical event, and were attempting to develop a museum, the GBHS "board elected not to pursue the Coast Hotel as a black historic site at this time," but "CCDC is respectfully put on notice that the Coast Hotel does in fact have a connection to the historic black community." The letter ended by saying that "in any event GBHS's interest in preserving the Coast Hotel is marginal" (Huff 2001b).

Huff's realization of the historical importance of the Coast Hotel occurred when she came across an advertisement for the hotel in a mid-1950s San Diego County telephone directory. An enlarged photocopy of the advertisement appeared on the cover of Huff's August 2001 report, stating that the hotel was "COLORED" (see Figure 4). According to Huff's report, the Clermont/Coast Hotel was historically significant because it was "the very first hotel in San Diego County to be officially recognized as segregated or 'colored only'" (Huff 2001a: 10). Huff pointed out in her report that unlike the Douglas Hotel, which allowed both African Americans and whites to rent rooms, the Clermont/Coast Hotel served only African Americans. Huff explained that "whites generally respected black-owned segregated hotels and steered clear of them whenever possible. To assist with this process, black owned or operated hotels like the Clermont were promoted as Colored, Colored Only" (Huff 2001a: 11).

Huff discovered through her research that Eugene and Mamie Deburn bought the hotel around 1922, and as Huff explained, "A black owned or operated hotel in San Diego recognized as 'black only' was unique" (Huff 2001a: 11). Huff noted that Charles T. Robinson bought the hotel in 1938 and that in 1945 the hotel became a black-segregated hotel; in 1945 the Clermont "was officially

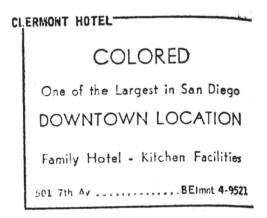

Figure 4 Clermont/Coast Hotel advertisement from the San Diego County Telephone Directory Yellow Pages (1957, p. 244).

identified as 'A Hotel for Colored People'" according to the county telephone directory advertisements (Huff 2001a: 13).

Some of the hotel's famous guests included the jazz luminaries Jelly Roll Morton and Charlie Parker (Huff 2001a). As a "family hotel" with "kitchen facilities," plus a tiny cafeteria offering its specialty of "fried chicken with rice & gravy," Huff (2001a: 13) noted that entertainers traveling with family members often stayed there. With declining segregation and the movement of African Americans out of downtown to southeast San Diego, the popularity of the place faded by 1960 (Huff 2001a).

The Historical Resources Board responded quickly to Huff's (2001a) latest report, and in a report dated September 6, 2001, used Huff's findings as the basis for recommending a city historical landmark designation for the hotel. The report summarized the history of the area, stating that in the "early 1900's the area around the hotel became settled by African Americans" and that in "the 1920's the area immediately surrounding the hotel was settled by numerous businesses owned by African Americans" (HRB 2001: 3). The report concluded that "based on the new information submitted by the Gaslamp Black Historical Society staff believes that the Clermont/Coast Hotel is a significant structure reflective of the African American settlement in central San Diego, and a documented remnant of the area's segregated era of development from 1920 to 1960" (HRB 2001: 4) (Figure 5).

Huff explained that the CCDC consultants "didn't look hard enough" for evidence about the hotel's past, missing what she found in phone directories (Millican 2001: B1). The advertisements listing the hotel as "Colored," Huff argued, were the evidence needed to counter the claims of those who had downplayed the existence of racial segregation in the city's history. Huff stated that the "Coast Hotel finally puts a face on segregation" and that when "you see the big ad in the Yellow Pages saying, 'hotel for colored people,' it really hits home" (Millican 2001: B1).

A *San Diego Union-Tribune* reporter asked Huff if preserving reminders of racial segregation merely serves to revive unpleasant memories of the past. In contrast to Andrew Young's focus on Atlanta's future rather than the past and its connections with discrimination, Huff explained that segregation was an important part of African American history and symbols of that history should be preserved. As with Doug Wilder's work to start a slavery museum and research center, Huff explained, "We preserve plantations, which were basically camps for breeding human beings. . . . We preserve those and have tourists

Figure 5 Exterior of the Clermont/Coast Hotel at the northeast corner of Seventh Avenue and Island Avenue, 2007. Photograph by author.

come through them. Likewise, with this, you are preserving it just to say, 'Hey, this is the way it was.' This hotel was a part of that, and we must recognize that." Scott Moomjian, the CCDC consultant, stated that the hotel was important if it was indeed the first segregated hotel in the city: "In my opinion, if further research is conducted and the Clermont was one of the first for colored people, as opposed to being one of the first advertised, I do happen to believe there is a great potential for significance" (Millican 2001: B1).

The former industrial and warehouse neighborhood containing the Clermont/Coast Hotel, with its large share of homeless people and social service providers, was renamed the East Village by the city as part of a drive to improve the image of the area. The CCDC planned for a mixed-use residential community with commercial and office space; to encourage families, the CCDC offered builders incentives to add a third bedroom to residential developments and planned for new parks (Kirkpatrick 2006). Property owners, residents, and merchants created the East Village Association in the early 1990s, and as the spokesperson for the organization explained, "We try to be eyes and ears for the citizens of the neighborhood and have been fairly active in trying to shape redevelopment policy" (Kirkpatrick 2006). The area was undergoing a major transformation with the construction of the ballpark, and condominiums in the new luxury hotel built adjacent to the ballpark, just several blocks south of the Clermont/Coast Hotel, had sold for $1.2–$9 million in 2004 (Engle 2004).

Because of the deterioration of the hotel's physical structure, the owners of the hotel opposed the historical landmark designation. As Arturo Zepeda (Millican 2001: B1), one of the owners, explained, "I have trouble with the concept of trying to preserve an eyesore. . . . It's a halfway house. . . . This building looks nothing like it did in its heyday." The East Village Association also voiced their concern about the poor condition of the building, stating that it served as "a magnet for undesirables" (Heller 2001: B1). Leslie Wade, spokesperson for the East Village Association, expressed opposition to the designation, explaining, "It's a wretched building in every way" (Heller 2001: B1). Five years later, Wade would repeat her concerns about housing for the poor, stating that "one of the problems we've had is trying to make sure we don't have a concentration of the very low-income housing in that area. . . . We don't want to look back in 20 years and see we created a ghetto" (Kirkpatrick 2006).

The characterization of the Clermont/Coast Hotel as an eyesore by Zepeda and as a wretched building by Wade echoed the remarks of Charles Tyson (1987: 2), the owner of the Chinese Mission who had argued that the mission was "a vandalized shell, the condition of which fails to do justice to the integrity of the congregation's history." Wade's concern about creating a ghetto can also be interpreted in racial terms because the word *ghetto* is often applied to low-income African American communities. In terms of the physical condition of the structures, the descriptions were accurate. Missing in these assessments, however, was an evaluation or appreciation of the social significance of the structures. Although the *Voice and Viewpoint* (Picou 1996: C9) referred to the 1950s Douglas Hotel as a "flophouse," the newspaper went beyond the physical condition of the hotel and recognized its historical importance.

On December 20, 2001, the day of the Historical Resources Board meeting to decide on the local historical landmark designation of the Clermont/Coast Hotel, the GBHS staged a demonstration in front of the hotel. A group of about thirty people shouted "Save our history" and "Keep these walls up" and then marched to City Hall for the Historical Resources Board meeting (Heller 2001: B1). At the meeting, a discussion occurred when city consultants contended that "colored" could have meant "Latino, Chinese, or other non-whites" (Heller

2001: B1). Carrol Waymon, the former professor at Mesa College who grew up in the community and called the city the "Mississippi of the West" back in 1968, refuted the claim that "colored" meant non–African Americans in the context of the Clermont/Coast Hotel. Waymon explained, "I was born in a colored society and reared in a colored community where we had colored hotels. . . . Everything was colored." Recognizing the research carried out by the GBHS and strong community support for the issue, the Historical Resources Board voted unanimously in favor of the historic designation.

In November 2005 the city placed a bronze plaque on the front of the hotel, proclaiming the historic status of the building. The building's new owners—Anthony Laureti, Larry Sidiropoulos, and Ashley Abamo—paid for the plaque and the installation (Stolz 2005: B3). The plaque states, "In 2001, the Clermont/Coast Hotel became the first building ever designated an African American site in San Diego. Preserved for its association with the era of racial segregation, it was one of the largest 'colored' hotels in downtown San Diego." Unlike the lack of widespread interest for the preservation of the Douglas Hotel, a number of city officials and civic leaders, such as Reverend George Walker Smith and former city council member George Stevens, who had represented the large African American constituency in southeast San Diego, showed their support for the historic designation and attended the unveiling of the plaque (Stolz 2005).

Documenting African American History

The GBHS's efforts convinced the CCDC to put out a "request for qualifications for historic consultant services" regarding a study of African American history in downtown San Diego. In 2002, the CCDC selected Mooney and Associates, a local planning and environmental studies firm, to carry out the research. The staff of Mooney and Associates worked to involve the San Diego African American community and contacted individuals and members of religious and civic organizations, such as the African-American Genealogical Association, the Catfish Club, and the Irving Jacobs Center, for interviews and their observations on the structures and sites that should be included in the study. These community contacts facilitated the collection of information and artifacts, such as "family histories, anecdotes, memories, and even photographs and documents" (Carrico and Jordan 2004: IV-1). The staff also examined the holdings of San Diego sources, such as the Historical Society, the County Tax Assessor's Office, the County Recorder's Office, and the County Superior Court. Other sources included the Sanborn Fire Insurance Map Collection, the National Archives at the Laguna Niguel Branch, and the Bancroft Library at the University of California, Berkeley. A final report was submitted to the CCDC in June 2004. With the identification and background of downtown buildings connected to African American history, the report was a critical first step toward preservation efforts and the establishment of an African American historic district.[7]

The Mooney report recommended that the area circumscribed by "F Street, 2nd Street, 17th Street, and Island Avenue and Commercial Street" (Carrico and Jordan 2004: VI-1) could be the basis for an African American Historic District (see Map 2). The majority of the structures were built in the 1880s through the 1920s, with the African American community's strongest presence in the first half of the twentieth century. The report described twenty-one structures that no longer exist and sixteen extant structures (although one has been demolished since the report's publication), including hotels, such as the Clermont/Coast Hotel; buildings that once housed African American–owned businesses, such as the Crossroad Tavern, formerly one of the city's major jazz clubs; and social centers, such as the Coliseum Federal Athletic Club (Carrico and Jordan 2004: VI-3).

The Mooney report concludes that the area "represents the surviving remnants and sites of the core of the city's downtown African-American community between 1900 and 1960. . . . Reflecting the residential, commercial, and institutional development of San Diego's African-American community, the buildings that comprise the district testify to the strong heritage and vibrant life of this once-thriving area." In its section on recommendations, the Mooney report proposes that "possibilities to explore include . . . [preserving] the major significant buildings within the areas designated as the thematic district. This could include all of the buildings listed as important and significant in the previous section" (Carrico and Jordan 2004: VII-1).

Of the Douglas Hotel, the Mooney report recognized the structure's central role in the social life of that era and concluded that "subsequently, the demolition of the Douglas Hotel came to symbolize the loss of structures and places representative of the downtown African-American community" (Carrico and Jordan 2004: V-45). Although the Douglas Hotel served as the primary symbol of the city's African American population in the historic core, the block containing the hotel was part of an area that had an even longer history as an African American neighborhood. As far back as 1887, the area contained residences and businesses that served the African American community, including a bar, a boarding house, and a billiards parlor (Carrico and Jordan 2004: V-40).

The Historical Resources Board held a public hearing on January 25, 2007, to discuss the adoption of the Mooney report for use by the city during the planning process as the basis for identifying historically significant properties affiliated with the African American community. As the report on the matter states, "An adopted survey would enable CCDC and HRB staff to identify significant sites during project review and to bring them to the HRB for individual designation proceedings" (HRB 2007: 5). The Historical Resources Board report recommended the adoption of the Mooney report and recognized the importance of the sites documented in the Mooney report and the number of sites already destroyed. The report explained that

> it is clear that the total sum of these resources reflects a strong association with broad and important patterns in national, state and local history. Because so many of the sites relating to the African American experience downtown have been demolished, the value of the remaining sites is heightened. Protecting them from adverse change through the adoption of the survey for planning purposes is of utmost importance. (HRB 2007: 5)

The Historical Resources Board report also stated that a "heritage walking tour and/or a plaque program" could be developed using the twenty-one sites listed in the Mooney report, although a historical district would require further discussion with property owners about the implications of such a designation as well as additional study of the general public interest in the establishment of such a district (HRB 2007: 5). By a unanimous vote, the members of the Historical Resources Board voted to adopt the Mooney report (HRB 2007).[8]

Conclusion: The Douglas and Clermont/Coast Hotels and the Chinese Mission

Although government policies since the 1960s have shifted away from supporting explicitly race-based inequality exemplified by urban renewal's "Negro Removal," race-neutral policies can lead to racialized results, as demonstrated by economic redevelopment and historic preservation policies in San Diego. The city's list of significant historic sites in 1986 did not include the Chinese Mission, the Douglas Hotel, or the Clermont/Coast Hotel. In fact, sites related to African Americans were completely absent from the list until community activists led a successful effort to include the Clermont/Coast Hotel in 2001, and relatively few sites related to Asian Americans were on the list until a campaign by Chinese Americans led to the addition of the Chinese Mission and other buildings and the designation of the Asian Pacific Thematic Historic District in the newly revitalized downtown.

The growth machine and the pursuit of profits threatened all historic structures as the urban core was remade into a corporate and entertainment center, but the experiences of African Americans and Chinese Americans demonstrated that the standard institutional processes involving historic designation in the city tended to overlook the history of racial minorities. It was not as though the Chinese Mission, the Douglas Hotel, and the Clermont/Coast Hotels faced destruction because they sat unnoticed and ignored in the rush to revitalize the area. The city commissioned formal studies on all three structures, and the studies concluded that the buildings were not architecturally or historically significant, a common finding for buildings related to racial minorities, as the 1986 list of historic structures makes clear. Although the study of the Douglas Hotel recognized the building as the preeminent social center for African Americans in the city in the pre–World War II period, this history was not considered sufficient grounds for preserving the building. As a result, the standard city procedures for redevelopment and historic preservation led to the demolition of the Douglas Hotel. As Larry Malone of the city's historical society noted, and the Mooney report confirmed, "We lost a jewel." As the struggles over the Chinese Mission and the Clermont/Coast Hotel illustrate, however, destruction was not inevitable; community members entered the redevelopment process and contested the images and historic value attached to these structures.

The CCDC's (1984) evaluation of the Douglas Hotel duplicated the justification of urban renewal projects that in an earlier era wiped out many ethnic communities, stating that "the block is extremely blighted" (p. 2). Galvanized by the destruction of the Douglas Hotel, African American activists used the successful effort to save the Chinese Mission and establish the Asian Pacific Thematic Historic District as a model for their campaign to conduct research to discover and preserve the remaining downtown buildings connected to African American history.

The San Diego cases illustrate a range of issues in the struggle over historic preservation. First, the effort by activists to create organizations that could serve to mobilize community members, raise funds, and lobby city officials proved to be a key factor in the successful efforts to save the Chinese Mission and the Clermont/Coast Hotel. Establishing the San Diego Chinese Historical Society and the Gaslamp Black Historical Society provided crucial support for the preservation efforts.

Second, as part of this effort, activists needed to educate and mobilize members of their community about historic preservation. As Larry Malone described the situation concerning the Douglas Hotel, the African American community was not involved in historic preservation at that time. Similarly, the Chinese Mission sat empty and in a state of disrepair, with the owner planning to demolish it. Dorothy and Tom Hom had gained experience in historic preservation, but it was through their work on the Gaslamp District, not with Chinese American structures. With an organized community effort, members of city agencies could be lobbied and educated about the historic importance of structures that did not receive recognition through the standard city evaluation process and about how such structures could contribute to the cultural value of the downtown area.

Third, the global mobility of capital and the potential for particular groups to attract international capital served to differentiate the tactics of Chinese Americans and African Americans. Although the presence of Chinese Americans and Chinatowns is seen as a potential draw for Chinese capital from the growing economies of China and Taiwan, as is the case in such cities as Vancouver, Toronto, New York, San Francisco, and Los Angeles, a similar situation does not exist for African capital. Clearly, Harlem has drawn capital investment, but Harlem is unique because of its historical claim as the nation's center of African American culture. As a result, the Gaslamp Black Historical Society focused on history and tourism rather than on any claims to attracting international capital investment.

Fourth, Asian American communities and commercial centers are seen as "foreign," and the ordinary inhabitants and everyday businesses of Chinatowns have been transformed in the opinion of the general public from "slums" to "exoticized" places of tourism (Lin 1995, 1998). In contrast, African Americans must contend with images of the "underclass" and crime-ridden "ghettos." Unlike the situation of Asian Americans, there is no model minority image that can serve as a counter. I suggest that African American neighborhoods have not achieved the transformation from "ghetto" to tourist site, as have Chinatowns. The ordinary inhabitants and everyday businesses of African American communities are not seen as contributors to tourism, as those of Chinese Americans are. Tourist destinations linked to African Americans are generally connected to major cultural and historical events— for example, Harlem and its status as the center of African American culture and the history of the Harlem renaissance, Memphis and blues music, Atlanta and the civil rights movement and Martin Luther King Jr., and the effort to establish a National Slavery Museum.

Finally, African Americans have achieved success in San Diego electoral politics, far outpacing Asian Americans in terms of elected officials, but the results of this effort have largely focused on southeast San Diego, where African Americans are concentrated today. Only recently, with the establishment of the Gaslamp Black Historical Society, have African Americans turned to the issue of historical preservation in the downtown area.

The successful efforts to save the Chinese Mission and the Clermont/Coast Hotel and the ongoing struggle to recognize African and Asian American history in San Diego's downtown area do nothing to change the overall growth machine strategy. These struggles are significant, however, because they attempt to prevent the removal of history and to reinsert a physical, cultural, and economic presence from their respective communities in the core of the city by contesting accepted notions of what is historically significant. At a time when city agencies are using millions of public dollars to rebuild and reshape downtown, the question is, Who benefits from redevelopment? This question clearly has class dimensions, as the benefits flow to downtown property owners and business interests rather than to low-income communities, but it has racial implications as well, as cities decide which parts of their histories will be preserved and celebrated.

4 Asian Americans and Multiracial Political Coalitions

New York City's Chinatown and Redistricting

REDISTRICTING IS THE REDRAWING of political district lines following each decennial census to reflect changes in population; the U.S. Constitution requires that districts be equal in population. Redistricting provides a unique opportunity to examine the relationship between race and politics because the 1965 Voting Rights Act requires the recognition and protection of the political rights of ethnic and racial minorities. As part of this process, however, a group must establish that it is a "community of interest," which is a population with shared social, economic, and/or political concerns (Feng et al. 2002; Hum 2002). This requirement compels groups that advocate for the use of race as a factor in redistricting to publicly and explicitly explain the political significance of race. Racial minority groups attempt to participate in the redistricting process because, historically, redistricting has often resulted in the fragmentation of their population into separate districts, diluting their political power.

An extraordinary opportunity for Asian Americans in New York City presented itself in 1990: the first redistricting that would occur after the 1989 change in the city charter that required an increase in the number of city council districts to enhance the political representation of minorities. Equally important, this round of redistricting followed the 1990 *Garza v. Los Angeles County Board of Supervisors* court decision, in which a federal court ruled in favor of the Latino plaintiffs (Kousser 1999). This ruling emphasized the political rights of racial minorities and the prevention of vote dilution. Following the court decision, the Los Angeles County supervisory districts were redrawn. Gloria Molina won the election in the district created to consolidate Latino voting strength, demonstrating the importance of how district lines are drawn. Molina was the first Latino elected to serve on the board in 115 years.[1] This convergence of advantageous factors would end several years later with U.S. Supreme Court redistricting decisions that would reduce the importance of race in redistricting.

Using information on the New York City council redistricting in the Chinatown area that took place in 1990 and 1991 and the elections that followed, I examine the dialogue among community activists as they debated their options when faced with district population requirements and the need to add neighboring areas. The proposals that emerged offered two distinct scenarios: linking Chinatown with middle-class whites to the west and south and taking advantage of past electoral support for Asian American candidates, or joining with predominantly working-class Latinos and African Americans to the east and north based on a history of multiracial grassroots political alliances.

The key issue that distinguishes the 1990 New York City council redistricting process from the San Diego economic redevelopment and historic preservation cases discussed in the previous chapters is that race explicitly framed the redistricting. This framework was based on the 1990 *Garza* decision, successful lawsuits brought by Latino and African American plaintiffs that led to an increased number of city council districts, and the active involvement of African American, Asian American, and Latino community groups from the start of the public hearing process. The multiracial members of the Districting Commission controlled the redistricting process, and it was their analysis and understanding of race and electoral politics that ultimately determined district boundaries. I argue that by creating a district that linked Chinatown with white neighborhoods and rejecting the proposed minority district that would have joined Chinatown with the Latino and African American Lower East Side, the commissioners viewed whites as a race-neutral group that would recognize the need for Asian American representation and would elect an Asian American council member. In contrast, commissioners viewed Asian Americans and Latinos as racial groups focused on racial representation and ignored the long history of whites working to disenfranchise minorities to preserve white power. When race was invoked by minorities during the redistricting hearings held by the Districting Commission, it was not a "biological" identity that was being referenced but rather an identity that incorporated the historical and contemporary experiences of a racial group in the United States, precisely what was ignored or misinterpreted by policymakers.

Changing Demographics in the United States and Race Relations

The Asian American population has grown rapidly across the United States, with 12.4 million, or 4.3 percent, in 2005, according to the U.S. Census Bureau (2006) estimate. However, even the major Asian American urban concentrations outside Hawaii are too small to form the majority of voters within electoral districts and to elect candidates without crossover votes. Therefore developing alliances with other groups is a crucial issue for Asian American political power, which raises the question, What forms the foundation for political alliances with other racial minorities and/or whites? Elevating the importance of this issue, the populations of major U.S. urban areas changed dramatically with the immigration of individuals from Asia, Latin America, and the Caribbean in the last several decades.

In changing from white-majority to "majority-minority" cities, demographic restructuring creates new possibilities in terms of the construction of multiracial alliances and growing power among disenfranchised minorities. At the same time, however, whites, as voters and elected officials, continue as the major political force in these regions, although that position is shifting with the growing electoral power of minorities.

Alliances among racial minorities have a long history as the "politics of prejudice" (Daniels 1974), and explicitly racialized government policies became embedded in economic, political, and social relations and channeled Asian Americans, Latinos, African Americans, and Native Americans into similar occupational, residential, and political urban spaces, creating common interests and concerns (De Genova 2006; Lipsitz 2006). In 1949, for example, Mexican American Edward Roybal used a grassroots alliance composed of Latinos, African Americans, Asian Americans, and whites to become the first Latino Los Angeles city council member in the twentieth century (Underwood 1992).

Racial minorities joining with whites to gain political incorporation is one of the dominant themes of contemporary urban politics (Browning et al. 1984, 1990, 2003), and it is based on a shared ideology of social justice, as in the civil rights movement (Morris 1984), or on the convergence of interests, such as Jews and African Americans joining to supplant entrenched white conservatives in the election of African American Tom Bradley as the mayor of Los Angeles in 1973 (Sonenshein 1993). The class and ideological divisions generated by the experience of new Asian immigrants and the problems that these divisions create for a coalition model were clearly demonstrated by the boycott of Korean stores by African Americans in Brooklyn in 1990 and the 1992 civil unrest in Los Angeles in which African Americans and Latinos targeted Korean immigrant entrepreneurs (Abelmann and Lie 1995; Kim 2000; Park and Park 2001). Antonio Villaraigosa had strong support from all racial groups in his 2005 Los Angeles mayoral victory, in which he defeated a white liberal incumbent, James Hahn. Although Villaraigosa's victory suggests broader support for candidates of color, the New York City Chinatown case reveals some of the limits of white crossover voting for minority candidates.

Asian Americans and Multiracial Alliances

The spatial representation of race in the form of residential segregation and the possibility of creating districts with race as a factor are the direct result of the history of economic, political, and social discrimination faced by racial minorities. These practices have been assisted by massive government subsidies and support for zoning and by financial policies that generated and supported segregated communities (Dreier et al. 2001; Jackson 1985; Massey and Denton 1993). The expression of that position through residential segregation patterns—with Asian Americans, Latinos, and African Americans facing greater levels of segregation, in that order (Logan 2001; Logan et al. 1996)—has literally positioned Asian Americans between whites and other racial minorities in metropolitan areas throughout the United States, such as Los Angeles and New York.

Crafting a district while considering the heterogeneity within Chinatown and the varied relations that Asian Americans have with other racial minorities and whites were dominant issues in the redistricting deliberations. Recognition of the importance of white-on-black oppression in the formation of the U.S. racial framework (Feagin 2006) has led to a growing debate over the position of Asian Americans within that structure (De Genova 2006; Park and Park 1999; Tuan 1998; Wu 2002). One discussion of Asian Americans as "between black and white" proposes that Asian Americans might become the next "whites" in order to preserve and maintain the cultural and political primacy of whites (Gans 1994) or to recognize the impressive economic gains made by Asian Americans and their depiction as a model minority. In contrast, others maintain that historical and contemporary patterns of discrimination continue to position Asian Americans as a racialized minority, generating shared experiences with other minorities (Lien 2001; Lowe 1996).

Clearly, the shared history of such issues as residential segregation, political disenfranchisement, and discrimination in the labor market illustrates the fundamental and central forces that operate to generate common experiences as racialized minorities that transcend group boundaries. At the same time, however, lumping all racial minorities together obscures the historical and contemporary circumstances that generate significant differences among the experiences of racial minorities (De Genova 2006). For example, although U.S. government practices have actively worked to disenfranchise and subjugate all minorities, African Americans experienced the power of the state through such policies as slavery and Jim Crow laws, Mexican Americans in the Southwest bore the loss of land following the Mexican American War and were forceably repatriated in the 1930s and 1950s, Native Americans suffered genocide, Asian immigrants were denied the right to naturalization, and people of Japanese ancestry were incarcerated during World War II. In addition, although the U.S. black-white racial framework and the fundamental ways in which racialization as minorities links the experiences of minorities are recognized, factors such as nativism and U.S. military incursions in Asia produce meaningful differences in the lived experiences of individuals at the neighborhood level for particular groups (Ancheta 1998; Okihiro 1994).

My focus in the New York City case is on relations between Latinos and Asian Americans, the two largest minority groups in Lower Manhattan. Latinos and Asian Americans share factors—such as recent large immigrant populations, a history as laborers in the United States, and their situation as language minorities—that have generated common experiences. Relations between Asian Americans and Latinos have been marked both by alliances, as in labor and the formation of the United Farm Workers by Filipinos and Mexicans in California (Almaguer 1994; Ichioka 1988; Scharlin and Villanueva 1992), and by conflict, as in the 1992 outbreak of civil unrest in Los Angeles and the destruction of Korean-owned businesses by Latinos (Navarro 1993).

Chinatown and the Lower East Side

The Lower East Side has historically housed the city's immigrants and working class and has served as the gateway and place of settlement for immigrants restricted by economics or race. Major groups included the Irish and Germans employed in the shipbuilding industry in the mid-1800s, followed by Italians and eastern European Jews in the garment industry in the 1920s; large-scale Puerto Rican migration to New York City was encouraged by labor recruiters in the post–World War II industrial expansion (Baver 1984; Mele 1994).

From the 1820s to the 1870s, Chinese men trickled into New York City, by land from the west and by sea as crew members of ships. Official counts list nineteen Chinese in 1870, with the population expanding rapidly over the next several decades, concentrating in the Chinatown area (Lin 1998). Beginning in the late 1880s, a series of U.S. immigration quotas and exclusionary policies targeting Asians slowed population growth, with the Chinese populace topping 6,000 in 1900 and 33,000 in 1960 (Waldinger and Tseng 1992). Chinese immigration rapidly increased following the Hart-Cellar Act of 1965, which eliminated the restrictive policies. The New York and Los Angeles metropolitan regions topped the list of favored destination points (Fong 1994).

Considering the extreme scarcity of land in lower Manhattan, Chinatown's proximity to the financial district, civic center, and increasingly popular residential and entertainment districts made Chinatown a valuable site for new, upscale development. Growing local and international capital investment by both Chinese and non-Chinese in Chinatown intensified the struggle between members of the growth machine, who view urban centers as places to maximize their real estate investments, and those who use these areas as places of residence, work, recreation, and services and are threatened by such investment (Logan and Molotch 1987). Economic development strategies directed at transforming downtowns into "corporate centers" based on advanced services and entertainment proceed not simply through free market forces but with major support from local and federal government policies (Dreier et al. 2001; Mollenkopf 1983, 1992).

The federal urban renewal program and interstate highway construction of the mid-twentieth century and local infrastructure projects—such as bridges, roads, and parks—established a clear pattern of destruction for Chinatown residents and other minority communities in New York City. These residents have absorbed a disproportionate share of the negative effects of such development, including displacement and the loss of affordable housing and living-wage jobs (Caro 1975; R. Chin 1971; Fitch 1993; Mele 2000; Schwartz 1993; Sites 2003; Smith et al. 1994). Asian Americans in New York City clearly understood the need to gain political power to influence government policies that directly affect economic development, housing, and employment opportunities. However, in contemporary Chinatown, Chinese Americans are active on both sides of the debate—as investors and developers and as working-class residents (Lin 1998).

The transformation and diversification of the economy is indicated by the increasing numbers of overseas and local Chinese banks, office building construction, and professional offices that house law and accounting firms (Hunter

College Neighborhood Planning Workshop 1992; Lin 1998). Rather than simply free market processes at work, however, gentrification of the Lower East Side and Chinatown has progressed with the aid of city government policies that favored and subsidized development, such as tax incentives, zoning variations, loans, and city staff assistance (Sites 1994, 2003).

New York City Redistricting

Districting Commission Hearings

In 1989, prompted by lawsuits charging racial discrimination and violation of the U.S. Constitution, the New York City Charter was amended to increase the number of city council districts from thirty-five to fifty-one, a change intended to increase the political representation of minorities. Working from 1990 to 1991, the Districting Commission created new council districts. As the redistricting process began, no Asian American had ever been elected to the city council or any citywide office. Because Chinatown and the neighboring Lower East Side contained the city's largest concentration of Asian Americans, the area offered the greatest opportunity for Asian American representation.

Significant political change through redistricting appeared possible with the increase in the number of council districts and the judicial climate favoring minority interests after the 1990 *Garza v. Los Angeles County Board of Supervisors* decision. Also, New York City had to submit its plans to the U.S. Department of Justice for preclearance because of procedures used to circumscribe the political participation of racial minorities, such as the use of literacy tests into the 1960s (New York City Districting Commission 1991b). One practical matter that favored minorities was the tremendous growth of the Asian American and Latino populations in the 1980s; and advances in computer hardware and software and the availability of demographic and political data (including a public access terminal provided by the Districting Commission) gave nongovernment groups the ability to carry out sophisticated data analysis.

Asian Americans in New York City directly linked efforts for political representation to local and national experiences of racial exclusion and hierarchy. From the earliest history of the United States, political practices have had racial consequences, particularly in the way such practices have been rooted in privileged access to power, rewards, and opportunities for whites (Lien 2001). During public hearings, Asian Americans enumerated the federal policies and practices that specifically disenfranchised and discriminated against Asian Americans, such as exclusionary immigration laws, the denial of naturalization to early immigrants, the incarceration of Japanese Americans during World War II, and gerrymandered districts. Community activists used the panethnic label "Asian American" when recognizing the common racialization of the diverse Asian ethnic groups and the ethnic-specific term "Chinese American" for particular individuals or events (Aoki 2002; Espiritu 1992; Saito 1998; Vo 1996, 2004).

Speaking at the redistricting public hearings, Rosa Koo (1990), vice president of the New York City chapter of the Organization of Chinese Americans, said:

> Historically, Chinese and Asian Americans have been ignored, misunderstood, discriminated, and denied the right to citizenship. WE are often the forgotten "other" in statistics, and, left UNHEARD outside the door by elected officials and other policy-makers.

Bill Chong, president of Asian Americans for Equality (AAFE), also emphasized the history of disenfranchisement faced by Chinatown residents in his presentation to the Districting Commission. He specifically mentioned the establishment of the Special Manhattan Bridge District without the input of Chinatown residents and the resulting zoning changes that AAFE believed would promote high-priced housing and office buildings in the Chinatown area, leading to "feverish speculation by investors and result[ing] in the displacement of hundreds of Chinatown residents" (AAFE, n.d.: 9–10). Chong (1990) stated:

> In 1981 the people of Chinatown learned a bitter lesson about political representation in our city. It began with a public hearing very much like tonight's at the community room of Hamilton Madison House just a few blocks from here. A special public hearing had been called by the local planning board, and hundreds of angry Chinese residents turned out to protest a controversial zoning plan that had been adopted.
>
> The zoning plan, called the Special Manhattan Bridge District, never had the support of our community. In fact, the community did not even know about the plan until it had been approved by the Board of Estimate. The entire public process had simply passed us by.
>
> A year later, in 1982, that painful experience was again repeated. More than 20,000 Chinese residents marched to the steps of City Hall to protest plans to build another jail in Chinatown. It was one of the largest protests by Asian Americans in recent history. Once again, the protests failed to turn the city's plans around.

Given the increased number of city council districts and the open redistricting hearing process, Chong (1990) expressed his hope for the enfranchisement of Chinatown residents: "After generations of exclusion from the political process, the 1991 election offers the first real hope of meaningful participation for our community."

Speaking before the Districting Commission, Margaret Chin, a city council candidate, F. H. LaGuardia Community College Chinatown Center administrator, and member of AAFE (a Chinatown social service provider), similarly voiced her hopes that the redistricting efforts would end exclusion.

> You have the power in your hands to make the dreams of thousands of . . . Asian American New Yorkers, to come true. . . . These new seats are like sixteen doors of opportunity swinging open for the minority communities of the City. . . . It is the opportunity for real representation for communities that have too long been under represented. (Chin 1990: n.p.)

Creating Chinatown's City Council District

Community activists agreed that uniting Chinatown within one district was the principal goal, ending the fragmentation and dilution of political power that occurred in past redistricting plans. As Margaret Fung, executive director of the Asian American Legal Defense and Education Fund (AALDEF, a New York City legal advocacy organization), explained:

> The voting strength of Chinese Americans has been diluted because Chinatown was divided into two state assembly districts. Moreover, Chinatown has also been split between two community board districts and two school board districts. This . . . has merely reinforced our community's inability to organize and develop a political cohesiveness. (Fung 1990: n.p.)

In developing criteria to define Chinatown, studies presented to the Districting Commission by the New York Chinatown History Project (1990) and AAFE (D. Koo 1990b) focused on population, housing, schools, social services, employment, industry, organizations, and commercial enterprises. The "core of Chinatown" was contained in eight contiguous census tracts (6, 8, 16, 18, 25, 27, 29, and 41), with Asian Americans making up more than 70 percent of the population in that area (D. Koo 1990b). AALDEF (Fung 1991) outlined a similar area.

With a city population of 7,322,564 (25.2 percent African American, 6.7 percent Asian American, 24.4 percent Latino, and 43.2 percent white), according to the 1990 census, each of the fifty-one districts would require a population of 143,579 (compared to 212,000 if there were thirty-five districts). The census counted 62,895 people in the eight tracts containing Chinatown, falling short of the district requirement by approximately 80,000.

The decision over which areas should be added to meet the population requirement was the fundamental issue that divided Chinatown activists. Two competing plans emerged in the debate; they offered contrasting alternatives for Chinatown and its relation to the predominantly Puerto Rican neighborhood to the north and east and to the white areas to the west and south. One plan emphasized "descriptive representation," electing someone with similar characteristics (Pitkin 1967)—in this case, the historic opportunity to elect an Asian American. The other plan supported a multiracial district based on similar political interests generated by the intersection of race, class, and neighborhood issues. The appeals from both groups to the commission went beyond traditional definitions of enfranchisement for racial minorities that focused on citizenship, voter registration, and voter turnout (Thernstrom 1987), and defined political power as the ability to elect officials who could enact policies on behalf of their constituents (Davidson and Grofman 1994; Guinier 1994).

Members of AAFE led the effort for a district based on descriptive representation. An Asian American elected to the council represented a genuine and concrete political gain, not merely a symbolic gesture, such as a city festival for diversity. Members of AAFE characterized redistricting and the upcoming election jointly as a pivotal moment that could mark the end of political exclusion, as Margaret Chin interpreted her reception at a community gathering.

> Close to a 1000 people showed up. . . . I've been to so many political functions . . . when candidates give a speech, there was a lot of noise. But this time . . . there was silence in the room. You could hear a pin drop. What I was talking about was that Chinese immigrants have been here for over a hundred years. When our ancestors came, we came under a lot of pressure from discrimination, oppression. I think for a lot of people in the audience, especially seniors and old timers, it brought out a lot of feelings and experiences with discrimination and lack of representation. This was an opportunity for us to really, finally, have some representation after all these years. In a sense it kind of captured the people's national sentiment. (Saito 1996b)

An Asian American elected official signifies representation in a variety of ways: a co-ethnic with a similar background and knowledge of and support for community issues, a source of political mobility into the mainstream, and a role model. Virginia Kee (1990), president of the Chinese American Planning Council, stated at a public hearing, "As a teacher, I can tell you that our young people must see their own faces in their government. If, in this decade, we are still without representation, then how can this city government work for us?"

Members of AAFE crafted a district where they believed an Asian American could win, using data from a number of elections involving Asian Americans. Because Asian Americans did not have the numbers to elect a candidate on their own, AAFE understood that a successful campaign would need to create a multiracial coalition of voters, and AAFE considered areas where such efforts had had a history of success. AAFE's plan followed the strengths of Chin, who was a member of Community Board 1 and who had been elected twice in the 1980s to the Democratic State Committee in that area. As Rosa Koo stated:

> For an Asian American to win, he or she must build on the strength of a coalition of voters supportive of, and proven to have elected, minority candidates in the past. . . . Our objective is not to look for districts where Asians did well. Our objective is to look for districts where Asians have won. (Koo 1990: n.p.)

With this in mind, AAFE (D. Koo 1990a) proposed that the core of Chinatown should be joined with areas to the west and south, that is, City Hall, Tribeca, and Battery Park City, stating that "Asian candidates have done better than white candidates in the area West of Core, where one would assume white candidates with a liberal agenda would traditionally be at their best." They ruled out the areas to the east of Chinatown because their data analysis showed that Asian American candidates did poorly in local elections.[2] Describing the social networks that linked the neighborhoods in the proposed district, Doris Koo (1990b) mentioned schools with high percentages of Asian American students, neighborhood services such as a senior citizen center and hospitals, and the growing number of Asian-owned businesses and manufacturers that provided employment for Chinatown residents.

An alternative to AAFE's plan was developed by a variety of community activists and service and civil rights organizations, including AALDEF, the Community Service Society, and the Puerto Rican Legal Defense and Education Fund (PRLDEF). Recognizing that no single ethnic or racial group in the area was large enough to constitute 50 percent or more of a district, residents formed an organization, Lower East Siders for a Multi-Racial District, which proposed a plan that would create a Latino, Asian American, and

African American district based on the needs and interests of low-income and working-class residents (E. Chan 1991).

The plan proposed a district with a racial majority-minority population, incorporating the bulk of their communities in the area, and considered population growth trends. The multiracial district group's analysis of the plan stated:

> The ethnic breakdown is as follows: Asians: 37%, Latinos: 34% and African-Americans 13% (total 84%). The district includes over 94% of the total Latino population below 14th Street, 96% of the Asian and 91% of the African-American population. In addition, it seeks to incorporate areas in which both Asian and Latino populations will continue to grow and expand. (Lower East Siders for a Multi-Racial District 1991: 4)

Elaine Chan (1991)—a member of the multiracial district organization, a city council candidate who withdrew from the race, and a coordinator for the Lower East Side Joint Planning Council (a housing advocacy group)—explained that "Asians, Latinos, and African Americans have had a historic working relationship on issues of common concern: housing, health care, immigration, day care, bilingual education, affordable commercial space, job training, and general quality of life issues" (p. 182). Chan stressed the long history of multiracial activism in the area and how that defined and reinforced a tightly knit political community.

> We represent more than thirty organizations on the Lower East Side that advocate for decent and affordable housing. Our plan, the United District, calls for a council district that closely resembles traditional Lower East Side boundaries as delineated by the parameters of Community Board 3. (Chan 1990: 253)

In addition, Chan refuted the assumption that Latinos would not vote for Asian Americans, noting that Latinos supported two Asian American candidates in the 1987 judicial race (Ohnuma 1991).

Offering her interpretation of descriptive representation versus community empowerment, Mini Liu—a member of the multiracial district group—said:

> Yes, we want minority representatives. But we want minority representatives who are accountable to the Asians and Latinos on the Lower East Side, not just Asian and Latino faces in City Council, representing white middle and upper class interests. (Liu 1991: n.p.)

Margarita Lopez—a housing activist since she moved to the Lower East Side in 1978 from her native Puerto Rico and a member of the multiracial district group—identified the battle over real estate and gentrification, the movement of higher-income residents into low-income neighborhoods with a concomitant increase in property values (DeGiovanni 1987), as one of the community's critical issues.

> The Lower East Side has a key geographic position in Manhattan. [It is next to] the financial center of the world. The Lower East Side is as close to Wall Street as you walking there with your own feet and you don't have to pay for transportation. . . . It's not just prime real estate, it's the dream of anyone who is a high executive. (Saito 1996c: 2)

Wing Lam (Saito 1996d)—a member of the Chinese Staff and Workers Association and supporter of the multiracial district plan—underscored the importance of housing as a factor uniting the residents of Chinatown and the Lower East Side, explaining that the "Lower East Side people know that if the developers can gentrify us [Chinatown], they can go east, we are the front line."

To receive public input, the Districting Commission held twenty-seven well-attended public hearings throughout the city in 1990 and 1991, and the commission outreach staff claims to have organized more than 400 meetings (Gartner 1993: 109). With its diverse demographics and political interests, Alan Gartner (1993), executive director of the Districting Commission, considered Chinatown "perhaps the most controversial area of the city for the Districting Commission" (p. 63). Gartner (1993: 67) explained that when the commission members created boundaries, they considered what they believed the majority of the Asian American community favored, that is, disengaging the Asian American and Latino populations. The commission stated that little data existed to show that Asian Americans and Latinos would jointly support a candidate. As Judith Reed (1991), general counsel to the Districting Commission, wrote in a letter to the Department of Justice, "Statistical analyses concerning political cohesion were inconclusive. The issue came to rest squarely in the realm of judgment" (n.p.). As a result, community testimony provided the critical evidence on community politics and a suitable district. In Gartner's (1993: 130) judgment, AAFE "became the dominant player in the Asian American community. . . . The careful and comprehensive presentations of AAFE's Executive Director, Doris Koo, impressed the Commission and staff" and the commission gave serious consideration to AAFE's data showing white support for Asian American candidates.

Crafting Multiracial Districts, Public Input, and the Chinatown District

The city's history of grouping more than one minority within the same district has involved primarily Latinos and African Americans and has provided inconsistent evidence for both conflict and crossover voting. Through his years of community work and research, Angelo Falcon—president of the Institute for Puerto Rican Policy, an organization that works to mobilize community members of all races in redistricting and to provide political data—intimately knew about the range of views within and among racial groups. As Falcon summed up the task, "The big issue was not locating the communities, that was easy. The question was the politics of it. The combined Asian and Latino communities, what would that give you?" (Saito 1996a). In the charter reform and initial redistricting hearings, testimony tended to favor separating the groups. As Betanzos (1989a) stated at a charter reform hearing about grouping Latinos and African Americans together in one district, "That's why I found the fact . . . of what was happening to specific Hispanic areas very important, because I really don't believe that lumping them together is meaningful at all" (p. 183). Similarly, Pauline Chen (1989), president of the Chinatown Voter Education Alliance, stated, "Do not force African Americans, Latinos, and Asians to compete with one another in the same district" (p. 3). Antonio Pagan (1990)—director of Coalition Housing, which builds low- and moderate-income housing, and a Puerto Rican candidate for city council on the Lower East Side—supported separate "Asian American" and "Latino" districts, stating that he was "emphatically in favor and supportive of the creation of a Chinese seat or Asian seat at this moment . . . but we want to be able to elect our own" (p. 213).

In other regions of the United States dealing with multiracial populations at that time, Latinos and Asian Americans successfully worked together, for example, in Oakland, California, to support the creation of separate Asian American– and Latino-influenced city council districts in 1993 (Fong 1995, 1998). On the other hand, the two groups worked together in the San Gabriel Valley of Los Angeles County to create state assembly and state senate districts that joined their populations in 1991 (Saito 1998). When Asian Americans examined the voting patterns in the San Gabriel Valley, they found that Latinos had supported Asian Americans candidates, whereas whites in the prospective areas had not, in contrast to the situation in New York; the white areas in San Gabriel Valley were also marked by hate crimes against Asian Americans. In addition, although clearly the San Gabriel Valley Latino and Asian American populations varied greatly, especially in terms of class and political ideology, the two groups had large professional middle classes that had forged a common political agenda. The more heavily working-class and low-income Asian American and Latino populations on the Lower East Side also had a history of political alliances, especially on the issue of political representation.

Having considered the local dynamics, Gartner (1993) explained, "Ultimately, the Districting Commission opted to craft a district designed to offer the only opportunity in the city to the Asian-American community to elect a candidate of its choice" (pp. 67–68). The Districting Commission joined Chinatown with areas to the west. As Gartner (1993) stated, "The Commission hoped that a strong Asian-American candidate, with the support of the white, liberal areas surrounding Chinatown, could be elected" (p. 68).

According to Judith Reed, however, others affiliated with the commission believed that public testimony clearly favored a multiracial district, contradicting Gartner's interpretation of events.

> Indeed, the commission's deputy counsel, Joseph Diaz, was so convinced that the public had indicated a preference for a lower Manhattan district that combined Latinos of the lower east side and Asians of Chinatown, that after one public hearing dedicated primarily to district 1, he mused: "Well, we know what the public wants, I wonder how the commissioners will respond?" (Reed 1992: 777)

This view was later expressed at a public discussion of Gartner's report on the redistricting process. As Margarita Lopez asserted, the new district ignored the evidence presented by the Lower East Siders for a Multi-Racial District that she believed clearly demonstrated Latino support for Asian Americans, such as the successful efforts of Latinos to increase the number of Asian Americans on Community Board 3 (Santiago, n.d.: 24). Lopez, who also supported the multiracial district, stated:

> It's not accurate, it doesn't reflect what happened . . . you don't know the precious history where the Puerto Ricans of our community were directly responsible for integrating the Community Board No. 3 with the Asian-Americans of the Lower East Side. In 1982, when I became a member of the Community Board No. 3, there only was only one Asian sitting on that Community Board. . . . It was the Puerto Rican community who organized an outreach effort to collect signatures and names of Asian-Americans that could become members of the Community Board No. 3 and Bill Chong, sitting right here, became one of them. (Santiago, n.d.: 24)

Elaine Chan, of the multiracial district coalition, also recognized past alliances between Asian Americans and Latinos and criticized the idea of whites as a race-neutral group. Chan declared, "I think there was a racist view that whites would vote for an Asian in an influence district, whereas Hispanics would not. There was an ignoring of history of the work that had been done between Asians and Hispanics on the Lower East Side" (Santiago, n.d.: 22).

The Chinatown District and City Council Elections

Approved by the U.S. Department of Justice on July 26, 1991, the redistricting plans joined Chinatown with areas to the west and created District 1, in which Asian Americans were the largest group, at 39.2 percent of the population, but only 14.2 percent of the voters. In contrast, whites made up 37.2 percent of the population but 61.5 percent of the registered voters, Latinos made up 17.4 of the population and 15.5 percent of the voters, and African Americans made up 5.8 percent of the population and 8.8 percent of the voters. On the Lower East Side, District 2 was created, with Latinos being 25.2 percent of the population and 18.4 percent of the registered voters, whites being 59.3 percent of the population and 71 percent of the registered voters, African Americans being 8.0 percent of the population and 8.1 percent of the voters, and Asian Americans being 7.1 percent of the population and 2.3 percent of the voters (Kovner et al. 1991b; New York City Districting Commission 1991a). In District 2, Antonio Pagan narrowly defeated incumbent Miriam Friedlander in the city council election following redistricting. Pagan campaigned on issues of community safety, Puerto Rican empowerment, and his work promoting affordable housing; his detractors argued that his efforts were intended to support the interests of real estate developers (Ferguson 1993; Morales 1991). Pagan's election increased minority representation on the council, a major goal of the Districting Commission (see Map 3).

In the Democratic primary, Freed emerged the victor with 42 percent of the vote, while Chin received 31 percent. Freed was elected with 53 percent of the vote in the 1991 general election, while Chin received 24 percent running on the Liberal Party ticket and Fred Teng received 23 percent. Teng, former board president of the Chinatown Planning Council and a Republican, received support from segments of the Chinatown business community. Although Asian Americans in Chinatown voted overwhelming for Asian American representation, as shown in an exit poll conducted by AALDEF (1992: 5), the results demonstrate the heterogeneity of the community (AALDEF 1992: 5): Survey-

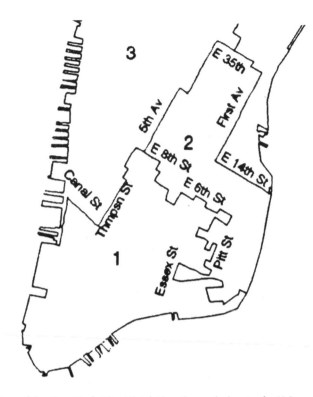

Map 3 Final submission of the New York City Districting Commission to the U.S. Department of Justice, July 26, 1991: Council Districts 1 and 2

SOURCE: New York City Districting Commission, 1991

ing 507 Asian Americans (predominantly Chinese) in Chinatown, 43.8 percent voted for Chin, 38.3 percent voted for Teng, 5.6 percent voted for Freed, and 12.2 percent declined to specify or voted for another candidate.

Factions in Chinatown did not divide neatly along racial and/or class lines but originated from a long history of a complex and often contradictory mixture of group and personal interests that carried over into the redistricting dialogue and elections that followed. From the perspective of many Asian Americans, District 1 was inextricably linked with AAFE and its council candidate, Margaret Chin, because the organization created and supported the general guidelines for the formation of the district.

AAFE originated out of efforts in 1974 to force contractors to comply with city policies on minority employment and hire Asian Americans in the construction of Confucius Plaza in Chinatown. Since then, AAFE has provided a range of community services, such as building and renovating affordable housing, filing the *AAFE v. Koch* lawsuit to counter gentrification, providing information and training to small business owners, and enforcing tenants' rights (AAFE, n.d.; *Harvard Law Review* 1989). In spite of AAFE's indisputable progressive and community roots, its critics charged that the group had become a developer intent on following its own agenda (Jacobs 1997), and unilaterally putting forth its redistricting plan reinforced that image. AAFE's support in 1982 for Chinatown garment subcontractors against workers and charges that it used a subcontractor that paid below-minimum wages supported the view that the organization had strayed from its original mission (Cho 1994; Lagnado 1991). Chin was also criticized for accepting campaign contributions from developers and garment manufacturers and for crossing a labor picket line in 1991.

Kathryn Freed, Chin's major opponent, was the former chair of Community Board 1 and an attorney with a history of working for tenants' rights and affordable housing. As *Village Voice* reporter Wayne Barrett (1991) contends, however, Freed also attended a dinner sponsored by the group that Chin was criticized for supporting because of its labor problems and Freed also received contributions from real estate interests and garment manufacturers.

Opponents of the AAFE plan asserted that the low-income inhabitants of Chinatown had little in common with the affluent whites to the west. Wing Lam, of the Chinese Staff and Workers Association, stated, "By merging with the west, AAFE essentially sold the poor and working class of Chinatown down the drain" (Bush 1991: 11). Economic restructuring and deindustrialization, with a shift from the production of goods to the production of services, have transformed major U.S. urban areas, including the loss of unionized manufacturing jobs, which provided living wages and benefits, contributing to increasing income inequality and poverty (Gladstone and Fainstein 2003; Mollenkopf and Castells 1991; Waldinger 1996). In the four decades before redistricting, New York City's manufacturing employment decreased by two-thirds from 1950 to 1989, a reduction of 680,000 jobs, and dropped from 30 percent to 10 percent of the city's employment (Mollenkopf 1992: 53–54).

Deindustrialization, however, which has had a substantial impact on Puerto Ricans because of their historically high participation rates in manufacturing, creates a range of both problems and opportunities for Chinatown's more heterogeneous population (Bailey and Waldinger 1991; Waldinger 1986, 1996). In

Lower Manhattan, garment factories and restaurants are the largest employers of working-class Chinese Americans (Kwong 1996). The exodus of manufacturing left empty buildings and lowered rents, which benefited garment manufacturers (Zhou 1992). The Chinatown Land Use and Planning Study (Hunter College Neighborhood Planning Workshop 1992) cautions, however, that increased office development threatens both restaurants and garment factories by driving rents upward.

Ken Chin, one of the founders of the Free Legal Clinic of Chinatown and a partner in his own law firm, was the only Asian American on the Districting Commission, and he supported the district (Gartner 1993: 204). Referring to the protection of racial minority groups by the Voting Rights Act, Chin explained that "it was the commission's job to protect Asians as a class. Not low-income people. . . . We were not empowered to carry out the class struggle" (Fitch 1991: 12). What Chin's emphasis on Asian Americans as a group overlooked, however, was the way class interests in Lower Manhattan were shaped by race in the neighborhood, as exemplified by the residential concentration of low-income minorities, the crisis in affordable housing intensified by city policies favoring gentrification, subsidies for major developers that contributed to a bifurcated economy with a decrease in living-wage jobs, declining social services, and an underfunded educational system (Abu-Lughod 1994).

Margaret Chin countered the claim that residents of Chinatown and the West Side did not share concrete interests by noting the issues of concern that joined the neighborhoods.

> A lot of them [on the West Side] send their kids to Chinatown schools. There is also a natural connection in terms of traffic problems and sanitation. When you talk about housing, everybody thinks that people on the West Side all live in luxury housing. Not true. There is government subsidized housing which has the same tenant issues as Chinatown. (Saito 1996b: 3)

The council election for District 1 did not have any compelling factors that would generate a multiracial alliance with whites, and Chin was unable to gain crucial West Side support for her candidacy. The influential SoHo Alliance argued that "problems on the West Side—overdevelopment, the waterfront, the West Side Highway, loft laws, historic districts . . . have little in common with Chinatown community's woes, such as the need for affordable housing, jobs and education programs" (Hester 1991b: 10). Racial minorities have formed alliances with white liberals to elect minority candidates in New York City, as when whites, Latinos, and African Americans joined together to replace Mayor Edward Koch and his divisive policies with African American David Dinkins in 1989. This was a period, however, marked by heightened racial tension, a political corruption scandal, and economic recession, important issues that promoted political alliances (Mollenkopf 1992).

The rapid growth of Chinatown received little campaign attention, although the long and often heated history of negotiations over the preservation of Little Italy continued as a major dividing issue. The Committee Against Anti-Asian Violence (CAAAV), a community advocacy group located on the Lower East Side, reported that white residents, merchants, and real estate developers in Little Italy and SoHo had used complaints to the police and city agencies and lawsuits to harass and close down Asian wholesale vegetable and fish merchants to restrict the growth of Chinatown (CAAAV 1998a, 1998b).

In discussing the problems associated with the Chinese vegetable wholesalers, one member of the SoHo Alliance noted the early morning noise and diesel fumes from the trucks that delivered their goods at "four o'clock in the morning" and left "their motors running" to power their refrigeration units. He believed that the wholesalers should relocate because the area was changing from manufacturing to residential and retail. Resonating with the late nineteenth- and early twentieth-century images of the Chinese as "unclean," he went on to say:

> I think there's a lot of cultures in this world and I have traveled all over the world. . . . There's certain cultures, they are very clean. . . . The Chinese I don't know about their history, but they did not learn about Pasteur's and Lister's laws. . . . SoHo used to be dirty, too, until we had the SoHo Partnership. That's why I should not get racist. . . . I don't want to get into stereotypes. They did not clean up the streets. And they leave all the lettuce and stuff just lying there, putrefying. They wouldn't clean up. (Saito 1999: 16)

Although it was not a major campaign issue, police brutality further divided whites and Asian Americans. Clearly, Asian Americans are concerned with crime; however, Asian Americans demand crime control without biased harassment. CAAAV was formed in 1986, working with Latinos and African Americans, to address this issue, including investigations of Asian Americans killed, beaten, or verbally abused with racial epithets by police (CAAAV 1996). Data in a 1994 national report showed that in New York City "the main perpetrator of suspected and/or racially motivated violence against Asian Pacific Americans is the police" (NAPALC 1991: 8).

Although New York City's Democratic Party has declined in power and its local structure is highly fragmented, it still exerts a strong influence on community politics, unlike politics in California, which is shaped by the reform movement (Jones-Correa 1998; Mollenkopf 1990, 1992). Considering the way ethnic and racial groups historically have used the party to gain power while keeping others out (Erie 1988; Glazer and Moynihan 1970) or have granted limited concessions to African Americans and Latinos (Mollenkopf 1990), it may have been unrealistic to expect West Side whites to forgo power to help Asian Americans in Chinatown. Freed gained the endorsement of a number of key Democratic groups, including the Downtown Independent Democrats with its critical base in the West Side and the Democratic district leaders of the assembly district in the area, whereas Chin received support primarily from the Village Independent Democrats (M. Chin 1991; Freed 1991; Hester 1991a). Because of Freed's support for low-income housing, employment issues, and support of multiracial coalition building, she received the backing of the Asian American Union for Political Action (1991), whose members included supporters of the multiracial district.

Deracialized Campaigns and the Election of Minority Candidates

White voters have elected Asian Americans to public office; some of the most prominent of these officials are Washington State governor Gary Locke and California congressmen Norman Mineta and Robert Matsui. What these three highly successful politicians have in common is that they established effective deracialized political platforms and campaign strategies. Joseph P. McCormick and Charles E. Jones (1993) examined the electoral approaches of successful African American politicians in areas controlled by white voters and pointed out the importance of a deracialized political agenda and campaign to build a broad base of support. In terms of formulating a political agenda, William J. Wilson (1990) explains that the emphasis should be on race-neutral programs, such as employment, health care reform, and education. In this way, politicians can enact policies that help all groups, including racial minorities, while avoiding white resentment of and backlash from policies specifically targeting racial minorities, such as affirmative action hiring programs and busing to end school segregation (Wilson 1990). Similarly, deracialized campaigns aimed at creating a broad base of support and coalitions among racial groups are built on nonracial issues and steer clear of explicit racial mobilization (McCormick and Jones 1993; Underwood 1997). McCormick and Jones (1993) acknowledge that race and racism remain factors in U.S. society and that using a deracialized campaign strategy "defuses the polarizing effects of race" (p. 76).

Deracialized agendas and campaigns are especially important for Asian American candidates because, outside Hawaii, they are much more likely to run for political office in areas or districts with small numbers of Asian American voters, compared to African American and Latino candidates who may run in districts with sizable voting blocs of people of the same race (Lai et al. 2001). In Washington State in 1996, voters elected Chinese American Gary Locke governor when the state was 89 percent white, the first of his two terms in office. The *Seattle Weekly* endorsed Locke, stating that he was "an extraordinary talent in government—idealistic, independent, a total master of detail, rooted in concern for the less advantaged" (1996: 12). The *Seattle Weekly* described Locke as an able administrator, "an acknowledged master of state programs . . . adept at dealing with polarized legislators and interests" (Brewster 1996: 11) and noted that his gubernatorial campaign stressed employment opportunities, education, and improving government efficiency. Previously, Locke had served in the state legislature after his election in 1982, and in 1993 he won election to the King County executive position.

When then-president Bill Clinton appointed Norman Mineta as secretary of commerce in 2000, Mineta became the first Asian American in U.S. history to serve in the cabinet. He also later served as secretary of transportation under President George W. Bush. Earlier in his political career, he had been appointed to the San Jose City Council in 1967, elected to the council in 1969, elected as mayor in 1971, and was a member of Congress from 1975 to 1995. Locally in San Jose and as a congressman, Mineta focused on a range of race-neutral issues, particularly transportation policy. As skillful as he was in dealing with issues of race, Mineta also dealt with the subject of partisanship, declaring after his selection as transportation secretary, "I believe that there is no more fertile ground for building a bipartisan consensus on what is necessary and right for our country than in the area of transportation policy. . . . There are no Democratic or Republican highways, no such thing as Republican or Democratic traffic congestion, no such thing as Republican or Democratic aviation and highway safety" (*San Francisco Chronicle* 2001: A1). This statement could also be understood in deracialized terms.

Robert Matsui began his political career in the Sacramento City Council, elected in 1971, and served until his election to Congress in 1978, where he served until his death in 2005. He was a senior member of the House Ways and Means Committee and, while in Congress, effectively worked on policies dealing with Social Security, international trade, and taxes. Diane Feinstein, U.S. senator from California, described Matsui as "a master of balanced, practical public policy" (CNN 2005).

The election of a Chinese American to the position of governor and of African Americans to the mayoralty in cities in the state suggests that voters have gone beyond race in Washington. However, as suggested by *New York Times* reporter Timothy Egan (2000) in his article on the 2000 election for governor, it is not that the importance of race has disappeared but that a different way of thinking about race has emerged. Although minority candidates, such as Locke, have experienced success, to attract voters they must run deracialized campaigns. As Egan (2000) explains, "But if the old racial order—of whites always on top—has eroded, a more complex one has replaced it. Now the system rewards nonwhites who know how to make the largely white electorate see in them what the voters see in themselves" (p. A1).

Locke understood that running a deracialized campaign did not mean that he must ignore race, because voters could clearly see his Asian American heritage. Instead of avoiding his racial identity, he used it in ways that reinforced American ideals and demonstrated that his personal biography and stand on policies placed him solidly within the mainstream. As Locke explained, "You can't hide your race. . . . My hair, my eyes, my skin color: people look at me and know I'm Asian" (Egan 2000: A1). Locke emphasized his family history, the story of immigrants and their rise from poverty. With degrees from Yale University and Boston University Law School, Locke campaigned on the importance of education, and as a former prosecutor for King County, his platform included a "tough on crime" message (Yu and Yuan 2001: 357).

While on the campaign trail in 1996, Locke spoke at the Organization of Chinese Americans national conference. He emphasized two important themes of his campaign that appealed to the "moderate and middle-class voter" (Yu and Yuan 2001: 357): personal responsibility and the importance of family, and limited government. Locke mentioned that his father nearly died because of injuries suffered during a robbery and that government medical and social services contributed to his survival.

I believe that each of us is defined by our background and our family experiences. And my background, and my family's experiences, have emphasized the meaning of values like hard work, education, the family, the meaning of personal responsibility, and that government can only provide an opportunity but cannot guarantee us success. It can only give us those opportunities and serves as a safety net. (Locke 2003: 360–361)

Talking about his achievements as the executive of King County, which contains a third of the population of the state, and in streamlining government, Locke (2003) said, "I'm proud of the fact that . . . I've been able to work with corporations to reinvent government by downsizing it and making it more efficient. We've added more police officers, we've focused on technology, and we've consolidated two governments" (p. 361).

Ron Sims, an African American who replaced Locke as King County executive, ran against Locke for the governor's position in 2000. During his political career, Sims also paid careful attention to race, recalling the advice he received early in his career as an elected official. Sam Smith, a Seattle council member and one of the senior African American politicians of his day, advised Sims to stay away from areas stereotypically seen as associated with racial minorities. "Don't you sit on no health and human services committee" (Egan 2000: A1). Instead, Sims became an expert on fiscal issues and on Pacific salmon, a high-profile issue in the Northwest. Sims noted that he could not completely escape race because, when his detractors wanted to call attention to race without explicitly invoking race, he was labeled by code words, such as "inner-city politician," despite the fact that he grew up in a predominantly white community in eastern Washington (Egan 2000: A1).

Mineta and Matsui knew all too well the effects of racial discrimination because both experienced incarceration in U.S. internment camps during World War II. Describing the sense of injustice felt by the internees, Matsui said, "We were treated as prisoners of war, really—not Americans. You have to imagine how we felt looking up at the guard towers, knowing that their guns were pointed not outward but in, at us. And I think that the stigma of being accused of disloyalty was even worse than being sent to camp" (Kitano and Maki 2003: 413–414).

Mineta and Matsui, along with U.S. senators Daniel K. Inouye and Masayuki "Spark" Matsunaga from Hawaii, provided key leadership and support that led to the passage of the Civil Liberties Act of 1988, which provided redress and reparations for Japanese Americans incarcerated in the camps. Deracialization became a part of their strategy in Congress as well in their effort to pass the act. Rather than promoting the act in narrowly defined terms, as redress for Japanese Americans, they framed it as a broader American issue of constitutional rights and equality and successfully gained support from a wide range of political, religious, and racial groups (Kitano and Maki 2003).

Even with the focus on constitutional issues, Matsui noted that he lost key supporters in his district back in Sacramento because of his involvement with the Civil Liberties Act.

> I had friends call me, people who had known me for twenty years, call the office and say, tell Bob not to send me an invitation to the next fund raiser because this shows that he has his own agenda and he doesn't represent me. We [Asian Americans in Congress] could have not pushed it and let it die, but we knew that it was too damn important. It transcended our own reelection.[3]

Based on their strong records serving their constituents, Matsui and Mineta overcame the opposition in their districts of those who opposed the Civil Liberties Act and went on to serve many more terms in Congress. Before leaving office, Mineta established the Congressional Asian Pacific American Caucus to support issues of concern to Asian Americans and Pacific Islanders.

Mineta skillfully brings together stories of his camp experience and political life to illustrate the extreme injustice and, in some ways, absurdity of incarceration in ways comprehensible to a broad audience. He often tells the story of the day that, as a 10-year-old boy, he and his family went to the freight yard to board the train that would take them to the Santa Anita racetrack, where they were put in converted horse stalls until being shipped to a camp in Wyoming. He arrived at the train station dressed in his Cub Scout uniform and carrying a baseball bat, glove, and ball. A soldier confiscated his bat because he considered it a possible weapon. While Mineta served in Congress, a man who had learned about his confiscated bat sent Mineta a bat signed by Hank Aaron and Sadaharu Oh, the home-run record holders of the United States and Japan, respectively. A story in the *San Jose Mercury News* reported that the bat was valued at about $1,500, which was above the $250 limit on gifts, and Mineta returned the bat (Wolfley 2001). Mineta sent a letter to the reporter declaring, "The damn government has taken my bat again" (Wolfley 2001). When Mineta left Congress in 1995, the owner of the autographed bat sent it back to Mineta (Wolfley 2001).

Candidates running in areas with high numbers of people of color face a different set of circumstances than candidates in predominantly white areas, as was the case with Locke, Mineta, and Matsui. Research on mayoral races in New

Orleans and Memphis, two cities with African American majority populations, examined the explanatory value of black-threat theory and deracialization in relation to the changing demographics of the cities, white voters, and the election of African Americans (B. Liu 2003, 2006; Vanderleeuw et al. 2004). Black-threat theory predicts a growing sense of black threat among whites as the African American population increases, resulting in less support for African American candidates by whites (Key 1949). Baodong Liu (2006), however, suggests that this theory developed during a time of explicit white supremacy and white control of elections. In places such as Memphis and New Orleans, where whites are now a minority of the voters and where white candidates have a difficult time winning elections, whites may see a vote for a white candidate as a "wasted vote" and instead support moderate African American candidates. Thus whites may join a biracial coalition when the African American candidate's agenda is perceived as incorporating the interests of whites and speaks to the importance of deracialized campaign strategies by minority candidates (B. Liu 2006). Deracialization can create problems for a minority candidate if the candidate's efforts to gain cross-racial support appear to alienate members of his or her minority group and result in decreased electoral support (Vanderleeuw et al. 2004).

Locke, Mineta, and Matsui won elections in areas with small Asian American populations, which I suggest makes it easier for Asian Americans to successfully run a deracialized campaign. Although not at the level of black threat, because the Asian American population is much smaller than the African American population nationally and is not a majority except in several cities and neighborhoods, I do suggest that the racial identity of candidates gains added importance when a minority population becomes significant. At this tipping point (Grodzins 1958; Lieberson 1980), the political importance of race is amplified when neighborhood interests and race create distinct communities, as in District 1 with the clear differences in issues expressed by the SoHo Alliance. As a result, whites see a minority candidate as inextricably linked to that community, whether or not such a connection actually exists, as opposed to a candidate who will represent the entire district. In the case of Margaret Chin, any failings of her campaign to win over white voters may have been unimportant in a council race explicitly framed by race, with the history of minority disenfranchisement in full public view through the lawsuits that generated the charter amendments and public discussion on the need for city council minority representation.

The first Asian American member of the New York City council was Taiwanese immigrant John Liu, whom voters elected in 2001 to Council District 20 in

Flushing, Queens, one of the most racially diverse areas of the city and an area that now contains the city's largest Asian American population (Matthews 2001; Virasami 2001). The district is 47.2 percent Asian American, 26.6 percent white, 18.6 percent Latino, and 3.8 percent African American, although as in District 1, whites are the majority of the voters (Logan and Mollenkopf 2003: 36, 39). Before the election, Liu worked as a manager at PriceWaterhouseCoopers, an accounting and financial services company. Among the top fundraisers of the city council candidates, Liu ran a deracialized campaign that stressed delivering basic city services. As Liu stated, "There is no Puerto Rican or Chinese or Italian way to pick up the garbage or pick up the snow.... The issues facing this district affect us all, and we will solve these issues together" (Logan and Mollenkopf 2003: 43). Liu's victory occurred in the same election as businessman Michael Bloomberg's successful bid for mayor, illustrating in part the benefit both candidates garnered by promoting the belief that successful businesspeople in private enterprise offer better management skills than career public officials. Considering the large number of Asian Americans in the district, Liu's racial and immigrant background certainly added to his appeal to the electorate, and he did not need to emphasize these factors in public statements.

Conclusion

The debate over what areas to add became the central dividing factor among re-districting participants, and it revealed the complexity and heterogeneity of the Chinatown community. The Districting Commission kept Chinatown intact within District 1 rather than fragmented among different districts, meeting an important goal of AAFE and the Lower East Siders for a Multi-Racial District. As Alan Gartner (1993) points out, Asian Americans also succeeded in keeping Chinatown whole in the new state assembly and state senate districts and in joining Asian American neighborhoods in Brooklyn, Queens, and Manhattan in a congressional district.

The Districting Commission joined Chinatown with areas to the west, creating in the 1990–1991 redistricting what commission members believed was a city council district that would support Asian American descriptive representation; however, the electoral reality was a district dominated by white voters. Council District 1 had an Asian American plurality population, but one that was only slightly larger than the white population. With 61.5 percent of the voters, however, whites dominated elections, compared to only 14.2 percent for Asian American voters.

The Districting Commission's assumption that white liberal voters would appreciate the need for minority representation in the district and vote for an Asian American candidate ignores the long history of active disenfranchisement of minorities in New York City through such practices as literacy tests, gerrymandering, and the lack of support for minority candidates by white-controlled political parties. The Districting Commission viewed whites as a race-neutral group who would not follow their own racial interests and characterized Asian Americans and Latinos as racial groups who needed to be put into separate districts. Increasingly in cities across the country experiencing demographic change, whites now participate in elections with viable racial minority candidates. As the election in Chinatown demonstrates, however, in areas with significant minority populations, whites remain reluctant to vote for minorities. The New York City case exhibits a very different electoral dynamic from the dynamics in such cities as Memphis and New Orleans, where whites are a numerical minority and a vote for a white candidate may be a wasted vote. Chinatown also presents a different situation from the one in Los Angeles when Tom Bradley was first elected mayor with the help of liberal Jewish voters who had been excluded from the power structure, along with African Americans, by conservative whites. As the dominant majority vote, liberal white voters in District 1 could elect a candidate of their choice without help from crossover votes. Therefore the need for a biracial coalition on the part of whites does not exist in the Chinatown district.

In addition to the reluctance of whites to vote for minorities, basic political issues hindered Margaret Chin's bid for the council seat. Although Chin attempted to build a campaign that went beyond Asian Americans and although white voters had supported Asian American candidates in previous local elections, Chin's campaign had apparently not laid the groundwork necessary to gain the endorsement of key West Side community leaders. Chin's campaign also failed to generate compelling issues that would win the support of a majority of voters.

In terms of issues reflecting the new constituency of the district, the result of joining New York City's Chinatown with affluent whites to the west is a district with more moderate politics than what would have been created if Chinatown had been joined with low-income and working-class Puerto Ricans and African Americans to the east. Issues such as affordable housing, jobs that pay a living wage, and police brutality are key issues of everyday life for low-income minorities but not for affluent whites.

In hindsight, the Districting Commission's reading of possible white support for Margaret Chin did not adequately consider interests within Chinatown, such as affordable housing and employment, that West Side residents did not share. Also, major concerns actively divided interests in the two areas, such as conflict over the expansion of Chinatown into the West Side. Clearly, many white voters crossed over, considering that Chinatown had a low voter turnout and only about 14 percent of the district's electorate was Asian American, but unlike Chin's election victories as Democratic Party State Committee representative in 1986 and 1988, apparently whites were reluctant to elect her to the much more significant position of council member.

Freed's efforts to gain Asian American backing and her support of working-class issues transcended narrowly defined racial and neighborhood politics and demonstrated the importance of building a larger, more inclusive base and a political platform that represented a range of interests. On the other hand, Freed's election was not a complete victory for backers of the multiracial district, even though some of its supporters had endorsed Freed, because the central concern that drove their plans was the preservation and reinforcement of the political community generated from the history of alliances in the Chinatown/Lower East Side region, a community fragmented by the boundaries of Districts 1 and 2.

The fact that Chin and Teng received a combined 47 percent of the vote in the general election demonstrated the strength of the candidates and the organizations that supported their efforts and was an indication of the growing political maturity and sophistication of Chinatown institutions. Considering that Chinatown had a low voter turnout, however, and that whites did vote for the Chinese American candidates, an argument could be made that the failure to elect an Asian American candidate was partly a result of the faulty political tactics of the Chinatown community. Rather than running multiple candidates, putting forward one candidate who would be supported by the entire community would avoid a number of issues that could weaken the electoral strength and political representation of Chinatown voters. Most basically, splitting the Chinatown vote would be avoided. One candidate decided upon by the Chinatown community would mean that they could put forward a candidate who represented the interests of Chinatown, chosen by that community, rather than running multiple candidates who would divide the Asian vote and give added importance to white voters, who would decide the winner among the various Asian candidates. In addition, a more positive campaign focused on one candidate rather than the negative barbs that accompany the battle for position among multiple candidates might encourage a higher voter turnout and gain more support for the candidate among all racial groups. Also, considering the high number of immigrants in Chinatown, existing efforts could be strengthened to educate residents about local politics, naturalize immigrants, register eligible citizens, and mobilize voters.

If one candidate is going to be chosen to represent the community, this raises another question: How would the selection process work? Considering the diversity of the residents and the range of political viewpoints supported by past candidates, the selection would not be an easy task. Such a tactic brings to mind the image of smoky backroom deals arranged by power brokers rather than the grassroots efforts by AAFE and the multiracial district group that guided the redistricting effort. Taking into account the significant issues and the long histories of conflict that divide the groups, selection of one candidate would be an extremely difficult task. Given that this is the district that Chinatown residents must deal with and that city council elections exist in the real world of highly competitive politics, I suggest that the Chinatown community needs to rally behind a single candidate. Creating a democratic process for choosing that candidate presents a challenge for community members.

5 Charter Reform and Redistricting in New York City's Chinatown, 1989–1991

LATINO AND AFRICAN AMERICAN PLAINTIFFS brought a number of successful lawsuits against New York City in the 1980s, charging racial discrimination and violation of the U.S. Constitution in city elections. The lawsuits led to the 1989 city charter reform, which eliminated the Board of Estimate and transferred many of its legislative duties to the city council, increased the number of city council districts from thirty-five to fifty-one, and established that redistricting would be carried out by a redistricting commission with its members appointed by the city council and mayor. After the charter reform, the New York City Districting Commission created new city council districts from 1990 to 1991, with the enfranchisement of racial minorities as one of the central redistricting goals.

In the November 5, 1991, New York City Council elections, in a district specifically crafted by the city's Districting Commission around Lower Manhattan's Chinatown to maximize the political strength of the city's largest concentration of Asian Americans, the Asian American candidates lost by wide margins to a white candidate. The defeat occurred despite overwhelming Chinatown voter support for the Asian American candidates (AALDEF 1992), continuing the city's history of never electing an Asian American to the council and demonstrating the uncertainty involved when racial minorities rely on white voters for empowerment. In contrast, the number of African Americans and Latinos on the council increased dramatically as a result of the election, increasing from nine (26 percent) to twenty-one (41 percent) (Gartner 1998: 35). With larger and more concentrated populations, districts could be created with strong Latino or African American majorities that did not depend on the support of white voters to elect officials.

In this chapter I examine charter reform, redistricting, and the council elections and the way in which these processes addressed the political concerns of Asian Americans. In particular, I examine how the discourse among charter reform and redistricting commission members revealed their understanding of race and its importance in the United States, and how this debate shaped reforms. I suggest that some commissioners failed to recognize the historical and contemporary existence of racialized outcomes embedded in a range of institutional practices and court decisions. As a result, some commissioners advocated political reforms that did not adequately recognize and address the racial consequences of city policies. I argue that, when attention was paid to race, charter reform commissioners focused primarily on the concerns of African Americans and Latinos, giving only nominal consideration to Asian American issues.

In terms of the national context for redistricting, policies and practices with racialized outcomes included the U.S. census and U.S. Supreme Court redistricting decisions that affirmed individual rights but not group rights and that considered harm against whites but not racial minorities. Local events in New York City included the 1989 charter reform, in which the number of city council districts was expanded to fifty-one rather than the sixty districts requested by a number of minority organizations; a charter reform process that Asian Americans claimed did not incorporate adequate input from their community; insufficient analysis of the impact of reforms on Asian Americans; and the city's census undercount. As a result, despite the various commissions' mandates to improve political access and representation for minorities, some of the key decisions proved to be obstacles for Asian Americans.

Casting a ballot is the quintessential symbol of democracy in the United States, but should government go beyond opening the polls to all? Abigail Thernstrom (1987) contends that government actions to empower racial minorities should be limited to ensuring access to voting: "The aim of the Voting Rights Act—the *single* aim—was black enfranchisement in the South. Obstacles to registration and voting . . . were the sole concern of those who framed the statute" (pp. 3–4). Thernstrom's call for limited government intervention, however, ignores the historical and contemporary practices that have produced institutional barriers that continue to hamper the political participation of racial minorities (Kousser 1999).

This debate on the role of government involvement regarding political activity and discrimination is based on two opposing conceptions of society. Thernstrom (1995) asserts in her discussion of U.S. Supreme Court redistricting cases in the 1990s that "at the heart of voting rights disputes ... is an argument about the nature of American society" (p. 931). The foundation of Thernstrom's argument is that political institutions are basically equitable and unbiased. In contrast, Cheryl I. Harris (1993) points out that white racial privilege is protected by and encoded in law and that the failure to recognize this form of institutional racism is a major obstacle to changes designed to address discrimination. Harris (1993) says, "The existing state of affairs is considered neutral and fair, however unequal and unjust it is in substance" (pp. 1777–1778). Harris (1993: 1777) explains that these privileges are not recognized as such but are instead seen as "natural" and "legitimate."

I suggest that the New York City case clearly demonstrates that the actions of the Charter Revision and Districting Commissions to enhance the political power of racial minority groups were constrained by the commission members' limited recognition of the way policies actively worked to privilege whites over minorities in politics. As Harris (1993) states, "The result is that the distortions in social relations are immunized from truly effective intervention, because the existing inequities are obscured and rendered nearly invisible" (p. 1777).

To address political inequality, research on the Voting Rights Act and the struggle to gain political power has focused on efforts to use the act to remove barriers to the right to vote, election systems and gerrymandered districts that result in vote dilution, the ability of groups to elect representatives of their choice, and the capacity of elected officials to enact policies on behalf of their constituents (Ancheta and Imahara 1993; Aoki 2002; Davidson and Grofman 1994; Guinier 1994). I focus on the factors leading up to and affecting a group's ability to elect a representative, one of the major indexes of political participation in the voting rights debate (Grofman 1998; Grofman et al. 2001; Kousser 1999; Thernstrom 1987).

Charter Reform and the 1989 Election for Charter Approval

New York City is divided into five boroughs, which ranged in size in 1980 from Staten Island, the smallest, with a population of about 350,000, to the largest, Brooklyn, with approximately 2.2 million (Benjamin and Mauro 1989: 1). Each borough elected to the forty-five member city council two at-large members in addition to members from districts. In *Andrews v. Koch*, African American and Latino voters in Brooklyn filed a lawsuit against the city, charging that the borough at-large election of council members went against the constitutional standard of one person, one vote. In 1981, a federal judge ruled in *Andrews v. Koch* "that the practice of electing two at-large council members per borough irrespective of the population of the boroughs violated the one-person, one-vote principle established by the Constitution" (Viteritti 1989: 29). The Supreme Court affirmed the ruling in 1982. Mayor Edward I. Koch established a charter commission in 1982; the commission recommended eliminating the at-large council seats, and city voters approved the change in 1983 (New York City Districting Commission 1991b: 15), reducing the number of city council members to thirty-five.

New York City's eight-member Board of Estimate, established in 1898 to guard the interests of the less populated boroughs against the larger ones, consisted of the mayor, comptroller, council president, and five borough presidents. The board had authority over such issues as budget approval, contracting, and land use (NYC-CRC 1990: 2). In 1981, residents of Brooklyn brought a suit against the city, charging that the Board of Estimate did not meet the equal protection clause of the Fourteenth Amendment. In 1986, Judge Edward R. Neaher, the same judge who ruled in the *Andrews* case, ruled in *Morris v. Board of Estimate* that the Board of Estimate was unconstitutional because it violated the one-person, one-vote principle of the Constitution. On March 22, 1989, the Supreme Court concurred, stating that, in the opinion of the Court, "the boroughs have widely disparate populations—yet each has equal representation on the board—the Court of Appeals for the Second Circuit held that this structure is inconsistent with the Equal Protection Clause of the Fourteenth Amendment. We affirm" (Mauro and Benjamin 1989: 53).

In response to the lawsuits and court decisions, two other charter reform commissions were established, the first in 1986, chaired by Richard Ravitch, and the second in 1989, chaired by Frederick A. O. Schwarz Jr. As the Charter Revision Commission Report (NYC-CRC 1990: 2) states, "The charter is New York's basic governing document. It sets forth the institutions and processes of the City's political system and defines the authority and responsibilities of elected officials and most city departments." Of the fifteen members of the second charter commission, six were "members of racial and language minority groups," although none were Asian American (Schwarz and Lane 1989: 8).

Under Ravitch, the Charter Revision Commission considered eliminating the Board of Estimate, but with the Supreme Court agreeing to take on the *Morris* case, Ravitch and Mayor Koch believed it best to suspend the work of the committee until the Supreme Court ruled on the matter. As a result, the commission's work was delayed. Once the Supreme Court had ruled on the case and although the commission would have to work quickly, the new chair, Schwarz, hoped that they would have a proposal ready for voters by the November 1989 election. Because a general city election would also be held during the November election, including a mayoral contest, Schwarz anticipated a large voter turnout. Speaking about public interest in the upcoming election and how this would contribute to increased attention to charter reform, Richard D. Emery, the attorney involved in the *Morris* case, stated that this is "the most exciting mayoral race in recent history" and that "this will force people to think about the City Charter" (Finder 1989b: B1).

Edward Koch, a Democrat, served as mayor going into the elections. First elected in 1977 following New York City's fiscal crisis of the mid-1970s, Koch did not reach out to white liberals. Instead, he used race in his attacks on African American leaders as part of a strategy to attract conservative white Catholics and Jews, and he used class to appeal to middle-class Latinos and African Americans by defending middle-class values and exploiting concerns about crime (Mollenkopf 1992). Koch was a three-term incumbent, but his popularity suffered greatly going into the 1989 election as news of corruption appeared in 1986 and 1987. The reports contributed to the suicide of a borough president and led to the resignation of a number of Koch's senior administration officials.

Koch's racial politics backfired when the city was struck by crises in the mid- and late 1980s. The times called for a leader who could bring the city together, not the divisive racial rhetoric that marked Koch's terms in office.[1] Manhattan borough president David Dinkins, an African American with deep roots in the area's Democratic Party, espoused liberal policies and worked to build cross-racial alliances. Dinkins defeated Koch in the September primary and went on to narrowly defeat Rudolph Giuliani, the Republican candidate, in the November general election, becoming the first and only African American to become mayor of New York City.

Once the Board of Estimate was found unconstitutional, Schwarz had another reason to support changing the charter as quickly as possible and aiming for the November 1989 election. Talking about the Charter Revision Commission's upcoming Friday meeting at the end of March, the first opportunity the commission would have to meet as a group and discuss the Supreme Court's ruling, Schwarz declared, "I think the decision we should make next Friday is that our aim is to proceed next November. . . . It's embarrassing to have unconstitutional government go on longer that it absolutely has to" (Purdum 1989: 1-1). Schwarz defended the decision to go ahead with the election rather than delay it, as requested by a coalition of African American, Asian American, and Latino groups, in an interview conducted after the commission's work was completed and just before the November 1989 election. Schwarz argued for the need for speed to correct an unjust situation, explaining, "We have an illegal, unconstitutional government, and we're under a court mandate to fix it. New York City should not be like Southern governors after the *Brown* decision, who stood in the schoolhouse door resisting changes in the law to reflect the Constitution" (Finder 1989a: 4-1).

The Charter Revision Commission put forth its final recommendation in early August 1989 and recommended eliminating the Board of Estimate, transferring its authority to the mayor and council, and increasing the number of council seats. A city vote of 55 percent in favor versus 45 percent against the changes approved the recommendations, and the U.S. Department of Justice notified Schwarz in a December 1989 letter that the charter revisions had been approved.

Charter Reform and Community Outreach

Members of the two charter reform commissions developed what they believed was an extensive outreach program to include a wide range of perspectives in the charter revision discussion. The commissioners also carried out a public education program designed to reach a broad range of the public to educate voters about the proposed changes. The two charter reform commissions held more than fifty public hearings and meetings to discuss possible changes; engaged in "hundreds of informal meetings with interested groups and individuals"; developed a "62,000 entity mailing list" and educational material in a number of languages, including Spanish, Korean, and Chinese; and sent press releases to "African American, Latino, Chinese and Korean newspapers and TV and radio stations" (Schwarz and Lane 1989: 46–49). The mailing lists targeted legal and community groups representing African Americans, Asian Americans, and Latinos.

To educate voters once the reform commission adopted the final proposal, the communications staff produced a free 16-page "Voters' Handbook on Charter Change." Two and a half million copies were printed in Chinese, English, and Spanish and distributed widely (NYC-CRC 1989: 23). Schwarz, speaking at a public meeting in 1989, stated:

> I think our outreach has been unparalleled, not only our public hearings, but the forums we've had, the letters we've read, the letters which can be stacked

up to the ceiling . . . and the extensive discussions we've had with people in all boroughs . . . fully reflecting the diversity of the city. . . . For example, just where I was yesterday, in the meeting in the morning with church leaders from Brooklyn and Queens, a meeting with the National Hispanic Business Conference, a meeting with Chinese and other Asian leaders. (Schwarz 1989b: 3–4)

A *New York Times* (1989: A22) editorial supported the outreach efforts of the committee, suggesting that the commission created the conditions necessary for public input from minority groups in the reform process. The editorial disagreed with the coalition of African American, Latino, and Asian American groups that sought to delay the vote.

They argue that tight deadlines have prevented minority groups from playing an adequate role in the charter process. If so, it's not for lack of opportunity. The commission went out of its way to solicit views, especially from minority groups. Since the Supreme Court's decision, it has held 29 hearings and meetings in all parts of the city and has heard from nearly 700 speakers. (*New York Times* 1989: A22)

Mario Paredes, a Latino member of the Charter Revision Commission, affirmed the outreach efforts while criticizing the response of community members, stating at a public hearing, "Let's be honest with ourselves. . . . Minorities, when they had a chance to raise their voice, they were not present" (Finder 1989b: B1).

Despite this strong effort to include the public in the deliberations, key leaders in the Asian American community viewed the revision process as exclusionary and protested the charter reform process in letters from community organizations (Fung 1989; Kong 1989). For example, in a group letter addressed to Chairman Schwarz, thirty-one Asian American community members stated that attempts to reach and inform their community occurred only late in the process.

The exclusion of Asian American communities from this process is exacerbated by the absence of any Asian American representative on the Charter Revision Commission, the lack of any translated materials until very recently, and the continued lack of outreach materials to our community organizations until the very end of this process. (Asian American Community Letter 1989: 1)

A community flier endorsed by eleven Asian American organizations, including the Asian American Legal Defense and Education Fund (AALDEF), the Chinese Staff and Workers Association, the Committee Against Anti-Asian Violence, and the New York Asian Women's Center, and nineteen individuals, such as Professor Shirley Hune of Hunter College and Fay Chew Matsuda of the New York Chinatown History Project, requested a one-year postponement of the city vote on the new charter, from November 1989 until November 1990, to allow for "an adequate opportunity to educate our communities about the charter revision proposals and assess their impact on Asian Americans" (AACR, n.d.). The flier discussed some of the problems identified by the group.

> The Commission held its first official meeting with Asian American groups very late in the process on May 16, 1989. The Commission said on May 16th that it wasn't planning to translate its proposals into Asian Languages. After community pressure, a Chinese translation was produced on May 31, 1989, the day of the first public hearing. A Korean Translation did not appear until late June, 1989. . . . In its latest proposal, the Commission has rejected the one demand that most Asian American groups have supported—enlarging the City Council to at least 59 districts. The Charter Revision Commission thinks that updating its mailing lists, publishing materials in English, and meeting with a handful of community groups on the eve of its public hearing is sufficient outreach to the Asian American Community. . . . We disagree. (AACR, n.d.)

A coalition of African American and Latino groups also favored an extension of the November 1989 vote to give voters more time to study the issues, especially because so many different alternatives had been offered in rapid succession. Ruben Franco, president of the Puerto Rican Legal Defense and Education Fund (PRLDEF), stated, "We're dealing with very, very complex matters. . . . We're putting together a government that is going to be with us for a long time to come, and we just don't think there has been a sufficient airing of the issues in our community" (Finder 1989b: B1). David R. Jones, director of the Community Service Society, said, "To go from bicameralism to unicameralism in six days was a bit much. . . . We went through about six different government structures in a quick series. The chance for the public to engage in any kind of debate about this is sharply truncated" (Finder 1989b: B1).

City council members may have favored voting as quickly as possible on the changes because they would gain new powers with the charter reform, and most African American and Latino members of the city council favored the November 1989 vote (Finder 1989b). The Charter Revision Commission was acting under a timetable established by a 1987 court ruling that the city had one year to make revisions once the Supreme Court ruled on the matter (Finder 1989b). In addition, the Charter Revision Commission would have had to go to the federal courts for an extension if it decided to extend the timetable. Because the state constitution allows city council elections only in odd-numbered years, the Charter Revision Commission members also hoped that if the November 1989 vote approved the charter changes, then new members of the fifty-one-member city council could be elected as soon as 1991, rather than later if the charter vote was delayed (Finder 1989d, 1989e).

Charter Reform and the Number of City Council Districts

The Charter Revision Commission's final report stated that the commission members' actions were guided by the "extremely high priority [given] to the fair and effective representation of racial . . . minority groups," exceeded "only [by] the requirement of population equality" (NYC-CRC 1990: 14). However, the Charter Revision Commission's decision in 1989 to expand the number of council districts from thirty-five to fifty-one, despite strong requests for a substantially larger number, was a key issue that shaped redistricting and limited efforts to address the disenfranchisement of Asian Americans. AALDEF (Fung 1989), the Chinatown Voter Education Alliance (Chen 1989), and the PRLDEF (1988) submitted testimony and proposals suggesting a minimum of sixty districts to decrease district population size, thereby improving the chances of creating districts that would enhance the political influence of minority communities.

Conducting an analysis for the Charter Revision Commission, Douglas Muzzio and Tim Tompkins (1989) noted that the number of city representatives had varied greatly in New York City's history, with seventy-three aldermen in the early twentieth century. Examining the five largest U.S. cities excluding New York (Chicago, Los Angeles, Philadelphia, Houston, and Detroit) and using 1984 population figures, Muzzio and Tompkins (1989) calculated that the cities had an average council size of 22 members, with 122,600 constituents per member (the largest, Chicago's 50-member council, averaged 60,101 constituents per member).

The Charter Revision Commission's final report stated that the council size was determined by an attempt to "balance four goals."

> (1) To enhance opportunities for minority voters to elect candidates of their choice, (2) to increase the number of minority Councilmembers, (3) to maintain a Council of manageable size in which all members can meaningfully

participate and (4) to increase Councilmembers' responsiveness by making their constituencies smaller, without making those constituencies so small as to foster parochialism. (NYC-CRC 1990: 11–12)

The Charter Revision Commission members discussed at length the percentage of a minority group within a district that was needed to elect a representative of their choice, and this became one of the key issues driving the calculation of the new number of council districts. Because the proposed charter reform plan had to be reviewed by the Department of Justice, this led to a discussion among the Charter Revision Commission members about what the U.S. department considered an acceptable percentage for minority representation. Frank J. Mauro, Charter Revision Commission director of research, explained, "The conventional wisdom that had emerged was that a district needed to be at least sixty-five percent minority to be considered a minority district to pass muster with the Justice Department. The Justice Department has denied that they use that fixed yardstick, that such a fixed yardstick exists, but it is generally known and referred to in some court cases as a standard" (Mauro 1989b: 142).

Mauro believed that the 65 percent figure was calculated on the basis of the lower electoral power of minorities as a result of the younger population of minority groups compared to whites, a large number of immigrants in those populations, and the history of disenfranchisement affecting racial minorities. Asian Americans and Latinos tend to be younger than whites and therefore have a smaller proportion of voting-age residents.[2] Also, Asian Americans and Latinos have a high percentage of immigrants, which means that large numbers are ineligible to vote until they become naturalized citizens. This is less of an issue for Latinos in New York because Puerto Ricans are citizens of the United States. Thus, as Mauro (1989b: 142) explained, 65 percent is reached by adding "five percent of the . . . citizenship difference; five to the age difference; and five to the participation difference," and although Mauro did not state a specific base number at this meeting, the base was most likely 50 percent.

Discussing fifty as a possible number of council districts, Mauro (1989b) explained that "the number fifty is an attempt to balance two issues, an attempt to balance minority representation with workability . . . a concern with creating a body that was in a workable range" (p. 178). As Chairman Schwarz later added in the discussion, a larger number of council districts creates the circumstances in which minorities' votes can count, but the election outcomes are not certain. Schwarz explained, "You're going to increase the percentage of districts where there ... are these high percentages of minorities in the districts and, therefore, you're going to give an increase in opportunity to win. It doesn't mean it's guaranteed" (Schwarz 1989c: 182).

Comparing the assumed Department of Justice benchmark of 65 percent with election data, Mauro (1989b: 143–144) explained that in his analysis of council elections, he found that there were twelve council districts that were 65 percent or more minority but that no district that was less than 80 percent minority had elected a minority representative. The 80 percent figure is a consequence of the lower voting strength of minorities. Mauro (1989b) explained that the "population percentage is not necessarily the citizenship population, isn't necessarily the citizenship voting age population and isn't necessarily the citizenship voting age population that registers and votes" (p. 179).

The 80 percent figure became an important benchmark for the eventual decision about the total number of districts. With their larger and more concentrated populations, districts could be drawn with African Americans and Latinos reaching 80 percent, but Asian Americans, with their smaller and more dispersed populations, could not reach this figure anywhere in the city. In the discussion leading to the decision on the number of council districts, Schwarz also emphasized the balance between the number of districts, recognizing the importance of a larger number for minority representation, and what is practical. Discussing the possibility of fifty-one districts, Schwarz (1989c) stated that "it looks from the numbers that that increases the numbers of districts with a sufficiently large minority population to increase the likelihood of minority elections. Further, it seems to do that for both blacks and Hispanics. Further, that we take into account, in choosing the number forty-nine for fifty-one, that we are also considering workability, and the desirability of not increasing the body so far that it may become less workable" (p. 186).

Mauro (1989a: 47) concluded that, compared to fifty-one districts, increasing the number to sixty districts would result in "only very marginal gains," "increas[ing] from fifteen to sixteen" the number of potential districts with at least 80 percent minority populations. Compared to thirty-five districts, Commissioner Amalia V. Betanzos, former head of the Puerto Rican Community Development Project and National Association for Puerto Rican Civil Rights, expressed her support for fifty-one districts. Betanzos (1989b) stated before the commission's vote to increase the council size to fifty-one, "I am convinced that staying at the fifty-one will enhance minority participation and still have a workable size for the Council" (p. 51).

During the charter reform discussions, Commissioner W. Bernard Richland (1989), attorney and adjunct professor at New York University Law School, stated that he was against the increase in the number of districts because "I suggest that the addition of a large number of new councilmen is a typical example of what, in classical economics, is known as the 'make work fallacy.' In more modern terms it's called 'featherbedding'" (p. 187). As part of his argument, Richland also believed that an enlarged council would dilute the power of already elected minorities. However, this view neglects the possibility of a greater proportion of minorities in a larger council or the opportunity to reverse the complete absence of Asian Americans on the New York City Council. In a May 6, 1989, decision on the number of districts, the commission voted 12 to 1 in favor of increasing the number of districts to either forty-nine or fifty-one districts, leaving the exact number to a future vote, with Richland casting the single negative vote (Schwarz 1989c: 185, 188). In the June 27, 1989, commission meeting, the members voted in favor of fifty-one districts (Schwarz 1989a: 52).

In testimony delivered at the hearings, Asian American community members stated that their concerns were not a central part of the discussion on the number of districts. Although Mauro (1989a: 48–49) specifically mentioned that, given the "substantial population growth" of Asian Americans, increasing the number of districts would enhance their political possibilities and although the analysis of minority populations included figures on Asian Americans, I suggest that, in general, Asian Americans were peripheral to the main discussion. Such figures as the 80 percent benchmark, for example, were meaningful only for Latinos and African Americans, with their larger populations and greater levels of residential concentration.

Testifying before the Charter Revision Commission, Gail Kong, vice president of the Chinatown Voter Education Alliance, emphasized that political data applying to other minority groups may not be appropriate for Asian Americans and that the application of such data may in fact work against the interests of Asian Americans.

> Analysis of data and policy discussion have relied upon consideration of voting patterns and positions of African Americans and Latinos. There has been almost no consideration of Asians in this work. . . . We disagree strongly with the Commission's assumption that a district must have at least 80% minority voters before a minority might be elected; at least, it does not necessarily apply to Asians.

This year 3 Asians were elected as community school board members in Queens County districts that could not possibly be 80% Asian. (Kong 1989: 1–2)

Offering an explanation of why the data analysis focused on African Americans and Latinos and did not adequately consider Asian Americans, Kong (1989) suggested that the consultants doing this work responded to the guidance offered by the charter revision commissioners. The lack of a commissioner actively supporting the interests of Asian Americans may have accounted for this oversight. Kong (1989) stated, "We think the test of your work should be turned . . . on the data analysis itself. . . . We believe a great deal depends upon the direction given to staff by Commission members. And we point out here that at that important policy level, there is no Asian Commissioner" (p. 1).

Discussing the issue of the size of the city council, Kong (1989) noted that the prospect for increased Asian American political representation should prevail over the argument against a larger council because it would be harder to manage and would be less responsive. Increasing the number of districts, "the difference, for us, is really significant."

> The argument that a larger Council is unwieldy is germane when discussing the difference between 22 and 130. But we believe it is much less persuasive when comparing 51 to 59 districts. Moreover, we believe the specific obligation to increase the likelihood of Asian representation is overriding and, in fact, might argue for a slightly larger Council, up to 61 or 65 districts, for example. (Kong 1989: 3)

As Alan Gartner (1993) later mentioned during the 1990–1991 redistricting process, "As he [Ken Chin, Districting Commission member] frequently noted, perhaps the presence of an Asian-American on the Charter Revision Commission would have led to that body to require more—and thus smaller—districts, thereby increasing the opportunity the Asian-American community would be represented" (p. 152). Ethnic representation on commissions and the impact of the number of council districts on redistricting were major issues that clearly affected Asian Americans.

The Racial Composition of the Districting Commission

The racial composition of the city council Districting Commission was a key issue for the Charter Revision Commission that revealed contrasting views on race and politics. Charter commissioner Betanzos (1989a) noted the importance of race in the future Districting Commission membership: "I wonder . . . if it would be possible to . . . have the nine members reflective of the ethnic and racial composition of the City, because I think the lines would be very different if it were that rather than nine white men" (p. 135). Discussing the phrasing of a racial requirement, Chairman Schwarz (1989c: 135) responded, "I think that's quite possible." Schwarz (1989c) went on to say that "the language . . . would be that a criteria for the body that does the redistricting, would be the effective representation of racial and ethnic minorities" (p. 136).

Later in the discussion, Commissioner Richland voiced his opposition to the consideration of race when selecting commissioners and discussed the problems involved in designating appropriate minority groups, including white ethnics.

> The native Afro American is not the same as the West Indian, is not the same as the black Puerto Rican, is not the same as the black Cuban. Now, which is the minority in that group? You get that all over the place. Asian, Chinese, Korean, Japanese, Vietnamese. These are groups that tend to move together, but don't have a real interest in common except the circumstance that there was space available. The same is true of white people that are present in an area that is dominated by Lubavichas and Satmars with whom they have nothing in common. . . . What do [you] mean by a minority, how do you describe it, how do you deal with it? (Richland 1989: 174)

Mauro, the commission's research director, and Schwarz explained that the Voting Rights Act defines which groups are classified and protected as "minorities." Mauro (1989b) stated that "the Justice Department doesn't look at every minority, it looks at certain protected classes" (p. 175). Chairman Schwarz explained that

> minorities have a hard time getting elected in New York City for lots of reasons. . . . We are not going to do something that's perfect, but we can move the ball along, and that's what we are trying to do to help with a subject which reflects historical prejudice, reflects issues of citizenship, reflects issues of poverty, reflects issues of age, and to try to construct a system which advances the ball of having the minorities of this City have a chance to, that is greater than now, to get elected, and I think we can and should. (Schwarz 1989c: 175–176)

The racial requirement for the members of the Districting Commission was approved by the commissioners, and the city charter (as amended through June

28, 1999) reads: "Chapter 2-A. Districting Commission, Section 50(b)(1). The commission shall have among its members . . . members of the racial and language minority groups in New York City which are protected by the United States voting rights act of nineteen hundred sixty-five, as amended, in proportion, as close as practicable, to their population in the city" (pp. 24–25).

In 1992, however, Richard Ravitch, chair of the first charter commission, who had resigned to run for mayor in 1988 (Finder 1989c), successfully challenged the use of "racial and ethnic quotas" on the Districting Commission in *Ravitch et al. v. City of New York* (Solomon 1990: 12). Ravitch asserted that appointments should be made "on the basis of merit and of politics, not on the basis of ethnicity" (Solomon 1990: 12). The district court ruled in 1992 that the requirement was unconstitutional, in part because it "does cause harm to innocent third parties" or, as Gartner (1998: 368) interpreted the ruling, "had the potential to harm innocent people who might be precluded by race from serving."

Redistricting: Individualism Versus Race-Based Group Identity

Justice O'Connor, in a landmark U.S. Supreme Court redistricting decision, *Shaw v. Reno* (1993), used reasoning similar to that of charter commissioner Richland, who had expressed concerns about imposing a group identity on individuals. In writing for the majority opinion against a majority African American district in North Carolina, Justice O'Connor explained that creating such districts supports stereotypes "that members of the same racial group—regardless of their age, education, economic status, or the community in which they live—think alike, share the same political interests, and will prefer the same candidates at the polls" (Kousser 1999: 270). Justice O'Connor stated, "Racial classifications of any sort pose risk of lasting harm to our society. They reinforce the belief, held by too many for too much of our history, that individuals should be judged by the color of their skin. . . . Racial gerrymandering, even for remedial purposes, may balkanize us into competing racial factions" (Kousser 1999: 393).[3]

The commentaries offered by Richland, Ravitch, and Justice O'Connor focus on individualism and minimal government regulation and correspond with the legal and political ideology of legal liberalism, which "emphasizes personal autonomy and freedom from governmental intrusion" (Ancheta 1998: 51). Richland and O'Connor, by emphasizing differences among individuals, ignore the historical and contemporary practices that have created common experiences and interests for these individuals as groups. This type of analysis omits the

inequality and discrimination embedded in U.S. society that racializes experiences and generates common interests among a heterogeneous population.
This understanding of unifying concerns contributes to a long history of panethnic and multiracial organizing around such issues as labor rights, electoral
politics, distribution of government resources and services, hate crimes, and
police violence, both locally in New York City and nationally (AALDEF 1987;
Aoki 2002; CAAAV 1996; Espiritu 1992; Louie and Omatsu 2006; Vo 2004).

Richland's dismissal of this history of discrimination and his emphasis
on individualism appears in his explanation of ethnic and racial residential
patterns: "These are groups that tend to move together, but don't have a real
interest in common except the circumstance that there was space available"
(Richland 1989: 174). Richland's assertion specifically disregards the history
of race-based practices used by local and federal government agencies, financial institutions, realtors, and neighborhood associations that contributed to
the creation of segregated residential and commercial areas (Dreier et al. 2001;
Massey and Denton 1993). At the time of the redistricting, following trends in
the United States (Logan et al. 1996), whites were the most residentially segregated group in New York City. According to the 1990 census, 84 percent of
whites lived in voter tabulation districts that were at least 50 percent of the
same racial group, compared to 68 percent for African Americans, 47 percent
for Latinos, and 9 percent for Asian Americans (Gartner 1993: 45).[4] The 2000
census data show that rates of segregation remain high and have been basically
unchanged in the New York metropolitan area since 1960 (Logan 2001).

Richland's analysis ignores how residential patterns are not merely the result of individual choice but rather are shaped by larger institutional factors.
Creating districts that consider race is a recognition of the complex relationship between community-situated factors, such as residential segregation and
political exclusion, and the way such factors are related to shifting and multiple
levels of ethnic and racial identity. Diverse groups, such as Chinese, Japanese,
and Koreans, organized at the more inclusive panethnic level as Asian Americans in redistricting. Richland (1989) further erases the practices of racial sub-
ordination and hierarchy when he adds the white ethnic groups Lubavitchers
and Satmars—Orthodox Jews with their origins in Russia and Romania—to
the discussion and asks, "What do [you] mean by a minority, how do you describe it, how do you deal with it?" (p. 174). Richland's and Justice O'Connor's
judgments on the political importance of race, framed by individualism, reso-
nate with Thernstrom's analysis of politics and redistricting and her attention

to individual and group attributes to explain the political involvement of racial minorities. Thernstrom's (1987: 53–62) focus on voting patterns, citizenship, age, and levels of cultural assimilation neglects government policies that directly contributed to a history of exclusion.

Chinese Americans in New York City's Chinatown recognized that their political interests were split along a number of lines, such as class and nativity. For example, a key community issue was the conflict between real estate developers' interest in gentrification and low-income workers' concern over jobs and affordable housing (Hunter College Neighborhood Planning Workshop 1992; Lower East Side Joint Planning Council 1984). Chinatown residents, however, also recognized their common subordinate political position as Chinese Americans and, even more broadly, as Asian Americans and people of color. During public hearings on redistricting, Asian Americans enumerated the federal policies and practices that historically have disenfranchised and discriminated against Asian Americans, such as exclusionary immigration laws, the denial of naturalization to early immigrants, the incarceration of Japanese Americans during World War II, and gerrymandered districts.

Community activists used the panethnic label "Asian American" when recognizing the common racialization of the diverse Asian ethnic groups and used ethnic-specific terms, such as "Chinese American," for particular individuals or events. Gail Kong, vice president of the Chinatown Voter Education Alliance, testified before the Charter Revision Commission.

> And we are a racial minority, which means that the inevitable burden of racism and discrimination persists with us. . . . I grew up in a California farm town, population 7,000, where one would expect that the residents, largely refugees from the Dust Bowl disaster, had precious little time to worry about discrimination. But they did find time to sign a petition barring my young, struggling parents from building their first home on the better side of town. That was even before World War II and internment. And all my Asian friends have a similar story. I am also frankly ashamed as a New Yorker, in liberal . . . New York City, that we're still under the jurisdiction of the Justice Department for our treatment of minorities. (Kong 1989: n.p.)

The emphasis on legal individualism, based on a consideration of individual rights, has historically worked in the United States to legitimate policies that supported the continued disenfranchisement of racial minorities by ignoring the history of racial exclusion in the political process. Disenfranchisement was further strengthened by recognizing potential harm to whites as a group and striking down provisions to assist minorities, as in the case of the charter provision on the racial makeup of the Districting Commission and the Supreme Court redistricting decisions, resulting in the continued support of the "possessive investment in whiteness" (Lipsitz 2006).

Census Undercount

The U.S. Constitution established the census to provide population information for the apportionment of congressional seats, and although determining the population appears to be a straightforward statistical exercise, politics and race have surrounded the census since its inception. Although avoiding explicit racial terms, guidelines for the census included racialized counting procedures with the infamous "three fifths" qualifier in regard to slaves while fully counting white indentured servants (Anderson and Fienberg 1999). The U.S. Constitution, in Article 1, Section 2, stated that the population "shall be determined by adding to the whole Number of free Persons, including those bound to Service for a Term of Years, and excluding Indians not taxed, three fifths of all other Persons." In 1868, Section 2 of the Fourteenth Amendment changed the counting process with regard to African Americans with the words "whole number of persons in each State."[5]

A comparison of the 1940 census with selective service registration of the same year showed that the census undercounted African American males from urban areas at a higher rate than it did white males, suggesting that rather than being random, the undercount varied by race and region (Anderson and Fienberg 1999). As Margo J. Anderson and Stephen Fienberg (1999) explain, the issue of the undercount changed from a methodological question for statisticians and demographers to a broader societal concern with the advent of the social movements for racial equality and social justice in the 1950s and 1960s. The census gained added importance as a major source of data in the study of discrimination and whether or not unequal racial and gender patterns existed in employment, education, and housing (Anderson and Fienberg 1999; Prewitt 2000c). The 1964 U.S. Supreme Court ruling in *Reynolds v. Sims*, involving districts in Alabama, established the one-person, one-vote principle in redistricting, requiring that districts be equal in population (Davidson 1992). Census figures are also used for calculating the distribution of federal funds to state and local governments. Considering the billions of dollars at stake for a range of programs, involving such vital areas as job training, transportation, social services, housing, and education, communities have a vital stake in the census figures (Prewitt 2000c).

The undercount received national attention when Daniel P. Moynihan, then director of the Joint Center for Urban Studies at MIT and Harvard University, helped initiate the 1967 Conference on Social Statistics held in Washington, D.C. The undercount of racial minorities concerned Moynihan, and he stated in the conference report that "the full enumeration of the American population is not simply an optional public service provided by government for the use of . . . sociologists, and regional planners. It is, rather the constitutionally mandated process whereby political representation in the Congress is distributed as between different areas of the nation" (Heer 1968: v). Conference organizer David Heer (1968: 10) explained that only recommendations approved by a minimum of two-thirds of conference participants would be noted in the conference report. The conference resolution, "Improving Enumeration of Negroes, Puerto Ricans, and Mexicans," commented on the serious racial implications of the undercount in terms of political representation and federal funding.

> Where a group defined by racial or ethnic terms, and concentrated in specific political jurisdictions is significantly undercounted in relation to other groups, then individual members of that group are thereby deprived of the constitutional right to equal representation in the House of Representatives, and, by inference, in other legislative bodies. Further . . . they are deprived of their entitlement to partake in federal and other programs designed for areas and populations with their characteristics. (Heer 1968: 174, 176)

The Census Bureau has used two methods to estimate the undercount: demographic analysis and the dual-systems or postenumeration survey. Demographic analysis uses data on births, deaths, migration, and other sources to create an estimate of the population. A dual-systems survey conducts a second survey after the census and then uses the two sources to develop an estimate of the population (Anderson and Fienberg 1999; Schenker 1993). According to Nathaniel Schenker (1993), the Census Bureau planned to use the estimates to evaluate the 1980 census undercount but not to make changes in the final figures. While preparing for the 1990 census, the bureau hoped to provide an estimate with an acceptable degree of accuracy to actually make an adjustment. In 1987, however, Robert Ortner, the undersecretary of commerce for economic affairs, announced the canceling of the postenumeration survey for the 1990 census because no adjustment would be made for the undercount.

Later in the year, Barbara Bailar, the associate director for statistical standards, resigned, as reported in the *Washington Post*, "because she believes Republicans in the Commerce Department had political motives in killing a plan to compensate for an expected severe undercount of Blacks and Hispanics in the 1990 census" (Anderson and Fienberg 1999: 88), groups that tend to register as Democrats. Testifying the following year before the House Subcommittee on Census and Population, Bailar stated that "first, adjustment is a correction operation that will make the census counts more accurate, and two, adjustment is technically feasible" (Anderson and Fienberg 1999: 91). Bailar also stated that "Dr. Ortner's arguments against adjustment are so seriously flawed and so inconsistent as to suggest utter indifference whether or not they are even believed" (Anderson and Fienberg 1999: 91). The secretary of commerce used the unadjusted 1990 census as the official census, rejecting the census director's recommendation that the 1990 adjusted census figures be used. The secretary explained, "I am confident that the political considerations played no role in the Census Bureau's choice of an adjustment model for the 1990 census. I am deeply concerned, however, that adjustment would open the door to political tampering with the census in the future" (Prewitt 2000c: 3).

Following the decision not to adjust the 1990 census, New York City and the state of New York, joined by other states and cities, such as California and Los Angeles, filed a lawsuit in 1988, *New York v. United States Department of Commerce*, in an attempt to compel the secretary of commerce to adjust the census. The lawsuit argued that the undercount would interfere with "both the efficacy of their votes and their entitlement to an equitable portion of federal funds" (*Harvard Law Review* 1995: 971). Through negotiations, the parties agreed in 1989 to establish an independent panel to review the decision not to adjust the census and to allow a postenumeration survey. In 1991, the secretary of commerce decided not to adjust the census, and a district court judge upheld that decision in 1993, stating that the plaintiffs failed to demonstrate that the decision was "arbitrary or capricious" (Anderson and Fienberg 1999: 156).

In 1994, the federal appeals court vacated the 1993 judgment, stating that by not adjusting the census using the postenumeration survey, the secretary of commerce did not make "an effort to achieve equality as nearly as practicable. ... The burden thus shifted to the Secretary to justify his decision not to adjust the census in a way that the court found would for most purposes be more accurate and would lessen the disproportionate counting of minorities" (Anderson and Fienberg 1999: 157). The case was argued before the U.S. Supreme Court in 1996, and the Court ruled unanimously in support of the secretary of commerce's decision not to adjust the census using the postenumeration survey, in part deciding that the decision followed the best available evidence. Anderson and Fienberg (1999: 163–164) suggest, however, that the opinion by Chief Justice William Rehnquist on the case demonstrates a misunderstanding of the dual-systems process and census. The 1996 Court decision ended the battle over the adjustment of the 1990 census.

Kenneth Prewitt (2000c: 7), director of the Census Bureau for the 2000 census, explains that an undercount results in injustice only if there is a systemic bias in the undercount, which he notes, is the case. He points out that the censuses from 1940 to 1990 show a clear differential between African American and white males through time, with African American males undercounted at a much higher rate. Nationally, the Census Bureau calculated that Asian Americans were undercounted in the 1990 census by 3.1 percent, Latinos by 5.2 percent, Native Americans by 5 percent, and African Americans by 4.8 percent, compared to only 1.7 percent for whites (Anderson and Fienberg 1999: 125). As Prewitt (2000c) explains, however, even with these systemic differences, adjusting the census results does not result in major changes with regard to the apportionment of seats in the House of Representatives and federal funding. Prewitt (2000c: 9) explains, "Changes in shares produced by adjusted counts are relatively small," but the reason there is so much concern over the adjustment is that the "political debate, however, often focuses on the large totals rather than the comparatively small changes in shares."

Making a similar point, Peter Skerry (2000: 122) notes that of the $185 billion in federal grant programs allocated in 1998, if the adjusted 1990 census were used instead of the unadjusted figures, for fifteen programs representing about 80 percent of the funds allocated, $449 million, or only 0.33 percent, would have been allocated differently. Skerry (2000) argues that adjusting the census adds its own potential errors, concluding that "the implications of the undercount have been overblown, the risks of adjustment have been underestimated" (p. 122).

The errors in funding as a result of the undercount, however, are not distributed evenly, and large cities with large populations of minorities disproportionately experience a loss in funding, which is substantial when added up year after year. David Dinkins—mayor of New York City in 1990—expressed concern about the loss of major federal funding based on population figures, stating, "At the Commerce Department, statistical grand larceny has become a way of life. . . . And the inevitable undercounting, under-funding and under-representation have become as certain as death and taxes" (F. Clifford 1990: A26).

The Census and World War II

Considering that the undercounted tend to be racial minorities in urban areas, groups that tend to register as Democrats, the decision of a Republican administration under Ronald Reagan not to use the postenumeration survey to adjust the census contributed to the view among racial minorities that the decision was based on political rather than statistical factors. U.S. government policies and institutions have created and enforced discrimination on such issues as residential segregation and immigration policies, generating well-founded suspicion and distrust among racial minorities toward government agencies, and the actions surrounding the 1990 census add to this history.

In the case of the Census Bureau, there was an egregious violation of trust between the U.S. government and its residents during World War II. Scholars suggest that the bureau provided confidential information from the 1940 census to the War Department to help locate Japanese Americans (Daniels 1982; Okamura 1981). Roger Daniels investigated this issue in 1975 and received a copy of a 1946 report from the Census Bureau written by John Vance Dobbin, who was employed by the bureau as a historian at that time. The report noted that Calvert L. Dedrick, the chief of statistical research for the bureau, went to California to assist with the internment of Japanese Americans. The Dobbin report stated that on Dedrick's arrival in California,

> he soon discovered that he did not have enough statistics and then followed a series of telegraphed orders to the Census Bureau to make special tabulations and maps. Various Divisions of the Bureau went into action and dispatched the needed data to Dr. Dedrick in record time. . . . Many special tabulations for the program of alien control by the War Department as well as for evacuation of the Japanese from the West Coast were prepared by the Bureau of the Census at the expense of the War Department. . . . The Census Bureau also provided special tabulations in the fields of agriculture and business for use in planning and executing the Japanese evacuation program. (Daniels 1982: 103)

In two press statements remarkable for their candor and forthrightness, Kenneth Prewitt (2000b: n.p.), head of the 2000 census, corroborated the Census Bureau's activity to aid the incarceration, stating that "in the spring of

1942, the Census Bureau cooperated with the war effort by providing special tabulations of the Japanese American population for counties and county subdivisions, and for some cities at the block level." Commenting on the legal and ethical status of the Census Bureau actions, Prewitt wrote:

> The record is less clear whether the then in effect legal prohibitions against revealing individual data records were violated. . . . However, even were it to be conclusively documented that no such violation did occur, this would not and could not excuse the abuse of human rights that resulted from the rapid provision of tabulations designed to identify where Japanese Americans lived and therefore to facilitate and accelerate the forced relocation and denial of civil rights. (Prewitt 2000a: n.p.)

In March 2007, Margo Anderson and William Seltzer made public documents from the U.S. Department of Commerce that they found while doing research on the Census Bureau. For the first time, the documents offered conclusive evidence that the Census Bureau released microdata containing information on seventy-nine individual Japanese Americans in the Washington, D.C., region, including names and addresses (Minkel 2007; Watanabe 2007). Authorized by the Second War Powers Act of 1942, which ended in 1947, the release of information to the Secret Service was legal, although it raises ethical issues and creates a sense of distrust between community members and government agencies. As Lane Hirabayashi explains, "People of color have always been suspicious of . . . federal agencies that collect information. . . . The historical pattern is that the data is used to the disadvantage of people of color without the money and legal resources to defend themselves" (Watanabe 2007: A18).[6]

New York City's Chinatown and the Undercount

As Prewitt pointed out, the size of the undercount is small in comparison to the total size of the population. For New York City's Chinatown, however, considering that immigrants (especially the undocumented), racial minorities, non–English speakers, and low-income residents of urban areas tend to be undercounted by the largest margin, the undercount would be much greater for the community. Before the 1990 census data were available, community members estimated that, based on the number of housing units and the average occupancy of those units, Chinatown contained 100,000 to 150,000 inhabitants, a population sufficient to create an Asian American majority district.[7] Recognizing that adjusting the census for the undercount is a highly partisan issue, because the undercounted tend to be Democrats (Rosenblatt 2001), Virginia Kee, president of the Chinese American Planning Council, stated, "We of the Asian American community have little faith that the 1990 census will be accurate. These figures should not be used to further stifle representation from this community" (Kee 1990: 66–67). Ken Chin, a member of the Districting Commission, reported that the Census Bureau suggested that New York City's Asian Americans were undercounted by about 18 percent (Chin 1991), a much higher percentage than the 3.1 percent undercount of Asian Americans in the nation as a whole.

According to the 1990 census, as shown in Table 2, the city's population was 7,322,564, and each of the fifty-one districts required a population of approximately 143,579 (compared to 209,216 if there were thirty-five districts, or 122,042 if there were sixty districts). The census counted only 63,414 in Chinatown. A high undercount in Chinatown meant that other areas (as it happened in this case, white neighborhoods) had to be added to meet minimum population requirements for a district. Commenting on the political repercussions of the undercount, Margaret Chin stated, "It was a tremendous undercount and there was nothing we could do about it. In the final scenario, they came down with a district but it was not the ideal district that we wanted" (Saito 1996b). During the 1990–1991 redistricting, the Districting Commission attempted to mitigate the problem by minimizing the population for District 1, which at 137,930 was the smallest of the fifty-one districts created.

Table 2 Racial composition of New York City, 1980 and 1990

Race/ethnicity	Percentage of city population		Number	
	1980	1990	1980	1990
African American	24.0	25.2	1,694,505	1,847,049
Asian American	3.4	6.7	239,338	489,851
Latino	19.9	24.4	1,406,389	1,783,511
White	52.4	43.2	3,703,203	3,163,125
Other (including Native Americans)	0.4	0.5	28,204	39,028
Total population			7,071,639	7,322,564

SOURCES: Data for 1980: U.S. Bureau of the Census, 1980 *Census of Population,* PC80-1-C1, Table 249250. Data for 1990 reported in the New York City Districting Commission newsletter, April 1991, no. 10, p. 2. African American, Asian American, and white data are from the non-Hispanic category.

This number is about 15,900 more than sixty districts would have required, a fairly significant number considering that the added white, middle-class individuals tend to be high-propensity voters.

Feelings of betrayal about the Census Bureau and the undercount were expressed at a public forum on Gartner's (1993) redistricting report, underscoring the belief that the government discriminates against minorities. Responding to criticism that ethnic communities should have taken greater responsibility to ensure an accurate census, Esmeralda Simmons, former member of the Districting Commission and director of the Center of Law and Social Justice at Medgar Evers College, cited U.S. government actions that stifled community efforts.

> E. Simmons: the idea that our communities did not get involved is very skewed because our communities were geared up to get involved until the INS [Immigration and Naturalization Service] decided to undo their commitment and do those raids immediately as the Census started. They said they wouldn't do raids. When they started doing raids, that was the end of the Census, and it was, in my opinion, deliberately timed. No one's going to sign up and say that they're here illegally and risk being deported. . . .
>
> Alan Gartner: The Secretary of Commerce who made this decision was [President George H. W.] Bush's campaign manager two elections ago.
>
> E. Simmons: Exactly. (Santiago, n.d.: 32)

As Simmons stated, "They knew the census was going on, and they understood that it would have a discouraging effect, but they went ahead and did it anyway" (Saito 2000).

Casting a Ballot

Because of New York City's history regarding the political disenfranchisement of racial minorities, the redistricting efforts were under the preclearance provisions of the Voting Rights Act because the U.S. attorney general had determined that New York had used a literacy test in violation of the Voting Rights Act. Also, with low voter turnout an indicator of obstacles to voting, the Census Bureau established that "fewer than 50% of the voting age residents in Bronx, Kings [Brooklyn], and New York [Manhattan] counties had voted in the 1968 presidential election," and in a lawsuit filed by the NAACP, a federal district court found that New York did not offer a required Spanish-language ballot (New York City Districting Commission 1991b: 8–9).

Barriers resulting from language and limited knowledge of the U.S. political system present additional challenges for immigrants. Even when immigrants manage to become naturalized citizens, register to vote, and appear at the polls, however, AALDEF reports that Asian Americans in Chinatown and other neighborhoods face other problems with a long history in the city. AALDEF (2006: 9) documented such obstacles as "interpreter shortages that led to voters being turned away; poll workers blocking interpreters from assisting voters or making disparaging or racist remarks about language assistance and Asian Americans; [and] poor and ineffective notices of poll site changes that led to voter confusion." In the 2004 elections, AALDEF poll monitors reported "poorly trained" and "racist poll workers," such as a poll worker who held Asian Americans responsible for slow lines, stating, "You Oriental guys are taking too long to vote" (AALDEF 2005: 1). The poll monitors also noted that voters whose names were missing from the voter lists could vote using provisional ballots, but when Asian Americans asked for such ballots, the poll workers refused to provide them (AALDEF 2005).

Even when poll workers attempted to be helpful, limited resources sometimes hampered their efforts. Poll monitor Claire Hsiang observed conditions at a Chinatown voting place during the 1996 school board elections. Because noncitizens can vote in New York City's school board elections, it is often an immigrant's first exposure to American-style democracy. Hsiang described the confused and hectic scene on voting day.

> There are only two interpreters, who are rushing back and forth, overwhelmed with demands for help. . . . More than 50 Chinese-speaking voters crowd the polling site. Unable to find their names in the rolls, election workers distribute affidavit ballots. . . . But these ballots are almost all in English and Spanish. . . . Unable to cast their vote, many start to leave. . . . I call the board a second time to report the lack of Chinese and English affidavit ballots. I have to shout to be heard over the bedlam of bewildered voters, agitated workers, and angry P.T.A. [Parent-Teacher Association] members. . . . A board representative . . . arrives. . . . He says, "Most sites only have three voters by now." The problem at this site . . . is the discrepancy between the actual number of registered voters and the number verified in the voter rolls. The book has only 54 names. P.T.A. members are incensed. They claim they had registered more than 500 parents and hand-delivered the registration forms to the board. (Hsiang 1996: 3)

The comment of the board representative that "most sites only have three voters by now," compared to the fifty at the Chinatown voting site, is telling. It shows that the effective grassroots effort by members of the PTA to mobilize residents is hampered by the city's election process, which is poorly equipped to handle the new voters, adding an obstacle that serves to disenfranchise Chinatown residents.

Conclusion

The New York City case demonstrates that the actions of the Charter Revision and Districting Commissions to enhance the political power of racial minority groups were constrained by the commission members' limited recognition of the historical and contemporary institutional barriers that actively worked to privilege whites over minorities in politics. Charter reform in 1989 and redistricting in 1991 were elements among a wide range of factors, both explicitly racial in character and outwardly race neutral and unconnected, that collectively contributed to political disenfranchisement. This constellation of local and national practices and policies that worked to exclude racial minorities from the political process constituted the "sedimentation" of political inequality (Oliver and Shapiro 1995).

More than 80 percent of the Asian American voters in Chinatown supported Asian American candidates in the 1990 city council election (AALDEF 1992: 5). The impact of those votes, however, was limited by the configuration of the district, its demographic profile, fifty-one rather than sixty districts and the population requirements for each district, the census undercount, and a range of other factors, such as the demographic and ideological makeup of the commissions, that framed electoral politics. Since the earliest history of the United States, when voting rights were limited to white men of property, political practices have had racial consequences, particularly in the way such practices have been rooted in privileged access to power, rewards, and opportunities for whites (Kousser 1999; Lipsitz 2006; Roediger 1994). Because of these procedures, racial privilege is in part developed and supported by the structure of political institutions. In other words, these institutions are not simply neutral instruments through which interests are contested and expressed (Crenshaw et al. 1995). As a result, the reform of political institutions is a key setting for the defense or contestation of inequality.

Asian Americans view membership on the city council and commissions as a step, however small, toward gaining a voice in politics to address state-sponsored and private exclusionary practices. City government is an important setting in which to contest and negotiate issues of class, race, and geography, particularly for Asian Americans and other minorities who lack the economic, social, and political resources to establish or become members of nongovernment organizations that exercise enormous influence on city policies and development projects. Historically, Asian Americans were absent from such New York organizations as the Regional Plan Association (which drew its membership from the city's elite bankers, developers, and corporate and foundation executives) or the Downtown Lower Manhattan Association (which included representatives of development, insurance, and finance interests).

The Districting Commission members' decision to link Asian Americans with whites and disengage them from Latinos did not adequately consider that political strategies were highly dynamic and contextual, adjusting to changing circumstances such as demographic characteristics, issues, candidates, and type of office. The public hearing requests by Asian Americans and Latinos for the separation of the groups were in part a recognition of the winner-take-all format of the political system that compels historically disenfranchised and underrepresented groups into direct competition with one another for a limited number of seats. Separating the populations was a strategy to maximize the potential for each group to elect community representatives, not necessarily an expression of antagonistic relations and opposing interests. Therefore, when the 1990 census figures ended the possibility of an Asian American majority district centered in Chinatown, the Districting Commission could have revisited the range of possibilities, including the creation of a majority-minority district, rather than adhering so strongly to the principle of separating racial minorities. Clearly, Asian Americans were divided over this issue, revealing the range of political interests and views concerning the composition of the district within the community. In the end, however, differences within the community could not be settled at the ballot box because a majority Asian American district was not possible, and when the Districting Commission created a district dominated by whites, the Chinatown debate was eclipsed by the dominant political voice, white voters. Elsewhere in the United States during that period, both the separation and joining of Latinos and Asian Americans had occurred. The groups successfully worked together in Oakland, California, to support the creation of separate Asian American– and Latino-influenced city council districts in 1993 (Fong 1995, 1998), and they also worked together in the San Gabriel Valley of Los Angeles County to create state assembly and state senate districts that joined their populations in 1991 (Aoki 2002; Saito 1998, 2006).

The second premise guiding the formation of the Chinatown district—that is, the belief that white voters would continue to support Asian American candidates—was extremely optimistic or else disingenuous, considering the long history of whites actively working to exclude minorities in New York City. As John Mollenkopf (1990) characterized the experience of African Americans and Latinos up to that point, "Collectively, blacks and Latinos are either excluded from the dominant coalition (as in the mayoralty or the Board of Estimate) or (as in the Council and Legislature) have been incorporated as a dependent, controlled and numerically underrepresented minority" (p. 78). Mollenkopf did not need to mention Asian Americans in this statement because Asian Americans have faced greater exclusion. The difference between whites voting for Chin for the position of local Democratic Party official and their voting for city council is that the city council is a much more powerful position in terms of city policy development and resource distribution. As John Logan and John Mollenkopf (2003) stated in their study of politics in New York City and Los Angeles about the reluctance of whites to support the multiracial coalitions that are necessary to elect minority candidates, "Of all the factors that impeded the closing of the immigrant minority representation gap, the persistence of racial polarization in urban politics may be the most important" (p. 48).

Finally, the belief that whites would vote for an Asian American reaffirms the notion of the group as a model minority and positions Asian Americans differently from African Americans and Latinos (Kim 1999). Although this seems like a positive characterization, accepting the belief that Asian Americans are the model minority and will receive white voter support weakens the political power of Asian Americans because it allows for the creation of the Chinatown district in which Asian Americans are placed with whites. As a result of the demographics of the district and the history of whites working to disenfranchise minorities, as suggested by community activists testifying at the Charter Revision and Districting Commission public hearings and the use of literacy tests, Asian American votes are submerged by white votes.

6 Latino Political Empowerment or Systemic Inequality

Redistricting in the Los Angeles Region, 2000–2002

DISCUSSING THE POLITICAL IMPORTANCE of redistricting, Maeley Tom (2001), an Asian American with twenty years of experience as a senior staff member in the offices of various California legislators, observed, "It amazes me that the majority of Californians barely notice or understand a process that would impact the political landscape of their state for a decade" (p. 1). Redistricting refers to the construction of new political districts by redrawing boundaries after each decennial census to reflect population changes. The configuration of districts directly affects the political power of racial groups, either by gathering members of a particular group within a district to concentrate their voting strength or by fragmenting a group by placing its members into two or more districts to dilute their political impact.[1]

The state legislature is the entity that carries out the redistricting of California's state senate, assembly, and U.S. congressional districts. This means that politicians control the process that directly affects their future political fates. Historically, politicians have not adequately considered the concerns of minorities. Even though Asian Americans, African Americans, and Latinos have all formed groups to participate in the process through research and advocacy, their efforts have not always reaped tangible benefits.

In the 2000 redistricting of state electoral districts in the Los Angeles region, a strong possibility for conflict existed among racial minorities, as each group attempted to influence redistricting in ways that would favor its community. A working relationship formed, however, among Asian American, Latino, and African American community groups and civil rights organizations, and I examine the factors that led to cooperation rather than conflict. Historically, redistricting has been a clear contributor to systemic inequality through the disenfranchisement of racial minorities. With increasing Latino electoral success, however, a substantial number of Latino officials were elected to the state legislature, and they were active in creating and supporting the 2000 redistricting plan. As a result, when the Mexican American Legal Defense and Educational Fund (MALDEF) filed a lawsuit against the final redistricting plan, it faced opposition to the suit from Latino elected officials, unlike in earlier redistricting battles when racial minorities were pitted against whites. I examine the dialogue that took place between MALDEF and the Latino politicians on the importance of race in politics and the consequences for redistricting and suggest that one's interpretation of race is influenced by one's position in the political structure and the interests related to that location. Ultimately, the case was decided in the courts, and the judges' decision echoed other court cases, such as *Shaw v. Reno*, and the arguments of the legislators, suggesting that society is entering a color-blind era and that racially polarized voting is no longer a major factor in society. I argue that that this move toward race-neutral public policy serves to disenfranchise minority voters in the redistricting process.

In terms of the factors framing redistricting, the 2000 census showed that Asian Americans made up 10.9 percent of California's population, African Americans 6.7 percent, Latinos 32.4 percent, and whites 46.7 percent. A comparison of the 1990 and 2000 censuses revealed different demographic trends for these racial minorities. Asian Americans increased by 38.5 percent, Latinos by 35 percent, and African Americans by only 4.3 percent. Moreover, African Americans declined as a percentage of the state's population (LaGanga and Hubler 2001: A1).

Two major changes affected the redistricting prospects of African Americans in Southern California. First, African Americans were moving away from areas of historically high African American concentration, such as South Los Angeles, to outlying multiracial regions, such as Riverside and San Bernardino counties. Second, Latin American immigrants were moving into the traditional African American neighborhoods. Where once districts could easily be drawn with African American majorities, this was no longer the case, as Latino immigrants and U.S.-born Latinos replaced out-migrating African Americans and became the majority population. Between 1980 and 2000, for example, the city of Compton went from 73.9 percent African American to 40.3 percent and from 21.1 percent Latino to 56.8 percent.[2]

The 1997 Los Angeles mayoral elections marked a turning point in the city's recent political history when Latinos, for the first time, surpassed African American voters in numbers. In that election, 15 percent of the voters were Latino, 13 percent African American, 4 percent Asian American, and 65 percent white (*Los Angeles Times* 1997: A27). In terms of redistricting, Latinos would like to expand their growing political clout, given their standing as the second-largest population in the state, their rapid growth, and their concentration in certain areas. As for Asian Americans, even though they are the fastest-growing population in the state, they are residentially dispersed. Thus they must find ways to maximize the few areas of concentration that exist. African Americans, meanwhile, are working to delay the possible decline in their political influence because of their out-migration and new residential patterns.

Establishing an Interracial Coalition

The Asian Pacific American Legal Center (APALC) in Los Angeles began organizing redistricting groups throughout the state in 1998, building on networks established through their 1990 redistricting effort, the 2000 U.S. census outreach, and their already extensive collaboration with other Asian American and Pacific Islander legal and community service organizations. A statewide organization, the Coalition of Asian Pacific Americans for Fair Redistricting (CAPAFR), emerged from these efforts and included nine regional groups.[3] Although APALC organized community groups in the 1990 California redistricting, the 2000 coalition strategy went far beyond the 1990 effort by including an analysis of all the assembly districts in the state, rather than just those with large concentrations of Asian Americans, and by building a broader network of community organizations. As CAPAFR noted in a summary of their redistricting activities:

> The year 2001 marked a significant year for Asian Pacific [Islander] American (AP[I]A) political empowerment. For the first time, APIA communities organized statewide to actively engage in the statewide Assembly redistricting process and create a statewide Assembly proposal. With the support and direction of the Asian Pacific American Legal Center, APIA communities in nine California regions came together under a single network, the Coalition of Asian Pacific Americans for Fair Redistricting. (CAPAFR, n.d.: n.p.)

MALDEF also organized on a statewide basis and held numerous redistricting educational workshops and gathered input from community members about their particular neighborhoods to be used in formulating districts. Amadiz Velez, MALDEF's statewide redistricting coordinator, described this outreach effort at the September 4, 2001, public hearing held by the assembly redistricting committee.

> We visited over 35 communities throughout California starting in [the] City of Calexico. Starting earlier this year we've done briefings with the community. We've shown them the technology. . . . We taught them the law to the extent that it interacts with redistricting. We have shown them how they can have an impact in their own community not just at the Assembly and Senate level and Congressional level but also at [the] Supervisor level and the City Council level. And people have really become more empowered by learning about this process. So the work we are today presenting is one that is based upon extensive, extensive outreach. . . . And I would also like to note that this is not exclusive. . . . Members of the entire public were always welcome to our meetings, and in fact people of all nationalities and ethnicities were present there. (Velez 2001: 70)

APALC targeted the San Gabriel Valley, which has one of the largest and fastest-growing Asian American populations in California. In conjunction with area residents, APALC developed an active regional group. Located just east of Los Angeles, the valley's population has been transformed by domestic and international migration, changing from a majority-white population in 1960 to a majority-Latino population in 1990. Asian Americans also enter the picture as a rising political force. Given the demographic shift, the locus of political power has changed. Latinos now form the main voting bloc. Latinos held all the higher elected positions in the area between the mid-1990s and 2001, when Chinese American Judy Chu was elected to the California Assembly. Today, Latino elected officials continue to dominate the west San Gabriel Valley political scene.

Given that migration and resegregation have created new multiracial minority communities, redistricting has become extremely complicated because drawing the optimal district for a particular group may conflict with the interests of other groups. What, then, explains the high level of cooperation that developed among the African American, Asian American, and Latino redistricting interest groups during the 2000–2002 process? I suggest that recent U.S. Supreme Court decisions that weakened the Voting Rights Act, a shared ideology of minority empowerment, and an awareness of personal and historical discrimination in everyday life and in the political realm contributed to an understanding of the need to forge an alliance among people of color.

The key legal decision that framed redistricting in 1990 was *Garza v. Los Angeles County Board of Supervisors.* In this case the federal court ruled in favor of the Latino plaintiffs, a victory that emphasized the political rights of racial minorities and the prevention of vote dilution. However, several U.S. Supreme Court decisions handed down since then, particularly *Shaw v. Reno* (1993) and *Miller v. Johnson* (1995), which ruled that race cannot be used as the "sole" or "predominant" factor, respectively, in redistricting, have dramatically altered the legal framework (Kousser 1999: 5). Community groups discussed the ramifications of these court decisions, speculating on the possibility that any use of race in redistricting might make a plan vulnerable to a lawsuit. Just as the California state legislature began its 2001 redistricting public hearings, another Supreme Court decision, *Hunt v. Cromartie* (2001), ruled that race could be considered, provided that it was not the "dominant and controlling" factor, clearing up the confusion over whether or not race could be used at all when drawing district boundaries (Greenhouse 2001: A1).

The Court decisions that reduced the relative importance of race simultaneously elevated "traditional districting principles," such as "compactness, contiguity, and respect for political subdivisions or communities defined by actual shared interests."[4] A number of factors led African Americans, Asian Americans, and Latinos to recognize the importance of working together to strengthen their influence in the redistricting process: the new legal framework that made race subordinate to traditional criteria; the complexity of the redistricting process, given the multiple ways that urban space can be divided into communities of interest; an understanding that the state legislature controls redistricting; and gerrymandering, which has historically fragmented minority communities.

Faced with these adverse conditions, the three groups established a dialogue from the beginning of the process, exchanging ideas, concerns, and information. Their common goal was to draw maps to support each other's interests. Stewart Kwoh (2001), executive director of APALC, explained, "It was . . . critical for us to have dialogue and collaboration with our counterpart civil rights organizations such as the Mexican American Legal Defense and Educational Fund, NAACP Legal Defense Fund, NAACP, the Southwest Voter Registration Education Project, the American Jewish Committee and many other community organizations" (p. 563). The handouts used by MALDEF in its community redistricting workshops stated, "The more leaders, organizations and members of the public the committee represents, the greater the clout of the committee and the community resources available to the committee. Furthermore, a unified minority community is more difficult for others to splinter or deny" (William C. Velasquez Institute, n.d.: 6). Priya Sridharan (2001), CAPAFR's statewide redistricting coordinator, declared, "In addition to being concerned about the voting rights of the Asian Pacific Islander American community, we are also very concerned about the voting rights and the potential disenfranchisement or political marginalization for other communities as well" (p. 98). Kathay Feng (2001a), project director of the Voting Rights and Antidiscrimination Unit of APALC, explained, "We have come together on the principle that each of our communities has the right to full political representation in accord with the Voting Rights Act. At the same time we are united in saying that no community should gain at the expense of another" (p. 47).

In the statements delivered at the state legislature's redistricting public hearings, African Americans, Asian Americans, and Latinos outlined the history of racial policies at various governmental levels that informed their present position on redistricting. An awareness of these policies contributed to the understanding that they shared a subordinate position as people of color in a society with continuing systemic inequality. Geraldine Washington, president of the Los Angeles NAACP and chair of the African American Community Advisory Committee on Redistricting, stated:

> We come before you today to voice the interests of the African American community in the current redistricting process. For some may view this as a political process, we see it as much more. The NAACP, as you know, is the oldest civil rights organization in the United States. We came into existence in 1909 in recognition of the fact that this nation had much work to do to correct injustices to its citizens who had borne the burden of enslavement and had their hopes dashed as the advances of reconstruction were displaced and replaced by Jim Crow. Impressing this nation to honor its commitment to all of its citizens, we became the vanguard of the Civil Rights Movement, and we were the foot soldiers in the establishment of the Voting Rights Act. (Washington 2001: 100)

Japanese American Thomas Ono, co-chair of the San Gabriel Valley group and a resident of Monterey Park, a city in the area, since 1977, recalled the events that shaped his understanding of race in the United States.

> I begin by sharing my background, for I believe it will help you understand the roots of my concerns. After the Second World War, my parents were released

from the internment camps and returned with nothing to Los Angeles, which remained largely segregated in its housing and employment. In 1948 I was born at the Japanese Hospital, Los Angeles, which was started in the 1920s because patients of Japanese ancestry were not accepted at other hospitals. My first residence was in a segregated neighborhood near Little Tokyo in the present skid row area of Los Angeles. . . . In the early 1960s there was a community controversy over the continued use of a racially restrictive covenant to preclude a black family from moving into Monterey Park. As a result, the Monterey Park City Council was the first to pass a resolution denouncing the enforcement of illegal race covenants. This encouraged Asian and Pacific Americans to move into Monterey Park. (Ono 2001: 138, 144)

Members of the African American Advisory Committee on Redistricting immediately followed the Asian American group at the public hearing. Coincidentally, but reinforcing the sense of shared purpose and history, Adrian Dove (2001) noted that his was the first African American family in Monterey Park that Tom Ono had mentioned. "That was my family. . . . The day that I moved in, some members of the Nazi party picketed my house in Monterey Park. . . . And a car pulled up and George Brown came . . . to my house and said, 'I'm the mayor. I'm going to stay at your house.' . . . That's how I met George Brown, and Al Song [Korean American], and the particularly strong leadership that represented that area" (pp. 162–163).

Larry Aubry, also a member of the African American Advisory Committee on Redistricting, summed up the spirit of cooperation.

We are currently working collaboratively because we feel that this is the way to do it, not because it's strategically the way to work, but because it's the [way] it should be done, through working collaboratively with MALDEF . . . with the Asian Pacific Legal Center, in crafting mutually acceptable redistricting plans. This is a very difficult task . . . we consider it critical to each group's realizing its own goals and objective, as well as collectively agreeing upon goals that benefit everyone else. Despite obvious barriers—political, cultural, attitudinal barriers, really—we believe that the needs of respective communities of color demand that we accept the challenge. (Aubry 2001: 116–117)

Having developed such perspectives, the level of cooperation based on shared goals among the Asian American, African American, and Latino groups reached an unprecedented level. In addition to constant communication among themselves, MALDEF, the NAACP Legal Defense and Educational Fund (LDF), and the National Asian Pacific American Legal Consortium co-produced a 94-page book, *The Impact of Redistricting in Your Community: A Guide to Redistricting*, which was distributed widely to community members at redistricting workshops.[5] The handbook offered useful information that defined and explained the importance of redistricting and discussed how community members could get involved in the process. The handbook stressed the importance of demographic change, the increasing numbers and percentage of people of color, and the importance of working for political representation. This last point was emphasized in the introduction: "The changing face of America raises important questions throughout our society, especially in electoral politics. Are minorities fairly represented at all levels of politics? Do we have an equal voice and an equal opportunity to elect representatives who consider our needs and interests?" (p. 3). The handbook included detailed sections on the Voting Rights Act; social, economic, and political factors that contribute to a community of interest; guidelines on how to organize at the community level; explanations of redistricting terms, such as "vote dilution" and "gerrymander"; and information for conducting a redistricting exercise to learn how to consider the many factors involved in the creation of a political district.

MALDEF, the NAACP LDF, and APALC also sponsored a one-day conference in May 2001 on the campus of the University of California at Los Angeles. Attended by community representatives from regions throughout the state, the conference included attorneys, demographers, and historians who provided information on redistricting. The conference featured hands-on redistricting workshops to help the participants learn more about the practical and legal aspects of redistricting; additional speakers from around the state and country spoke on historical, demographic, and legal aspects of redistricting.[6]

The California Districts

In writing about redistricting, a *Los Angeles Times* reporter observed, "Many members [of the state legislature] admit [that it] is their most self-serving, interest-conflicted and partisan ritual: carving new political boundaries for themselves and Californians" (Ingram 2001b: B7). Cruz Reynoso, former associate justice of the California Supreme Court, spoke at a 2001 Sacramento MALDEF redistricting conference and began his comments by noting, "Democracy is where people choose their representatives. And redistricting is where representatives choose their people" (Gonzalez 2001: 30).

In a remarkably candid discussion reported by the *Orange County Register* on August 26, 2001, Congresswoman Loretta Sanchez explained that congressional members hired Michael Berman as the primary redistricting consultant. As it turns out, one of the districts named in MALDEF's lawsuit was that of Congressman Howard Berman, the brother of consultant Michael Berman. Sanchez explained:

> She and the rest of the Democratic congressional legislation went to [Michael] Berman and made their own deal. Thirty of the 32 Democratic incumbents have paid Berman $20,000 each, she said for an "incumbent-protection plan. Twenty thousand is nothing to keep your seat," Sanchez said. "I spend $2 million (campaigning) every election. If my colleagues are smart, they'll pay their $20,000, and Michael will draw the district they can win in. Those who have refused to pay? God help them." (Quach and Bunis 2001)

Democrats controlled the 2000–2002 redistricting process because they had a majority in the state assembly and state senate and the governor was a Democrat. Republicans, however, did have several powerful tools at their disposal to attack a plan they disliked, as they had done in the past. In 1982, Republicans used a statewide referendum to challenge a Democratic plan, compelling the governor and state legislature to rework the plan. In 1991, when the Republican governor and Democratic-controlled legislature disagreed on the plan, a special committee of judges carried out the process. Also, because Republican governors had appointed all the state supreme court justices, a Democratic plan that landed in the court would face a difficult challenge. And with Democrats and Republicans battling for congressional seats around the country, federal intervention under a Republican administration was a possibility (Ingram 2002: 2).

If the Democrats developed a plan that Republicans supported and if it passed with two-thirds of the vote in the legislature, it would become law. State senator Don Perata, chair of the Senate Committee on Elections and Reapportionment, explained, "Our goal is for a status quo reapportionment. . . . I think if we do it right, we will have a bipartisan plan that will not be challenged by a statewide referendum or in the Supreme Court" (Ingram 2002: 2). To ensure Republican support for a plan, the current number of Republican congressional districts would have to be maintained. Because Democrats would get the new congressional district added through reapportionment and had won four seats from Republicans in the 2000 elections, they would also back a plan that would preserve their recent gains (Ingram 2002: 2).

After the preliminary plans were revealed in the first week of September, a *Los Angeles Times* editorial concluded that the map was aimed at protecting incumbents.

> Consider the havoc that the Legislature is causing . . . through the congressional redistricting plan. . . . The same sort of gerrymandering occurs in the state Senate and Assembly plans as well—all in the name of party politics, to keep as many incumbent Republicans and Democrats as happy as possible. . . . As a result, the plans shatter the concepts of community of interest and compactness of districts, with a few exceptions, and largely thwart the desires of Latinos and Asian Americans to win additional seats in Congress and the Legislature. (*Los Angeles Times* 2001: B14)

Later that month, after minor adjustments, the state legislature passed the redistricting plan and Governor Gray Davis signed it into law. Davis declared, "The maps produced this year are fair and balanced" (Ingram 2001a: B12). In contrast to the governor's assessment, a statement written in bold letters in the middle of the January 2002 cover of the *California Journal* proclaimed, "Redrawing California: An Incumbent Protection Plan." John J. Pitney Jr., a professor of government at Claremont McKenna College, called the plan "a classic incumbent gerrymander" in the feature article (Cannon 2002: 10).

Redistricting and Politics in the San Gabriel Valley

Media discussion on redistricting and incumbency protection primarily focused on the creation of safe seats for Democrats and Republicans. Although protecting seats was clearly an important issue, the debate ignored equally important changes and struggles that occurred within these so-called safe seats, as demonstrated by the electoral battles in the political districts covering the San Gabriel Valley. Democrats dominate this area for the most part, and incumbents were astonished by challenges from members of their own party. Although Latinos are the majority population and major political force in the region, Asian Americans are gaining numbers and winning elections, working both with and against Latinos.

Primarily a white-majority area in the 1950s, Latinos and Asian Americans overcame restrictive covenants to enter the working- and middle-class communities in the region. Domestic and international migration transformed the population, and the 1990 census showed that one city in the area, Monterey Park, became the first city in the continental United States to have an Asian

American majority, with 57.5 percent. Native-born Japanese Americans were the first Asian Americans to enter the region in significant numbers, but Chinese immigrants and Chinese Americans are now the largest Asian ethnic group. The region continues to attract Chinese immigrants and Chinese Americans as a result of its emergence in the 1980s as a regional center of commerce and services for Chinese immigrants; the region contains one of the largest concentrations of Chinese-owned businesses in the country (Fong 1994; Horton 1995; Li 1999; Tseng 1994).

Bordering Monterey Park to the north and east are the cities of Alhambra, Rosemead, and San Gabriel, which also have significant numbers of Asian Americans, and their numbers continue to grow, as shown by the 2000 census. Diversity in the Asian population in the region has also increased, with Vietnamese Americans now greatly outnumbering Japanese Americans and with growing Filipino and Korean populations. In general, as the Asian American population grows, whites have decreased dramatically in number, illustrating Philip Ethington's findings that whites have tended to "flee the growing diversity of the metropolis" (Ethington et al. 2001: 2) or at least have chosen not to move to these areas. Latinos, predominantly Mexican Americans, are at about one-third of the population in these four cities, as shown in Table 3. As a percentage of the population, the proportion of Latinos has remained about the same in Alhambra but has declined in the other three cities.

The West San Gabriel Valley contains one of the highest concentrations of Asian Americans in California, the state with the largest number of Asian Americans in the country, and because of these numbers and a significant middle-class segment with resources that can be used for politics, the West San Gabriel Valley is seen as a place of great potential for electoral success. Already, Asian Americans are making inroads on local school boards and city councils. The political reality, however, is that this concentration of Asian Americans exists within a much larger Latino population that now controls electoral power in the region. Therefore an Asian American must have significant Latino support to be elected.

Electoral victories for Asian Americans and Latinos in the region did not automatically follow demographic change. Instead, electoral success occurred through a multipronged strategy that involved building a political base with strong grassroots organizations to generate resources, mobilize voters, and support and develop candidates, coupled with dismantling systemic political barriers (Calderon 1991, 1995; Horton 1995). Activists in the region established

Table 3 Racial composition of Alhambra, Monterey Park, Rosemead, and
San Gabriel in 1980, 1990, and 2000

	Percentage of population				
	African American	*Asian American*	*Latino*	*Native Hawaiian/ American Indian*	*White*
Alhambra					
1980	1.0	12.7	36.9	0.3	48.7
1990	2.0	38.1	35.0	0.4	24.3
2000	1.7	47.2	35.5	0.8	13.8
Monterey Park					
1980	1.2	34.8	37.8	0.4	25.5
1990	0.6	57.5	29.6	0.3	11.7
2000	0.4	61.8	28.9	0.8	7.3
Rosemead					
1980	0.2	9.2	56.5	0.6	33.1
1990	0.6	34.3	48.5	0.5	15.9
2000	0.7	48.8	41.3	1.0	8.0
San Gabriel					
1980	0.7	8.8	37.2	0.9	52.3
1990	1.1	32.4	35.4	0.5	30.4
2000	1.1	48.9	30.7	0.9	17.4

SOURCES: 1980 Census of Population, v. 1, Table 59; 1990 Census of Population and Housing,
Summary Tape File 3A; Table DP-1, Profile of General Demographic Characteristics, 2000.
NOTE: Table DP-1 categories for 2000 figures: One Race: Black or African American,
American Indian and Alaska Native, Asian, Native Hawaiian and other Pacific Islander;
Hispanic or Latino and Race: Hispanic or Latino (of any race); White alone.

the West San Gabriel Valley Asian Pacific Democratic Club in 1985, one of the
first panethnic Asian American political groups in the region. Geared toward
educating the community, supporting issues, and backing candidates, the group
served as the main organizing body for the 1990 redistricting effort in the San
Gabriel Valley. The group eventually dissolved in the mid-1990s, partly a victim
of its own success as other organizations in the region developed to support
Asian American candidates and issues and some of its members went on to win
political office. Judy Chu, for example, was elected to the Garvey School Board
in 1985, the Monterey Park City Council in 1988, the state assembly in 2001,

and the state Board of Equalization in 2006. Mike Eng, a founder of the Asian Pacific Democratic Club, was elected to the Monterey Park City Council in 2003 and to the state assembly in 2006.

Ranking as one of the most important national victories in overcoming political barriers was the historic 1990 lawsuit, *Garza v. County of Los Angeles*, led by MALDEF, against gerrymandering and the fragmentation of Latinos. The San Gabriel Valley, with its large Latino population, became the center for the Los Angeles County Board of Supervisors district that was created to consolidate Latino political power. Gloria Molina, who was elected to the state assembly in 1982 and the Los Angeles City Council in 1987, was elected to the County Board of Supervisors in 1991; she joined a number of other Latino elected officials representing the San Gabriel Valley.

In the redistricting of state districts that occurred in 1990 and 2000, the boundaries of the 49th California State Assembly District were drawn to contain the four contiguous cities of Asian American concentration, reversing the fragmentation of these cities into multiple assembly districts, as in previous redistricting plans. The coalition among African Americans, Asian Americans, and Latinos in 2000 had its roots in the 1990 redistricting, which was the first major effort by Latinos and Asian Americans to work as partners.

Going into the 1990 redistricting, the four cities were divided into three assembly districts, and Asian Americans quickly reached consensus on the need to unite these cities into one district. Because the total population of the four cities was too small, at 231,600, to create an assembly district and thus an additional 140,000 people had to be added, Asian Americans faced the same dilemma as did Asian Americans in New York City's Chinatown—join with whites or with Latinos. Should the district join with cities to the north that had growing Asian American populations but white majorities that were largely Republican? Or should they join with cities to the east and west that were inhabited by Latino Democrats? After months of debate, Asian Americans decided to try to join with Latinos because of shared issues, such as immigration, bilingual education, and racial discrimination. Working against attempting to include cities to the north was an alarming number of hate crimes against Asian Americans, and unlike in Lower Manhattan, voter data showed a reluctance of white voters to support Asian American candidates.[7]

Negotiations began between the two groups, and one of the major concerns Latinos expressed was the fate of incumbent Xavier Becerra, the Latino Democrat who represented the assembly district and lived in Monterey Park. Recognizing the growing electoral strength and electoral success of Asian Americans, uniting the four cities of Asian American concentration might pose a threat to the incumbent. Latinos also acknowledged that Asian Americans had supported Latino candidates in the region through political donations and votes. Latinos and Asian Americans understood the history of gerrymandering in redistricting that had fragmented their communities in the past. When then-speaker of the assembly Willie Brown candidly stated that "the desires of incumbent lawmakers will come first as the Assembly draws new district lines," this reinforced the need for the two groups to work together rather than be pitted against one another (Weintraub 1991). Latinos and Asian Americans finally agreed on an assembly district for the area that would unite the four cities, forming an Asian American influence district that would still retain a significant Latino majority. This would create the conditions for the eventual election of an Asian American to that district in 2001.

The San Gabriel Valley: Challenging an Incumbent Congressman

Redistricting created "safe" districts in terms of political parties, but as the 2000 primary election for the 31st Congressional District in the San Gabriel Valley showed, major upheavals within a party could still occur. Matthew Martinez, a Democrat and 18-year incumbent, was challenged in the primary by fellow Democrat Hilda Solis, who had risen through the ranks as a Rio Hondo Community College trustee, assemblywoman for the 57th District, and, at the time she ran, state senator for the 24th District, the first Latina elected to that body (Rodriguez 2001). As the *California Journal* noted, "Some politicians . . . criticized Solis for targeting a colleague to further her own career" (Rodriguez 2001: 29), and, as noted political analyst Harold Meyerson stated, "Incumbents are hardly ever challenged by serious candidates from their own party—and almost never challenged by fellow office-holders from their own party" (Meyerson 2000: n.p.). Ironically, Martinez, who was elected to the Monterey Park City Council in 1974, beat a Democratic incumbent in the 1980 assembly primary in his first run for state office (Simon and Olivo 2000: B1).

Detractors of Martinez pointed to his lackluster record in Congress and his frequent absences from his district. In fact, Martinez's sister, Helen Lujan, a local school district board member, backed Solis and stated that "this is the first time I will not be supporting my brother. . . . We see Hilda, and we don't see Matthew" (Simon and Olivo 2000: B1). As Martinez explained his time away from his district and in Washington, D.C., "How can you be present when you're busy working for the district?" (Simon and Olivo 2000: B1). His supporters noted his long record of service, good staff members in the district who provided able assistance to his constituents, and reliable votes for labor issues. Yet labor unions were divided in the race, as were elected officials from the region, with support for both candidates.

Solis had a strong record of pushing issues dealing with the environment and labor. Her interest in these areas was rooted in her upbringing in the San Gabriel Valley, which was the site of eight major landfills, mining pits, and groundwater contaminated by the rocket fuel ingredient perchlorate. Her father was an immigrant from Mexico who worked with the Teamsters Union, and her mother was an immigrant from Nicaragua who worked on an assembly line (Rodriguez 2001). Solis won by a surprisingly large margin in the primary, with 62 percent of the vote (Rodriguez 2001). Although the record would show that the seat passed from one Democrat to another, this misses the importance of the change to the region and the replacement of an official that Meyerson (2000) described as one who "has no significant . . . achievements to point to" with another official who "has made important contributions to virtually every single progressive cause." After his loss in the primary election, Martinez unexpectedly changed his party affiliation from Democrat to Republican and criticized Democratic leaders for a lack of support (Simon 2000). A *Los Angeles Times* analysis of his vote found that he voted with Democrats 18 percent of the time on issues divided by party after the primary election, as compared to 92 percent of the time in the previous year (Simon 2000).

The San Gabriel Valley: Crafting the 49th Assembly District

Solis's victory left an open seat in the state senate. Gloria Romero was the 49th Assembly District representative, elected in 1998 with strong support from then–speaker of the assembly Antonio Villaraigosa. A former professor at California State University at Los Angeles, Romero had a long history working with organized labor and was elected to the Los Angeles Community College Board of Trustees in 1995. Romero ran for the state senate seat in a special election and won in 2001, leaving an open assembly seat. This set the stage for Judy Chu, who had run for that assembly seat twice before, losing each time, the last time in 1998 to Gloria Romero. Romero recognized the importance of Asian American votes and donations, and Chu clearly understood the need for Latino support and votes. Competitors in 1998, the two supported one another in 2001, and both emerged as victors, setting the stage for redistricting in 2000–2001.

Asian Americans wanted to ensure that the four cities remained intact to preserve the core of their electoral strength, but they preferred that the district shift east and north to shed parts of the Eastside of Los Angeles, which lay to the west of Monterey Park. Although this would not greatly alter the number of Latinos, it would bring in Latinos living in multiracial communities with more experience voting for Asian Americans in local elections, compared to the Eastside, which had shifted from a multiracial area in the first half of the twentieth century to a primarily Latino community.

One of the major factors guiding redistricting was to keep communities of interest intact so that areas sharing common political, economic, and social issues would remain within the same district. Areas of the Eastside in the 49th Assembly District fell under the political jurisdiction of the city of Los Angeles, and freeways separated the region from the cities in the San Gabriel Valley. As a result, the political orientation of some of the residents of the Eastside looked more to the west and the city of Los Angeles than to the east and the San Gabriel Valley, providing a reason for detaching parts of the Eastside from the 49th district.

Unlike the discussion in 1990, when cities to the north were ruled out because of their white Republican residents, even though they had growing Asian American populations, the political scene had shifted by 2000. The Asian American population continued to grow dramatically, and Asian American candidates were gaining support from white voters. Unlike previous Asian Americans elected to office, who tended to be U.S.-born, the newest wave were often immigrants with high levels of formal education (obtained in their countries of origin and/or in the United States), middle-class professionals, and former urban residents in their countries of origin with experience in civic activities.

Immigrants entering politics could take advantage of existing Asian American political networks and organizations in the San Gabriel Valley, speeding up the political acculturation process. For example, Charlie Woo, a wealthy immigrant from Hong Kong who is prominent in the Los Angeles business community as one of the leading toy manufacturers in the country, established Chinese Americans United for Self Empowerment (CAUSE) in 1993. Through educational programs, voter registration, and leadership development, CAUSE is "dedicated to promoting APA [Asian Pacific American] civic and political participation" and changed its name in 2003 to the Center for Asian Americans United for Self Empowerment to reflect its larger panethnic focus (CAUSE 2006). The organization of Chinese American Elected Officials serves as an information and networking organization and also sponsors educational events. APALC, located in downtown Los Angeles, organized the 1990 and 2000 redistricting efforts, and its educational, research, and legal activities have established its reputation as one of the most effective organizations in the nation working on Asian American issues. Developing projects through multiracial coalitions drives APALC's efforts, as its redistricting efforts have demonstrated.

In the decade after 1990, the number of Asian Americans elected to office in the region increased from six to twenty (Winton 2001a: B1). Commenting on the growing number of elected Asian Americans in the region, Don Nakanishi, professor and director of the Asian American Studies Center at UCLA, stated, "What we're seeing in the San Gabriel Valley reflects a larger trend of Asian Americans becoming more involved in politics" (Winton 2001a: B1). On the subject of increased Asian American political activity, David Lang, a political consultant who has worked with a number of Asian Americans running for office, said, "The number of Asian American candidates is exploding. . . . Chinese Americans running for office used to be news in the San Gabriel Valley. Now we're talking 10 to 15 candidates every election cycle" (Winton 2001a: B1). Marina Tse, an activist on education issues from Monterey Park who had been appointed to the state board of education and who was an immigrant from Taiwan, observed, "Now is the time for politics. . . . New immigrants initially had to take care of the family, their business. Now they are looking to contribute to the community (Winton 2001a: B1). Offering a similar explanation, University of Southern California scholar and political commentator Sherry Bebitch Jeffe noted, "The immigrant generation is not as visible in the political process because of the length of time it takes to become politically socialized," but Jeffe expressed her surprise at the growing success of Asian immigrants in politics, saying that she was "just astonished" (Watanabe 2003: B9). The recent success of Asian immigrants is no surprise, however, given the history of community volunteer work and appointments to city commissions on the part of Asian immigrants. The cluster of small cities in the San Gabriel Valley affords many opportunities for election to local school boards and city councils and serves as a training ground for elected officials who wish to run for higher office.

An analysis by CAPAFR showed that the 49th District was under the population requirement established by the 2000 census results by 44,496, which left room to add new areas. In an early proposal, CAPAFR suggested the addition of Arcadia, a city that demonstrated the remarkable demographic and electoral changes occurring in the area. In 2000, the city of Arcadia was 45.4 percent Asian American and 40.1 percent white. Sheng Chang was elected to the council in 1994, Annie Yen was elected to the school board in 2001, and John Wuo would later be elected to the council in 2002.

The state legislature's redistricting committee released the preliminary maps of the districts to the public at the end of August, right before the Labor Day weekend. On the following Wednesday and Thursday (September 4 and 5, 2001), public hearings were held in Sacramento by the legislature's redistricting committee. Despite the short notice, African Americans, Asian Americans, and Latinos analyzed the plans over the holiday weekend and joined together at the hearing to speak on the proposed plan. Kathay Feng stated:

> Today we are gathered here together. You may see that we have three organizations represented sitting together, and I think it's a momentous occasion for the Coalition of Asian Pacific Americans for Fair Redistricting, the African American Redistricting Committee, as well as the Mexican American Legal Defense and Education fund to be sitting together to present a unity map that you see here today. (Feng 2001a: 43)

Feng spoke about the underrepresentation of the growing Asian American population in the state legislature, noting that "our community is currently 13 percent of the State's population. We are the fastest-growing population in this state, yet there are only four representatives of API [Asian Pacific Islander] descent elected to the entire state legislature of 120 representatives" (Feng 2001a: 48). Feng recounted the history of the 1990 redistricting effort of Asian Americans and the importance of the effort to keep the Asian American communities in the South Bay and the San Gabriel Valley intact within their respective districts. Feng emphasized the success of this effort, stating, "Through our advocacy, both were configured to hold our communities whole. The impact was the eventual election of two Assembly members of Asian Pacific American descent. One was George Nakano from the South Bay, 53rd Assembly District in 1998 and the second was Judy Chu from the 49th in 2001" (Feng 2001b: 146).

Latinos and the 49th Assembly District

Amadiz Velez, an attorney and redistricting coordinator for MALDEF, spoke about the importance of the growing Latino population for California, the result being an additional congressional seat in the 2000 reapportionment of districts based on changes in population in the nation. Velez stated, "Had it not been for the growth in the Latino community there would be no 53rd Congressional seat in California today. 80 percent of the new residents of this state are Latino" (Velez 2001: 71). He went on to say that he had expected the proposed congressional, senate, and assembly district maps to reflect this increase in population. "Greater population would seemingly mean greater representation in our community," particularly "in Los Angeles County [where] the Latino population grew by over 800,000" (Velez 2001: 71, 72). Los Angeles County had shown the largest population gains in the state over the past decade, growing by just over 1 million residents. This was more than twice the number gained in the areas second and third in growth, Orange and San Diego counties, which each grew by just over 400,000 residents, and Riverside County, the area of fourth-largest growth, which grew by about 352,000 residents (Yu and Ichinose, n.d.).

Denise Hulett, the national redistricting coordinator for MALDEF, spoke next, stressing the importance of the legality of the plans, saying, "Our top priority of course is enforcement of the Voting Rights Act" (Hulett 2001: 73). Examining the legislature's proposed congressional, senate, and assembly plans, Hulett explained that they looked "to see whether the Latino vote was diluted," and she stated that the Latino vote was "diluted primarily in Los Angeles County in all three plans." Hulett then discussed the issue of voting patterns, citing the research of redistricting expert Morgan Kousser, who had earlier served as a research consultant for MALDEF in the 1990 *Garza v. Los Angeles County Board of Supervisors* case to see whether voters in the state and Los Angeles County had become "color blind when we entered the voting booth" (Hulett 2001: 76). Hulett stated that the research showed that "we absolutely have not, unfortunately" (Hulett 2001: 76). Continuing her discussion of voting patterns and comparing white and Latino voters, Hulett referred to the research of Claudine Gay and pointed out that "Latinos and Anglos vote very differently in Los Angeles County" and that, according to the data, "we think that the evidence is there to support a finding of continued and marked racial polarization in Los Angeles County" (Hulett 2001: 76).

Later in the September 4 hearings, state senator Richard Polanco asked for MALDEF's analysis of the proposed 49th Assembly District. Polanco and state assemblyman Marco Firebaugh repeatedly questioned MALDEF's support for the proposed 49th Assembly District and the decrease in the Latino population, an apparent contradiction in comparison to MALDEF's concern over the way the Latino population had been reduced and/or reconfigured in other districts

(Polanco 2001). Representatives of MALDEF explained that one of the issues they looked at was the population trend over the next decade, when the district maps would be in effect, stating that the Latino population was not growing in the San Gabriel Valley, whereas Latinos were rapidly increasing in other areas of concern. Assemblyman Firebaugh, noting the number of elected Latino officials that have represented the 49th, said, "In the last special election a non-Latino won that district," and he asked whether MALDEF was concerned about the drop in Latino population because "that may dilute the ability of [the] Latino population in that district to elect the candidate of its choice" (Firebaugh 2001: 87–88). MALDEF representatives again stated that their concern was areas in southeast Los Angeles where they believed additional districts could have been created with Latino-majority populations. MALDEF representatives also acknowledged the importance of the San Gabriel Valley for Asian Americans and expressed their support for a district that recognized the growing Asian American population.

In reply to Senator Polanco's question about the issue of vote dilution and the decrease in the Latino population in the 49th Assembly District, Velez stated that "our analysis shows that the Latino population in that district has been diminishing . . . in . . . particular cities which are Rosemead, San Gabriel and Monterey Park and the City of Alhambra has had very, very little [Latino] growth . . . as opposed to . . . the Asian American population" (Velez 2001: 80–81). Velez explained that fewer Latinos were moving to the area because "they simply cannot afford to live in these areas like they once could" (Velez 2001: 82). In contrast, in the southeast part of Los Angeles County, Velez said that "what we feel is that the Latino community deserves and is entitled to a new additional district in Los Angeles County that will be an area of high growth. . . . These are cities that undeniably have grown tremendously in the Latino community" and "that is why we have decided to give greater voice to [the] Latino community in the southeast cities" (Velez 2001: 81, 82).

Hulett noted the demographic trends and recognized the importance of the 49th District for Asian Americans. Hulett explained that the 49th "is not a district that Latinos can hang onto for the rest of the decade" and that, recognizing the growth of the Asian American population and issues of representation, "we were frankly very pleased that we could find a way to, in Los Angeles County, create two new Latino districts . . . without diminishing the growing Asian population and their ability to influence the outcome of an election" (Hulett 2001: 83, 84).

The Final Redistricting Plan and the San Gabriel Valley

In the 49th Assembly District that was approved, the demographic character-istics of the district did not change dramatically from the previous district, with 46.63 percent Latinos, a 6.37 percent drop from 1991; 39.11 percent Asian Americans, an increase of 2.95 percent; 12.10 percent whites, a 3.39 percent increase; and African Americans and Native Americans each remaining at less than 1 percent of the new electoral district's population.[8] However, the char-acter of the district was altered because it became situated squarely within the San Gabriel Valley, having shed the areas of the Eastside. Also, San Marino was added to the district, whereas Arcadia was not, but because San Marino has an Asian American plurality, it was a positive addition for Asian Americans. San Marino borders Alhambra and San Gabriel to the north and, as one of the most affluent communities in the Los Angeles region, was highly coveted by elected officials because of the potential funds that could flow to their cam-paigns. The 2000 census showed the dramatic growth of the Asian American population, now the largest in the city at 48.6 percent (from 32.1 percent in 1990), followed by whites with 44.6 percent and Latinos with 4.4 percent (see Map 4). San Marino voters elected the first Asian American to the city coun-cil during the redistricting process in March 2001. Matthew Yuan-Ching Lin, an immigrant from Taiwan and an orthopedic surgeon with an office in Al-hambra, came to the United States in 1973 to complete his medical residency. Lin later served as mayor, a position filled by a council member chosen by the other council members. The election of Lin showed the growing strength of the Asian American electorate and the willingness of whites to support an Asian American in the region.

In contrast to the assembly district's new boundaries, which respected the Asian American and Latino base of the incumbent Judy Chu, the boundaries of the new state senate and congressional districts fragmented the Asian American population in the San Gabriel Valley. The final plan divided the four cities with the heaviest concentration of Asian Americans into three state senate districts (21, 22, and 24) and two congressional districts (29 and 32). Monterey Park was split between the two congressional districts, disregarding traditional political boundaries and exacerbating vote dilution.[9]

To use their limited resources most effectively, APALC and CAPAFR focused their redistricting efforts on determining where the boundaries of the assem-bly districts would be, because these districts encompassed smaller areas than state senate and congressional districts in terms of population requirements

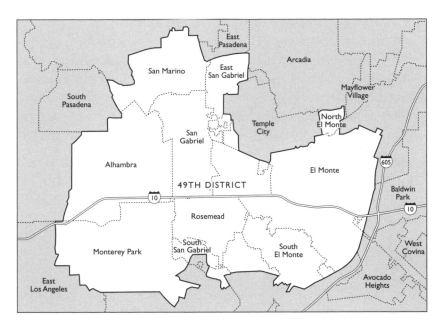

Map 4 Forty-Ninth Assembly District
<small>SOURCE:</small> California State Assembly

and thus gave Asian Americans the best opportunity for forming a district in which they would have an influential vote. Because they analyzed only assembly districts, APALC and CAPAFR did not consider filing a lawsuit based on the fragmentation of the Asian American population in the redrawn congressional and state senate districts in the San Gabriel Valley. However, at the last public hearing held by the state legislature before the plans were approved, Kathay Feng requested, "We do ask that you revisit the Senate and congressional con-figurations which have carved this west San Gabriel Valley area up into so many pieces as to create a virtual glass ceiling for our community's representation at these higher levels of government" (Feng 2001b: 349).

There were four African Americans from the Los Angeles area in the assembly and two in the state senate when redistricting took place. Alice Huffman, of the NAACP, testified:

> We believe that the lines that are drawn in these districts are critical to our sur-vival. We assess the potential of maintaining African Americans in these districts over the next 10 years and we examine the likelihood of the new lines drawn if

it would pit one minority group against another. We firmly believe that it was not the intent of the Voting Rights Act to ever cause ethnic warfare. The Voting Rights Act is to protect all ethnic groups, and so we are looking very carefully at lines that could pit us against each other. We want to recommend some adjustments in the lines in Los Angeles that we think will strengthen the African American base in those districts and will not harm our Latino and Asian sisters and brothers. (Huffman 2001: 365–366)

By paying attention to preserving the Asian American concentrations in areas such as Gardena and Torrance and by designing districts that enhanced African American voting strength while recognizing the growing presence of Latinos, among whom were a large number of noncitizens who could not vote, the African American elected officials suggested minor alterations in the plan that took the concerns of all minority groups into consideration.

In 2007, looking back at the 2000 redistricting process and the working relationship between African Americans and Latinos, Antonio Hernandez, then with MALDEF, stated that the groups worked together to make sure that the districts they proposed did not harm African Americans (Meyerson 2007). Connie Rice, with the NAACP Legal Defense Fund at the time of redistricting, asserted that "Latinos have bent over backward not to take African American districts" (Meyerson 2007: M1). Antonio Gonzalez, of the Southwest Voter Registration Education Project, one of the key groups that has worked to increase the electoral clout of Latinos through voter registration and get-out-the-vote drives, explained about working with other minority groups: "Over the years . . . there's been a prudent consensus that you try to work it out so that everybody has what they perceive as a critical mass or representation. It's in everyone's interest that communities be represented" (Meyerson 2007: M1).

MALDEF's Lawsuit, *Cano v. Davis*

On October 1, 2001, MALDEF filed a lawsuit, *Cano v. Davis*, against the redistricting plan. The lawsuit alleged that the boundaries of two congressional districts—one in the San Fernando Valley, the other in San Diego—were drawn to reduce the number of Latinos in each district to protect white incumbents. The lawsuit also stated that an additional state senate seat with a Latino majority should have been created in Los Angeles County. Antonia Hernandez, MALDEF president and general counsel, declared, "It is unacceptable and illegal to jeopardize the voting rights of historically disenfranchised minority voters. The district lines compromised the basic principles of community and the electoral process and are illegal" (MALDEF 2001: n.p.).

The lawsuit pitted MALDEF against the Latino state legislators who supported the plan. Unlike past political battles in which racial minorities opposed whites or in which conservative minorities disagreed with liberal minorities, this struggle was between traditional progressive allies. I suggest that the conflict between MALDEF and Latino state legislators revealed how their contrasting public stances on the contemporary role of race in electoral politics were shaped by the complex set of interests and goals of each group and the constituencies they served. The MALDEF attorneys, as representatives of a civil rights organization, were advocating for districts based on their understanding of the historical and current importance of race in politics in general and redistricting in particular, using one of the main tools available to them, a lawsuit.[10]

In opposition to MALDEF's insistence on the continued importance of racially polarized voting, the Latino state legislators spoke of a new era in politics and white support for Latino candidates and issues. This position, I suggest, was influenced by the legislators' belief that the districts in question were represented by officials who had strong records supporting the interests of their Latino constituencies. Also influencing this position, the legislators needed to consider the way the new districts would affect their political careers, how their stance on the lawsuit would be interpreted by voters, particularly non-Latino voters, and how their working relationships with their colleagues in the state legislature would be affected.

In a *Los Angeles Times* editorial, Latina state senators Martha Escutia and Gloria Romero (2001: B13) voiced strong opposition to the lawsuit, describing it as "frivolous and racially divisive." Escutia and Romero noted that the new plan maintained or strengthened thirteen state senate and U.S. congressional seats held by Latinos and created a "new heavily Latino congressional district . . . in Los Angeles County" and that twenty-three of the twenty-six Latino state legislators had voted for the plan. Commenting on Latino electoral success and what this means in terms of race, politics, and democracy, Escutia and Romero noted that Latinos have been elected in "non-Latino areas," thereby demonstrating that

> more and more, California is reaping the benefits of multiracial coalitions. The voice of Latinos in California is stronger because electoral politics and

issues are no longer just about race. . . . Latinos need not limit themselves to only seeking office in "safe" Latino district. We should not relegate ourselves to only a few court-imposed barrios. Our success lies in proclaiming that the Latino agenda is (and should be) the American agenda. . . . But, ultimately, we trust the voters. Most citizens cast their votes the American way—they vote for the most qualified candidate, regardless of race or gender. All we have to do is compete for votes the old-fashioned way: by earning them. (Escutia and Romero 2001: B13)

Demonstrating the divided views among Latino progressives but also the reality of how politics works and the importance of backing longtime allies, Dolores Huerta, co-founder of the United Farm Workers—perhaps the iconic organization for Mexican American activists of the 1960s generation—submitted a statement on behalf of the defendants in the MALDEF lawsuit. Huerta specifically praised Congressman Howard Berman of the San Fernando Valley district named in the lawsuit, stating that he "has always been one of our most effective political supporters" (Huerta 2002: 1). Also at stake for Huerta was the fate of legislation that at that time was working its way through the state senate and assembly. The legislation would give "farm laborers the right of mandatory mediation in deadlocked contract negotiations" and was strongly opposed by large growers. The bill, characterized by the *Los Angeles Times* as "a triumph [for farm workers] unprecedented since the passage [in California] of the 1975 agricultural labor relations law" (Jones 2002: A1), was signed by Governor Gray Davis on September 30, 2002.

On June 12, 2002, the three-judge federal district court upheld the redistricting plan and dismissed the MALDEF lawsuit. In terms of the lawsuit's charges of vote dilution and racially polarized voting, the court opinion stated:

The essence of any successful vote dilution claim must be that the ability of a minority community to elect representatives of choice is adversely affected. . . . However, if a district is drawn in which Latinos constitute a plurality, non-Latino voters have shown that they are willing to vote for Latino candidates, and Latino candidates receive a majority of the overall vote with some regularity, then the most basic and necessary dilutive effect is lacking. . . . Latino candidates win elections in the territory that constitutes CD 28, and they do so with the support of non-Latino voters. (*Cano v. Davis* 2002: 85–86)

The court opinion discussed the statement by assembly member Juan Vargas in the San Diego region concerning the $20,000 paid by Congress members to the consultant Michael Berman to create districts that would protect incumbents, and the judges decided that no harm to Latinos occurred in the redistricting and that the new districts did not support "a system that perpetuates racial discrimination." The judges explained:

> Vargas asserts that many of the incumbent members of the California delegation . . . paid $20,000 per person to obtain the services of the legislature's chief map-drawing consultant, Michael Berman. In exchange, he contends, Berman took steps to render their districts less susceptible to potential challengers, both partisan and ethnic. Plaintiffs admit that they do not allege that defendants were motivated by racial hostility. . . . Although we assume, for summary judgment purposes, the truth of plaintiffs' intent evidence, and their charge that the legislature sought to limit the number of Latino voters in the two districts at issue, given the background and record of California's 2001 redistricting, the evidence does not support an inference that the legislature intended to marginalize a racial group politically through invidious discrimination, or invidiously to maintain a system that perpetuates racial discrimination. (*Cano v. Davis* 2002: 80–81)

The judges did not see incumbent protection as a problem because "the protection of an incumbent . . . [is] a well-established legitimate districting criterion" (*Cano v. Davis* 2002: 27). In summary, the judges concluded that the redistricting plan was legal because it considered a range of traditional redistricting criteria, including "ensuring adequate representation for Latinos and other minority groups," "advancing partisan interests," and respecting existing political entities, such as "city boundaries" (*Cano v. Davis* 2002: 27, 33, 81, 85–86).

After Governor Davis approved the districts, the *California Journal* included a debate on the redistricting process, with one article written by the senate redistricting staff and consultants and another by MALDEF. The state senate addressed the Michael Berman controversy, stating that the "California Senate contracted with consultants. . . . As explicitly allowed in their Senate contract, these same consultants were sought out and hired by the California Democratic congressional delegation (all 32 Democratic members signed contracts) to submit a redistricting proposal to both houses of the Legislature. All roles were clearly disclosed and approved in advance" (Senate Redistricting Staff and Consultants 2002: 41).

Focusing the discussion on the role of race in politics, the state senate article asserted that MALDEF's interpretation was rooted in the past and no longer applied to today's electoral scene. The article explained that MALDEF's position "represents a long out-of-date perspective on the law and California politics" and that "MALDEF is stuck . . . in a 20-year 'time warp' regarding California's openness to electing Latino candidates" (Senate Redistricting Staff and Consultants 2002: 38, 42).

In MALDEF's *California Journal* article, they stressed the self-interest of politicians protecting themselves and how this negated Latino legislator support for the plan. The article stated that "the most-often cited justification for the plans is that many of the Latino legislators approved the maps. Again, with the exception of a handful of principled legislators who were offended by the process, the driving issue behind each legislator's vote was incumbency, not the rights of voters; the incumbents who were protected voted in favor of the plans" (MALDEF 2002: 40).

Contrasting Interpretations of the Significance of Race

The organizing and advocacy efforts of MALDEF, APALC, and the NAACP LDF, on the one hand, and the actions of the state legislators and federal district court judges, on the other, reveal contrasting interpretations of the significance of race in contemporary California politics in general and the redistricting process in particular. None of the groups believe that racial discrimination has disappeared. MALDEF, however, thinks that voting tends to be racially polarized, that Latino political influence may be diluted in districts that do not favor them because of this polarization, and that these issues should be directly addressed through the redistricting process. In contrast, Escutia and Romero and the federal district court judges assert that voters have largely gone beyond race, and they point to the votes garnered by Latino candidates from non-Latinos as evidence of this trend.

Latino elected officials, such as state senators Gloria Romero and Richard Polanco, and non-Latino officials, such as Congressman Howard Berman, clearly have impressive records in office. Tireless and effective advocates, they have written and supported important legislation on behalf of their Latino and non-Latino constituents. Considering their exemplary performance in office, supporting the redistricting plan was support for effective representation. As part of the evidence submitted by the defendants, they used an expert report by Gary Jacobson, a political science professor at the University of California at San Diego. Jacobson's report explained that senior members of the House of Representatives, such as Filner and Berman, are effective representatives because of the importance of seniority, a resource that would be lost if they were replaced.

> It is my opinion that legislative activity, efficiency, leadership, and effectiveness increase with tenure in that body. . . . It is part of the conventional wisdom about the House that influence and effectiveness increase with tenure. One reason is that more senior members are more likely to gain the formal positions of authority—chairs or ranking members of committees or subcommittees or formal party leadership posts—that enhance members' ability to shape public policy. (Jacobson 2002: 5)

MALDEF's primary goal was to analyze demographic and political data in order to develop districts that would give Latinos an effective and influential voice as a voting bloc. Whether Latino voters in fact chose to vote for Latinos or non-Latinos was not MALDEF's concern. Critics of MALDEF's lawsuit who argued that the white incumbents in the disputed districts have long records of supporting Latino issues were arguing a completely different point. In terms of substantive representation (Hero and Tolbert 1995)—that is, officials who support policies and the distribution of resources to reflect the interests of their constituents—if Latinos voted for white incumbents because of the incumbents' records, that would not contradict MALDEF's position in favor of developing districts that enhance the voice of Latinos.

MALDEF's point is that given the complexity of district boundaries and the multiple interests within them, elected officials necessarily respond to varied and often conflicting voter concerns. As the proportion and voting power of Latinos, or any other group, increase in a district, elected officials and especially candidates who wish to win office must pay attention to that group. As the demographic makeup of the district changes, the interests of the constituency may also change. Although an elected official may be Latino, if the vote is numerically dominated by whites, then that official will have to respond to interests that may be quite different from those in a predominantly Latino district.

Conclusion

Simply citing the election of Latinos as evidence that voters have gone beyond race essentializes and trivializes the category "Latino" by suggesting that the election of a Latino, regardless of his or her political ideology, record, and abilities, is an adequate indicator of political empowerment and the decreasing importance of race in elections. In terms of class, nativity, political ideology, and religion, Latinos are a heterogeneous group, and these differences are reflected in their voting patterns, making a "Latino vote" and a "Latino politician" complex and problematic categories (Nagler and Alvarez 2004). In a district dominated by Latino voters, the voters can work out their differences at the ballot box. In districts where the number of Latino voters is small, however, other voters and issues enter the picture, which decreases the opportunity for the discussion of issues considered important by Latino voters.

As this case study makes clear, an individual's or a group's racial or ethnic membership does not always predict their economic interests and ideologies. Asian American, African American, and Latino civil rights and community redistricting organizations were able to work together during the 2000–2002 redistricting process in Southern California because they had a common goal—to develop districts that could take minority political interests into consideration. These groups understood the history of racial gerrymandering that had fragmented their communities and diluted their political power. They also understood that politicians are focused primarily on getting reelected and on maintaining good working relations with other members of the state legislature. Furthermore, the two major political parties, given their desire to maintain or increase their political power with each election, do not always have the interests of racial minorities uppermost in their minds.

The critics of MALDEF's lawsuit note that non-Latinos have gone beyond race and do vote for Latino candidates, but these critics have not acknowledged the fact that Latino voters have also gone beyond narrow nationalist thinking and will vote for non-Latinos, as demonstrated by the 2001 and 2006 elections of Chinese Americans Judy Chu and Mike Eng in the 49th Assembly District. This voting record demonstrates that Latinos are willing to judge candidates according to their records.

I would characterize this phenomenon, not as one that goes "beyond race," because race remains a critical part of the analysis that voters make, but rather as one in which voters give careful consideration to candidates' overall records and political agendas—agendas that include racial issues (Abrajano et al. 2003). Judy Chu's electoral success, for example, reflects her ability to appeal to particular groups, such as Chinese Americans and Asian Americans, as well as to whites and Latinos. She has a long record of supporting issues important to all residents in the region, such as education and health services, and the distinct ways in which such issues affect particular groups, such as bilingual education and English-only policies. Prominent Southern California Latino officials, including Congresswomen Loretta Sanchez and Hilda Solis and Sheriff Lee Baca, endorsed Chu during her campaign. As Solis explains, "The voters are growing more sophisticated in their choices. . . . Judy . . . is a bridge-builder with different groups. She is more than Asian American. She's dynamic, and she has helped the Latino community numerous times over the years" (Winton 2001: II-4).

Redistricting is an arena in which contrasting views on the political implications of race are put forward by various groups and are acted on and given material form in the shape of the districts produced. Not only are districts a product of the debate on race, but they also shape future race relations by creating conditions that may promote or discourage coalitions among groups. Residents within the same district have a reason to work together to lobby their shared representative. By fragmenting groups and placing them in separate districts, this basis for an alliance is removed. Dividing up concentrations of Latinos into separate congressional districts removes a political basis for collective action at the local level. When district court judges adhered to traditional redistricting criteria in *Cano v. Davis*, they perpetuated the practice of disenfranchising minority communities.

As Morgan Kousser (1999) points out in his analysis of various U.S. Supreme Court decisions on redistricting, "Partisan, personal, and ethnic advantage were the real 'traditional districting principles' in North Carolina [*Shaw v. Reno*]" (p. 4). By "ethnic advantage," Kousser is referring to whites who continue to strive to disenfranchise African Americans in the South. Even though the situation in California is demographically different from the situation in the South, with larger numbers of Latinos and Asian Americans, some of the same factors are nevertheless at work. *Shaw v. Reno* reduces the ways in which race can be considered in redistricting, negating the *Garza v. Los Angeles County Board of Supervisors* ruling that emphasized race. Judges ignore voting patterns that clearly demonstrate continued patterns of racially polarized voting and base rulings on a belief that society has entered a color-blind era. In California, the state legislators control redistricting, and "incumbent protection plans" weaken the political influence of racial minorities. Considered together, court decisions and redistricting plans are part of a long history of factors contributing to systemic inequality in the United States. The significant cooperation achieved by African Americans, Asian Americans, and Latinos during the 2000–2002 California redistricting process, however, demonstrates that racial minorities are actively involved in the effort to change this historical pattern of political inequality. The alliance that contributed to the shape of districts in the San Gabriel Valley and the election of Latino and Asian American officials demonstrate real gains in the region.

7 Conclusion
Race in the Contemporary Era

Minority Elected Officials: Crafting Racial Images and Deracialized Campaigns

In Washington State in 1996, voters elected Chinese American Gary Locke as governor at a time when the state was 89% white, the first of his two terms in office. In his campaign Locke talked about being the child of poor immigrants, and in his inaugural address he noted that his grandfather had worked as a houseboy less than a mile from the capitol grounds. Locke said, "It took a hundred years to go one mile, but it's a journey that could only take place in America" (Egan 2000: 1A).

Los Angeles Mayor Antonio Villaraigosa, a Mexican American, declared during his 2005 inaugural address, "What a beautiful country. I am proof that the United States is a country of opportunity and liberty. In what other country of the world could I be in front of you as mayor of a great city?" (McGreevy and Garrison 2005: A1). Recognizing his roots in the nearby Eastside of Los Angeles, a collection of multiracial and immigrant neighborhoods of primarily working-class and low-income Latinos, Villaraigosa's speech echoed Locke's mention of the short journey in terms of geography but the long journey in terms of race and equality. Villaraigosa stated, "It may be a short way from City Terrace to City Hall, but, fellow Angelenos, we all know what a vast distance it truly is" (*Los Angeles Times* 2005a: A36). Stressing the American ideals of family and perseverance in difficult times, Villaraigosa went on to talk about his mother's life: "A true story, like those of countless Angelenos, past and present. A story of working hard, of loving your kids, of having a clear picture of a better future in your mind's eye and driving for it with a sense of ferocious purpose" (*Los Angeles Times* 2005a: A36).

The stories of Locke and Villaraigosa without a doubt epitomize the immigrant success story and the social and political progress of racial minorities in the United States. Their life stories are testaments to the possibility of assimilation and the expansion of the mainstream to include Asian Americans and Latinos, as Alba and Nee (2003) have claimed. Locke's opponent in the 1996 Democratic gubernatorial primary was Norm Rice, mayor of Seattle and an African American. A Chinese American and an African American as the principal contenders in the primary in a state in which whites are the vast majority of the voters seemingly supports the idea that race no longer hinders minority candidates. Indeed, the election of minority candidates to political office is often noted as a clear indication of a color-blind society (Thernstrom and Thernstrom 1997). A deeper look into the lives and campaigns of Locke and Rice, however, reveals the subtle yet powerful ways that race continues to operate and influence politics.

We have clearly not entered a color-blind era in electoral politics, because race remains a highly influential force when voters enter the privacy of the voting booth. Candidates, both whites and racial minorities, understand that voters of all races continue to consider the race of candidates when voting. As a result, as the electorate becomes more diverse and as racial minorities seek office in areas with white voters, candidates must deal with race in ways that they believe will appeal to a wide spectrum of voters. For racial minorities, this usually means carefully crafted deracialized campaigns, but not the absence of race. Understanding that voters are cognizant of their racial identities, minority candidates must frame race in ways that overcome the reluctance of whites to vote for minorities.

Locke, speaking to an overwhelmingly white electorate, talked about the Chinese immigrant history of his family. His personal narrative emphasized positive racial images of Asian immigrants and Asian Americans as the model minority, countering the persistent negative stereotypes of the Chinese, in particular, the devious perpetual foreigner. His story touched on some of the cherished ideals of American society, such as hard work and perseverance to overcome difficulties and the openness of society, linking his life with the stories of mainstream America and the beliefs in individualism and assimilation. This was not going beyond race but understanding how to frame his race in ways that would be acceptable to voters. As Locke said, "You can't hide your race . . . people look at me and know I'm Asian" (Egan 2000: A1).

Norm Rice has had great success in politics, but as an African American, he has had to deal with a different set of stereotypes than Locke. A *New York Times* article described his performance in office in positive terms, stating that Rice was "one of Seattle's most successful mayors. Under Mr. Rice, the city rebuilt its downtown and improved its schools, the job and housing markets boomed, crime plummeted and tax revenue rolled into city coffers" (Egan 2000: A1). In the gubernatorial primary, Rice focused on the issues and did not discuss his personal biography, as Locke did, even though Rice commented, "I have a great story about how my family came to America. As good as Gary's. We just happened to have different travel agents" (Egan 2000: A1). For Rice, his decision was framed by the understanding that equivalent images of African Americans did not exist. There was no model minority image to counteract negative labels attached to African Americans, such as the undeserving poor or the underclass, and mentioning race might bring attention to such negative images rather than his impressive record as mayor.

Ron Sims, an African American, won election to the Metropolitan King County Council and the King County executive position to replace Gary Locke after Locke's election as governor. As with Locke and Rice, Sims's success in politics seemingly offers proof that race no longer matters in elections. Yet Sims has noted the ways in which race has shaped his campaigns and political platform. When opponents of Sims wished to attack him, one method was to make race salient. Using code words to bring attention to race without using racial terms, his detractors labeled Sims an "inner-city politician," although Sims was born in Spokane and grew up in eastern Washington in a white community (Egan 2000: A1). Understanding that race would be an issue in his political career, Sims heeded the advice of a senior politician and focused on important race-neutral concerns, such as fiscal, transportation, and environmental issues. For Locke, Rice, and Sims, their success is based on analyzing how race works in society and on using that knowledge to craft images of their political and personal lives that support core American values, build reputations as outstanding public officials through their skill and performance in office, and develop race-neutral policies rather than depend on voters going beyond race.

Beyond doubt, the election victories of candidates such as Gary Locke and Antonio Villaraigosa signal a major change in voting patterns. Although the race of a candidate may be of less importance today, the careful way each candidate dealt with race in his campaign demonstrates that race still matters. The importance of race in politics means that the configuration of districts directly affects candidates' political campaigns and chances of winning elections. As the number of white voters increases, Asian American candidates in New York City's Chinatown or Latino candidates in Southern California face the obstacle of being labeled the Asian or Latino candidate, and running a deracialized campaign becomes more important. For officials such as Gary Locke, Norm Rice, and Ron Sims, who serve primarily white populations, once they were in office, focusing on nonracial issues did not affect their ability to serve their constituencies. For candidates and elected officials in places such as New York City or Southern California with large minority populations, however, officials who must win the favor of white voters to remain in office face the pressure of establishing and supporting a race-neutral political agenda and may have to modify their support of policies that address the unique interests of racial minorities.

Latinos in Southern California

In Villaraigosa's winning 2005 mayoral campaign against a white incumbent, James Hahn, Villaraigosa stressed that he would be a representative of all residents, regardless of race. Villaraigosa understood that he would have the support of Latinos because he had already laid a foundation of service in the community. What he needed to win was votes from African Americans and whites. In the election, a *Los Angeles Times* exit poll (2005b: A19) showed that 84 percent of Latinos, 50 percent of whites, 48 percent of African Americans, and 44 percent of Asian Americans voted for Villaraigosa. In his failed run in 2000 against Hahn, Villaraigosa's percentage of votes from whites was 41 percent, and he managed only 20 percent from African Americans. Villaraigosa became the city's first Latino mayor since 1872, joining in city office a number of other Latinos, including Alex Padilla, the first Latino city council president since 1868, and Rocky Delgadillo, the first Latino city attorney since 1851 (McGreevy 2005: A1).

These wins individually, and especially collectively, signal a major shift in the electoral power of Latinos and the ability of Latino candidates to appeal to non-Latino voters. These successes do not simply represent progress on the path of assimilation, however, because it is unclear whether the candidates have reached a political glass ceiling or whether Latinos will gain even higher elected positions. Although clearly both Latinos and whites are diverse groups with complex voting patterns and although whites show electoral support for Latino candidates, which was an important factor in the judges' decision in *Cano v. Davis*, racially polarized voting remains. The Latino vote for Villaraigosa was 34 points higher than the white vote in the 2005 victory, and in the 2006 Democratic primary vote for state attorney general, 71 percent of whites voted for Jerry Brown, the former California governor and mayor of Oakland, whereas 74 percent of Latinos voted for MIT-educated Rocky Delgadillo (*Los Angeles Times* 2006: A10). Delgadillo is the first Latino Los Angeles city attorney in more than 150 years, but it remains to be seen if whites will elect him and Villaraigosa to higher offices, as with Margaret Chin in New York City and her repeated failure to win a city council seat in Manhattan after victories for a lesser elected position.

Latinos have not transcended their ethnicity, because all Latino candidates continue to be labeled as such, no matter how they attempt to frame themselves as representatives of all groups. After Villaraigosa's victory, for example, he was featured on the cover of *Newsweek* (May 30, 2005) with the caption, "Latino Power: L.A.'s New Mayor—And How Hispanics Will Change American Politics." By focusing on his Latino identity and the growing number of Latinos, the headline downplays Villaraigosa's successful effort to build a broad base of support among voters. At the same time, however, it is the changing demographics of the city and state and the rising Latino population that make Villaraigosa special. As a friend of Villaraigosa commented about the *Newsweek* coverage, "Antonio was upset. . . . To have that headline, after he'd worked so hard to run a campaign saying he is Latino but would be the mayor of all of L.A. But if it weren't for Latino power he wouldn't have been on the cover of *Newsweek*. So it cuts both ways" (Bruck 2007: 44).

In terms of ethnic politics and eventual integration into American society, the route of Mexican Americans is sometimes compared to the trajectory taken by Irish Americans (Rodriguez 2005). One major difference, however, is that although the first Latinos entered the United States long before the first Irish immigrants settled in the country, Latinos are still seen as newcomers and as nonwhite. True, Latin Americans continue to immigrate in large numbers, unlike the Irish and other European groups, but I would argue that, like Asian Americans, Latinos—even those who have been in the United States for generations—are seen as the perpetual foreigner, marked as people of color in a way that European Americans are not (Tuan 1998). Just as Ron Sims's opponents labeled him an inner-city candidate when they wanted to interject race into politics, in the 2000 election, Villaraigosa's first attempt at running for mayor, Hahn used racial images, such as graffiti and illegal drugs, in his negative attacks on Villaraigosa (Ayon 2001).

Villaraigosa operates in a political climate that stresses color-blind policies, especially with California voters passing the anti–affirmative action Proposition

209 in 1996, and he must present issues without framing them in terms of race. At the same time, however, through his personal experiences and knowledge of history as a Latino from the Eastside of Los Angeles, he is acutely aware of the significance of race. For example, on the night of the June 2, 1998, primary elections, Villaraigosa, the speaker of the state assembly at that time, visited the campaign headquarters of Gloria Romero, who was running for the state assembly in the 49th District. Both Villaraigosa and Romero shared a long history in the labor movement, especially with the United Farm Workers. It was early in the evening, and the initial vote tally had Romero's opponent, Judy Chu, ahead, although as more precincts from East Los Angeles reported later in the night, the vote would change in Romero's favor and she would go on to win in the general election.

The room was packed with campaign volunteers, staff, and other supporters, many wearing bright red United Farm Workers T-shirts. Surrounded by a wall of red shirts, Villaraigosa gave an impassioned speech in Spanish, and the crowd roared its approval of his talk of victory and electoral power. Villaraigosa grew up speaking primarily English, and he was not fluent in Spanish (Hernandez 2005), and many who wore the red T-shirts were not members of the United Farm Workers. As I stood in the crowd at Romero's campaign headquarters and listened to Villaraigosa speak, I could see and feel the power of the Spanish language and the union as potent symbols of struggle and success for Mexican Americans and Latinos in California. Villaraigosa also included Spanish in his mayoral inaugural address, clearly a way to be inclusive, recognizing the Mexican history of the city and the large number of Latino immigrants in the region. It was in Spanish that he declared that his life personified the American dream. "I am proof that the United States is a country of opportunity and liberty" (McGreevy and Garrison 2005: A1). Using the Spanish language in public, however, also carries political risk. Jaime Regalado, a noted analyst of Los Angeles politics, remarked, "If he is perceived as a bilingual-bicultural candidate, that will turn off Republicans or more traditionally conservative Democrats" (Hernandez 2005: A1). Proponents of English-only policies and practices criticize Villaraigosa's public use of Spanish, but this ignores the history of the country and the common use in schools and communities of languages other than English among the early immigrants, including those from Europe, Latin American immigrants eagerly filling English-as-a-second-language classes for adults, and the rapid acquisition of English by the children of immigrants. Villaraigosa's use of Spanish acknowledges that we live in a global society in which being bilingual or multilingual is a critical resource, and his personal life underscores the understanding among immigrants and their children that English is the language of the nation and the key to integration into society.

Translating Villaraigosa's claim to be a public official for all residents means that he pays careful attention to the unique needs of all communities, including those defined by race and ethnicity, and does not focus simply on so-called race-neutral policies. Racial minorities have built community institutions, such as museums, because mainstream organizations have not adequately addressed issues related to these communities, just as race-neutral historic preservation practices have ignored buildings related to the history of Chinese and African Americans in San Diego. Villaraigosa has a long history of supporting Asian American issues, and in 1999, for example, he was a featured speaker at the opening of a new building for the Japanese American National Museum in Los Angeles. He proudly stated that as a member of the state legislature, he helped pass legislation to provide funds for the museum.

The historical and contemporary government actions that have shaped Villaraigosa's childhood Eastside neighborhood are a clear reminder of the ways in which public policies give race meaning in the United States (Acuna 1984, 1996; Diaz 2005; Valle and Torres 2000). At the museum opening, Villaraigosa talked about his childhood in the nearby Eastside, just a few miles across the Los Angeles River, and that he remembered listening to his mother tell the tragic story of her good friends and neighbors who were rounded up by the government and sent to internment camps during World War II. From his mother's personal experience, Villaraigosa learned about the impact of race on those who lived around him. Internment was an egregious example of racism and violation of constitutional rights by the U.S. government, and adding to this injustice, as revealed decades later, staff at the Census Bureau used confidential census data to "facilitate and accelerate the forced relocation and denial of civil rights" (Prewitt 2000a, n.p.). Villaraigosa's life story was a reminder of the shared history of Mexican Americans and Japanese Americans, from their work as laborers in the agricultural fields to the restrictive covenants that created neighborhoods such as the Eastside peopled with racial minorities.

Sedimentation of Inequality:
Racial Effects of Race-Neutral Policies

Melvin Oliver and Thomas Shapiro (1995) contend that to understand the effects of systemic discrimination on capital accumulation, it is necessary to take into account the range of government policies that have "promoted homesteading, land acquisition, home ownership, retirement, pensions, education, and asset accumulation for some sectors of the population and not for others" (p. 4). Taken together, these factors contribute to the "sedimentation of inequality" (p. 51). It is not simply the individual factors that people bring to the marketplace that matter; the way that government policies structure opportunities must also be taken into account to understand racial differences in terms of wealth. As William J. Wilson (1980) suggests, however, government actions have undergone a transformation, from blatant racism to race-neutral policies. No longer do the issues raised by Oliver and Shapiro have such a prominent role in shaping people's life chances. The events that influenced the Eastside, such as the World War II incarceration of Japanese Americans, restrictive covenants that confined Latinos and Asian Americans to communities such as East Los Angeles, and interstate highways constructed to eliminate minority communities, would not occur in today's color-blind world, according to supporters of race-neutral policies.

Contemporary policies may appear to be race neutral and fair on the surface, but, as Cheryl Harris (1993) points out, such policies may in fact support racial outcomes because of the history of systemic racism in society. To understand the contemporary effects of race in the area of economic development that contribute to the sedimentation of inequality, current policies should be examined within the context of past and present actions that contributed to development and residential patterns in the United States. Segregation in the 1800s and early 1900s confined racial minorities to specific downtown areas. Federal mortgage policies and highway construction spurred development in the suburbs in the post–World War II era but explicitly reserved these areas for whites, enforcing segregation and the trend of minorities inhabiting urban areas and whites populating the suburbs. The growing political power of the suburbs and the downsizing of federal government programs resulted in a shift of resources to the suburbs and disinvestment in urban areas. With the effort to revitalize the cities, the urban renewal and highway construction programs of the 1950s through the early 1970s wiped out many multiracial and minority neighborhoods and forced the displaced residents into segregated areas. Now, as public and private funds pour into downtown areas across the country in a renewed effort to turn downtowns into corporate centers, cities such as San Diego are attracting affluent residents and new development to the urban core. Infrastructure projects to support this growth, such as highways and oil pipelines, produce health problems, destroy housing, and tear apart neighborhoods. As a result, low-income and minority residents face displacement and the problem of finding a new place to live, which in Southern California and New York City involves some of the most expensive housing markets in the country.

Community Activism and Infrastructure Projects

Events in Villaraigosa's boyhood community in the Eastside neighborhood of Los Angeles illustrate the impact of development on minority communities. The area has one of the highest concentrations of freeways in the region, and their construction destroyed close-knit communities and erected permanent barriers dividing neighborhoods, eliminated badly needed housing, displaced residents, and filled the air with carcinogenic diesel emissions. In the successful grassroots effort to block the construction of a state prison—which would have been the state's first erected in a "downtown urban" area—in the Eastside in the 1980s and early 1990s, part of the political education of the Mexican American women who led the effort came from the multiple displacements they had experienced during the construction of freeways (Pardo 1998: 53). The women working on the prison issue formed an organization called the Mothers of East Los Angeles (MELA), and Juana Gutierrez, one of the MELA leaders, explained why she grew suspicious of government development efforts.

> One of the things that really upsets me is injustice, and we have seen a lot of that in our community. Especially before, because I believe our people used to be less aware, we didn't assert ourselves as much. In the 1950s they put up the freeways, and just like that they gave us notice that we had to move. That happened twice. The people complied because the government ordered it. I remember that I was angry and wanted the others to back me up, but no one wanted to do anything. (Pardo 1998: 73)

Mary Pardo (1998: 75) points out in her study of MELA that the women developed an understanding of how their individual experiences reflected "group interests." Unlike the perspective of liberal individualism, the members of MELA recognized that they did not exist solely as individuals but instead collectively faced shared issues as working-class Mexican Americans. MELA later participated in the successful effort to block the construction of a toxic waste incinerator in the nearby working-class community of Vernon. Attacking the toxic waste incinerator and prison were not the results of narrow, self-interested NIMBYism ("not in my backyard"), as supporters of the projects attempted to characterize the protestors, but an awareness of the history of "dumping" projects in low-income areas that communities with more resources and political clout have resisted (Pardo 1998: 63).

MELA also participated in protests against the construction of an oil pipeline through Los Angeles in the 1990s. At a community meeting, a woman asked why the pipeline should go through the city rather than along the coastline. The pipeline representative replied, "'Oh, no! If it burst, it would endanger the marine life.' The woman retorted, 'You value the marine life more than human beings'" (Pardo 1998: 132). In the final route of the pipeline, "89% of the census tracts have a higher percentage of minorities than the city average," but the pipeline representatives explained that the pipeline follows existing railroad and freeway routes (Martin 1997: B1).

As Aurora Castillo, another MELA leader, declared during discussion of the oil pipeline, "We just don't want all this garbage thrown at us because we are low-income and Mexican American" (Pardo 1990: 5). When the oil pipeline representative declared that the proposed pipeline route followed major transportation corridors, planning seemingly based on nonracial and rational principles, this ignored the way that earlier transportation routes were explicitly designed to act as barriers between white and minority communities or to wipe out minority communities, as when the urban interstates were used by local officials to "get rid of local 'niggertowns'" (Frieden and Sagalyn 1991: 28). Proposing to build the oil pipeline along the same transportation routes may appear to take advantage of existing infrastructure without regard to race, but doing so builds on past inequities and contributes to the disproportionate number of environmental hazards in racial minority communities (Bullard 2000, 2005; Pulido 2000).

Economic Development and Historic Preservation

Current economic development and historic preservation politics are guided by commissions and boards whose members clearly make an effort to avoid policies that contribute to racial inequality. Just as the oil pipeline officials believe that following established transportation corridors is based on race-neutral factors, because policymakers do not recognize the racial implications of their decisions, their actions may produce results with negative racial implications, as clearly demonstrated in the San Diego cases. To their credit, the San Diego Centre City Development Corporation (CCDC) carried out research to assess the importance of the Douglas Hotel, the Clermont/Coast Hotel, and the Chinese Mission, but the research failed to uncover or recognize the cultural and historical importance of the structures for their respective communities or for society in general.

The CCDC responded to the lobbying efforts of the Chinese American community and worked to preserve the mission and supplied a valuable piece of land for its new location. The Historical Resources Board, based on research carried out by the Gaslamp Black Historical Society (GBHS), declared the Clermont/Coast Hotel a local historical landmark in 2001, the first ever in San Diego associated with the history of African Americans. It also sponsored a comprehensive survey of downtown African American history and structures when the GBHS petitioned the city for action. The Historical Resources Board adopted the report in 2007 for use in the planning process in downtown San Diego. Although, on the one hand, these actions show a city willing to cooperate in important and meaningful ways, these examples also demonstrate that it takes extraordinary effort among people of color to mobilize and lobby for city actions that are institutionalized in city commissions and boards and carried out on a routine basis for whites in the city.

Structures and property owned by all, regardless of race, may be threatened, as demonstrated by the 2005 U.S. Supreme Court *Kelo v. New London* decision, which upheld a city's use of eminent domain for redevelopment purposes. A structure's economic contribution to an area's appeal as a site of tourism and entertainment is likely to be more important than historical value in the decision to preserve or demolish a building. The lists of historic structures for San Diego and Los Angeles and the results of the city of San Diego's research on the Douglas Hotel, the Clermont/Coast Hotel, and the Chinese Mission, however, clearly demonstrate that city agencies serving the public are less likely to recognize the social and historical importance of structures related to people of color.

Redistricting

In addition to development struggles, critical redistricting battles have focused on Villaraigosa's childhood neighborhood, the Eastside of Los Angeles. The 1990 *Garza v. Los Angeles County Board of Supervisors* court decision and the redistricting that followed addressed the fragmentation of Latino communities and vote dilution by joining East Los Angeles with Latino populations to the east, north, and south, followed by the election of Gloria Molina, the first Latino elected to the Board of Supervisors in more than a hundred years.

The 2000 redistricting of state assembly districts removed areas of East Los Angeles and added areas from the San Gabriel Valley to the 49th District. Although these changes resulted in only a slight demographic change, with a small decrease in the Latino population and a slight increase in the Asian

American population, by adding areas in the San Gabriel Valley while eliminating the predominantly Latino East Los Angeles area, the shift in population altered the politics of the new district. One of the major differences is that voters in the San Gabriel Valley are much more familiar with local elected officials, who gain experience in the area's numerous city councils and school boards and later run for state assembly and state senate seats. Thus the new boundaries create a district that is more favorable to San Gabriel Valley–based candidates and the many Asian Americans emerging from these locally elected positions. Recognizing the decrease in the Latino population in the region in relation to the Asian American population and the importance of this region for Asian Americans, because it was one of the few areas in the state that had such a high concentration of Asian Americans, Latino as well as Asian American statewide redistricting coalitions supported the new configuration for the district. The Latino redistricting group believed that other areas in the state offered better opportunities for Latinos and focused on those areas, even though the group faced opposition by some Latino elected officials who wanted to enhance the electoral chances of Latino candidates in the San Gabriel Valley.

Judy Chu, a former school board member and Monterey Park City Council member, was elected to the 49th District in 2001, and she reached the maximum allowed by term limits in 2006. Mike Eng, a Monterey Park City Council member and an established community activist as well as the spouse of Chu, won the Democratic primary election and general election to replace her. The recent election of Mike Eng shows the importance of redistricting and of creating districts that enhance the political power of minorities. Although the consolidation of the Asian American community in Eng's assembly district played a key role in his election, this same community was fragmented into three state senate and two congressional districts created in the 2000 redistricting for the region. Monterey Park was divided up into two congressional districts, violating the traditional redistricting standard of respecting established political boundaries. The new districts seriously diluted the political power of the region, including the Asian American population. One of the immediate effects of the new district boundaries in this era of term limits in California politics is the difficulty created for an assemblyperson who wishes to run for a state senate seat. If the assemblyperson has strong support from voters in his or her district, part of this base is eliminated in the state senate district because the assembly district is fragmented at the senate level.

Court decisions in such cases as *Shaw v. Reno* and *Cano v. Davis*, limiting the use of race in redistricting, have weakened the voting rights of racial minorities and their ability to shape districts in ways that enhance their political power. The decision in *Shaw v. Reno* demonstrates that translating voting rights issues into public policy is highly complex and subject to varied interpretations of the U.S. Constitution and federal policy. The close 5–4 vote in *Shaw v. Reno* shows the split among the Supreme Court justices and illustrates that such issues are not objective matters that will be decided in the same way by any fair and impartial individual. These court cases and the efforts of the statewide redistricting coalitions in California underscore the importance of supporting and strengthening existing legal and community organizations—such as the Mexican American Legal Defense and Educational Fund, the Asian Pacific American Legal Center of Southern California, the Asian Law Caucus of San Francisco, the Asian American Legal Defense and Education Fund of New York, the Committee Against Anti-Asian Violence of New York, and the NAACP Legal Defense Fund—and of building new ones to work for social justice and political equality.

The Voting Rights Act was renewed in July 2006, but even with strong support from President George Bush, who was eager to court minority voters, the approval process generated bitter debate in Congress and opposition from some Republicans who wanted to eliminate some sections of the act, such as the provision for bilingual voting material. Reflecting a focus on individual rights and a disregard for systemic discrimination that gives race meaning in contemporary America, Congressman Steve King, a Republican representing western Iowa, stated that "the party is engaged in group politics. I reject the idea of doing that. We are all created in God's image. He draws no distinction between race, skin color or national origin. It's an insult to him for us to do so in our public policy in America" (Wallsten and Neuman 2006: A15). Similarly, Congressman Dana Rohrabacher, a Republican from Orange County, stated that "what unites us is English. This is multiculturalism at its worse" (Neuman 2006: A20). In contrast, recognizing the diversity of the country and the effort of immigrants to participate in electoral politics, Congresswoman Linda Sanchez, a Democrat from southeast Los Angeles, noted that her mother, who is an English teacher, occasionally prefers a Spanish-language ballot to better understand the complicated measures on the ballot.

Rohrabacher's statement that "what unites us is English" ignores the reality that the 2000 census reveals: we remain a nation divided by race. A powerful indicator of this divide is that segregation driven by whites who seek all-white neighborhoods continues at high levels. Racial segregation in Los Angeles County "has been increasing faster than integration since the 1960s" and "whites have had the freedom to settle wherever their wealth enables them to purchase a home. They have used that freedom to flee the growing diversity of the metropolis, either by moving out of the county completely or by retreating to its edges" (Ethington et al. 2001: 1–2). Racial segregation also continues at high levels in the New York City metropolitan area, and although African Americans have experienced a gradual decline in segregation in other parts of the country, John Logan (2001: n.p.) noted that "New York is an extreme case, one of very few where there was no improvement in black-white segregation in the last two decades."

Latinos and Asian Americans have experienced more residential mobility into the suburbs than African Americans, but the areas they have moved into often show a pattern of desegregation followed by resegregation (Ethington et al. 2001; Logan 2001). As with Monterey Park and other cities in Los Angeles County, areas that experienced segregation as all-white enclaves created through exclusionary policies and practices, these areas went through a period of integration as the policies were challenged and Latinos and Asian Americans moved in during the 1970s and 1980s. These areas now experience resegregation as whites greatly decline in numbers. New York City Charter Revision Commission member Bernard Richland explained the development of ethnic enclaves as the result of individual preference; although for many the concentration of services, stores, and entertainment serving a particular group is appealing, Richland's statement ignores the racial practices that continue in the real estate industry. A study by the National Fair Housing Alliance found that "illegal practices [including] denial of service, steering, illegal comments, and the use of schools as a proxy for the racial or ethnic composition of neighborhoods and communities" were common among workers in the real estate industry (NFHA 2006: 2). Rather than talking directly about the racial composition of a community, the report explains how "good" or "bad" schools become a substitute for race (NFHA 2006: 12). In this so-called color-blind era, many whites are very aware of race and prefer to live in all-white communities (Ethington et al. 2001).

Election Systems

Institutional processes configure political opportunities, and although African American, Latino, and Asian Americans share a subordinate position in a racialized political hierarchy, the New York City redistricting and charter reform process and the council elections that followed demonstrated that different political opportunities were created for these groups because of distinct demographic and political characteristics. The charter reforms focused primarily on the situation of African Americans and Latinos. Districts could be created in which these groups, with their large and concentrated populations, formed an effective voting bloc. Although such reforms have increased the number of Latino and African American elected officials in New York City, as well as in other cities across the United States, using a "one size fits all" strategy treats all racial minorities as the same and fails to take into account the particular histories and political and demographic characteristics of Asian Americans.

In New York City, Asian Americans joined in their support of Chinatown united within a council district. However, a majority Asian American district was impossible because of the limitations imposed by the census undercount, the smaller number of districts than requested by Asian American groups created during the charter reform process, and the dispersed and relatively small Asian American population. John Logan and John Mollenkopf (2003: 47) note that in the New York City council primary elections, candidates can win with a plurality of the vote, whereas in Los Angeles, if no candidate wins a majority, a runoff is held in the general election between the two top candidates. If New York changed to the Los Angeles model and added an additional feature, an "instant runoff" that allows voters to list their preference for candidates and that allows their votes to be transferred, this might help overcome the issue faced in District 1 with multiple Chinese American candidates fragmenting the Chinese American vote.

The Voting Rights Act of 1965 was designed principally to enfranchise African Americans in the South. With much larger and more highly segregated populations—compared to Asian Americans—African Americans, Latinos, and whites in New York City have been better served by single-member districts, as the New York City Council elections demonstrated. In New York City and much of the United States, in areas where the more dispersed populations of Asian Americans—and to a lesser degree, Latinos—make such districts problematic, alternative election systems could be considered (Aoki 2002). Such systems would allow greater opportunity for smaller and more dispersed populations to elect candidates of their choice. As Lani Guinier (1994) points out in her discussion of the problems associated with single-member districts, group interests may not coincide with district boundaries, gerrymandering plays a prominent role in redistricting, and the dominance of the majority voters can lead to a "tyranny of the majority" in which the votes of the minor-ity are unproductive. Judith Reed served as legal counsel to the New York City 1990 Districting Commission, and in a law review article following the pro-cess, Reed drew on the work of Guinier and discussed the limitations of single-member district elections for the Lower East Side. Reed (1992) concluded that alternative election systems should be considered, such as cumulative voting, a voting system in which voters can cast as many votes as there are open seats in districts with multiple representatives. Thus voters can strategically use their votes by spreading them among the candidates or by using all their votes for one candidate, and more readily form alliances with other voters based on shared interests.

The Myth of Whites as Race Neutral

The members of the New York City Districting Commission emphasized racial boundaries and labels for Asian Americans and Latinos and past white support for Asian American candidates. The commission's analysis assumed that whites would recognize the merits of Asian American political representation and would support a qualified Asian American candidate. This viewpoint, however, does not adequately consider the racial interests of whites and the active sup-port of white racial privilege through the historic and contemporary practices of political exclusion used by whites against racial minorities. Certainly whites have joined with racial minorities to elect minorities, but this scenario pri-marily occurs when progressive whites need allies to supplant an entrenched group (Browning et al. 1984; Sonenshein 1993), not when they are a voting majority, as in District 1. To suggest that Asian Americans will be the "next whites," following the pattern of acceptance of formerly nonwhite groups, such as southern and eastern Europeans (Gans 1994), favors an assimilation model of political integration that ignores the "color line" and the fundamentally different racial experiences of Native Americans and groups from Asia, Latin America, and Africa. Successful politicians, such as Gary Locke and Antonio Villaraigosa, win because they run carefully sanitized, deracialized campaigns in which race is mentioned in ways that support accepted notions of assimila-tion and a color-blind society.

There is a fundamental difference between, on the one hand, ignoring the impact of race on campaigning and enacting outwardly color-blind policies that have a negative impact on people of color and, on the other hand, cam-paigning to build a multiracial coalition and enacting policies that are described as race neutral but have positive consequences for everyone. City officials can recognize the importance of issues that affect all residents, such as improving transportation systems, health care services, and employment opportunities, reducing pollution, and combating crime. Government programs can have unequal racial outcomes, as demonstrated by the history of displacement of communities of color by infrastructure development, vastly different levels of quality in public schools in affluent versus low-income neighborhoods, or concern over racial profiling by police officers. A different scenario is offered by policies that are important to all residents, such as the quality of public education or immigration regulation, but that consider the issues of particular groups, such as bilingual education or immigration reform. Villaraigosa's support for funding for the Japanese American National Museum recognizes that major public cultural institutions that are supposed to represent the public may neglect minority communities. Thus, assisting the Japanese American National Museum is a way to bring the history and culture of this community into public view, where it can be noted and appreciated by all, not an attempt to isolate or separate a community from society as critics of ethnic- or race-specific activities contend (Schlesinger 1998). Although support for the museum targets a particular group, living-wage ordinances offer an example of a race-neutral effort that helps racial minorities. Baltimore's city council passed the first living-wage ordinance in the United States in 1994, and in the decade that followed, 123 cities, counties, school boards, and other governing bodies passed similar ordinances (Luce 2005). Such changes can work to improve the condition of all affected workers, but considering the high number of people of color in the jobs covered by these ordinances in cities such as Los Angeles, these policies have a positive effect on minority workers.

With the increasing heterogeneity of the Asian American community in terms of such factors as class, nativity, and political ideology, is race a viable category for the construction of districts? Race remains important because whites at times organize to develop policies to protect white racial privilege. As a result government policies are shaped by race and ethnicity in ways that negatively affect minorites and become embedded in economic and political relations. (Lien 2001; J. Wong 2006). In accord with the history of political and economic exclusion faced by Asian Americans locally and nationally, AALDEF's exit poll showed that Asian Americans in Chinatown voted overwhelmingly for Asian American representation, and although some whites crossed over to support the Asian American candidates, most did not.

The racial politics of Lower Manhattan demonstrate that what it means to be Asian American, Latino, or white is highly situational, with personal meaning emerging from local contexts while also linked to larger social and economic factors. Race is not simply an identity tied to a racial label. Voters in the city council elections considered neighborhood issues, such as the personal histories of the candidates and the local organizations that supported them, changing community demographics, efforts to slow the growth of Chinatown, and gentrification. Voters also placed these local concerns within a larger context, connecting the issues to factors such as the history of political exclusion faced by Asian Americans in the city and nation, the global flow of capital and economic development, and city policies supporting gentrification in Chinatown.

Political reform, such as New York City's charter revision, is supposed to enfranchise minorities, as were government efforts to address civil and political rights in the 1960s. However, as George Lipsitz (2006) asserts in his discussion on the contradiction between civil rights legislation and the public policies that obstruct its implementation, the national discourse on issues of discrimination reveals the connection between a civil rights dialogue ostensibly about inclusion and fairness and the production, support, and extension of white privilege. As Kousser (1999) points out in his analysis of the U.S. Supreme Court redistricting decisions in the 1990s, such as *Shaw v. Reno*, the Court used "the Reconstruction Amendments to protect powerful whites rather than much less politically potent minorities, employed the language of equality and integration to promote inequality and exclusion, and established racial and partisan double standards while pretending to be colorblind and nonpartisan" (p. 377).

The serious and sustained efforts of Asian Americans to preserve their history in San Diego and to gain political access in Los Angeles and New York City demonstrate the difficulty and complexity of gaining access to and modifying institutions that have historically excluded racial minorities. Mari Matsuda (1995: 66) discusses the contrast between lived experiences and deeply held beliefs; she cites the contradiction faced by the Nisei who volunteered for military service during World War II while they and their families were locked up in internment camps, yet still believed in U.S. "constitutional democracy." By "looking to the bottom," as Matsuda (1995: 63) suggests, at those who have experienced oppression and exclusion, Asian Americans reveal their interpretation of society and struggle for inclusion and their commitment and desire to become a part of American society. Their efforts signify a continued belief in the possibility of inclusion and equality, in contrast to those who see political mobilization along racial and ethnic lines as a sign of the balkanization of American society (Huntington 2004; Schlesinger 1998). Looking up from the bottom also reveals the impediments, layer upon layer, that contribute to the sedimentation of political inequality. Recognizing these impediments, the community members who participated in the redistricting struggles in New York City and the Los Angeles region and in the historic preservation and economic development plans in San Diego are driven by the hope that conditions can be altered and improved and that the United States can address the American dilemma of racial inequality that has existed through the centuries.

Notes

Chapter 1

1. A third issue, which is not a major focus in this book's case studies, is that race-neutral policies may ignore the existence of people who are actively and purposefully working to create and support racial inequality in society. Therefore, although individuals and groups work to implement race-neutral policies, the policies may not effectively counter the actions of those implementing discriminatory policies.

2. Areas of emphasis in Gordon's (1964) work include cultural assimilation, which involves adaptation to the customs and culture of mainstream society, and structural assimilation, which involves integration into society's political, economic, and social institutions.

Park's view of assimilation theory is currently seen as conservative in its support of the status quo because it suggests that nothing need be done to address discrimination in society for structural assimilation to occur. When Park first introduced the theory in the early 1900s, it was a progressive counter to biologically based theories of race that established a hierarchy of racial groups and supported the exclusion of so-called inferior groups (Omi and Winant 1994).

3. As research on the construction of panethnic identities among Asian Americans, Latinos, and Native Americans demonstrates, organizing for political purposes along racial and ethnic lines continues to occur in contemporary society, creating larger, more inclusive identities and organizing practices (Cornell 1988; Espiritu 1992; Nagel 1997; Oboler 1995; Okamoto 2003; Padilla 1985).

4. Alba and Nee also widen the analytical focus to include changes in the mainstream, not just racial minorities. They point out that Gordon and others saw the mainstream as culturally homogeneous and as incorporating new groups while remaining unaffected by such groups. In contrast, Alba and Nee suggest that assimilation

involves changes in both the mainstream and the immigrants and their descendants and that the mainstream is being reworked by this process of incorporation.

Based on the impressive economic and social gains that Asian Americans have made in present-day U.S. society, some social scientists have suggested that Asian Americans may follow the racial trajectory of southern and eastern Europeans and move from a nonwhite to white racial category (Gans 1994). Alba and Nee believe that additional groups will not be added to the "white" category; instead, they believe that the racial mainstream has expanded beyond white and that additional groups, such as Asian Americans, are included. Of major importance for Alba and Nee's discussion of this change is the federal government's enforcement of civil rights; also important is expansion of the economic, educational, and residential opportunities that allow the advancement of racial minorities without posing a major threat to white interests.

In a landmark multigenerational study of Mexican Americans, Edward Telles and Vilma Ortiz (2008) found a complex situation involving educational and occupational gains and losses through generations that calls into question assimilation theory's assumption of progress.

5. Contemporary works emphasize this multiracial aspect of race relations and racial formation (Camarillo 2004; Chung 2007; De Genova 2006; Jones-Correa 2001; Kim 2000; Logan and Mollenkopf 2003; Ong et al. 1994; E. Park 1996; E. Park and Park 1999; Sanchez 2004; Sanjek 1998; Wild 2005) rather than the traditional focus on African Americans and whites, as reflected historically in the nineteenth-century writing of Alexis de Tocqueville (1969) and Gunnar Myrdal's (1944) mid-twentieth-century report or in later works by William J. Wilson (1980) and Andrew Hacker (1995).

Demonstrating the malleability of racial judgments, with the onset of the Great Depression, Molina (2006: 10) describes how government agencies used changing racial images to describe "Mexicans as an economic burden," and "the inferiority of Mexicans soon became 'indisputable,'" thus serving to legitimize the change from assimilation efforts to "repatriation drives" to clear Los Angeles of Mexicans.

6. In a key analysis of Asian American politics, Glenn Omatsu (1994: 21) emphasizes the importance of Malcolm X and the black liberation movement for the understanding of the centrality of "oppression and power" for activists. Omatsu explains how this perspective informed the Asian American movement and the 1968 student strike at San Francisco State University, led by a multiracial coalition of African American, Asian American, Latino, and Native American students (Umemoto 1989). For a contrasting view, see Susan Koshy (2001) and her discussion of Asian Americans and attempted alliances with whites.

7. The 1965 Immigration Act abolished national quotas set at a time in the early 1900s when eugenics was influential and immigration was largely limited to northern and western European countries. The change in immigration policy dramatically altered immigration patterns; whereas immigrants primarily came from Europe before

the 1965 act, Latin America and Asia became the major sources of immigration following passage of the act. This change contributed to the demographic transformation of urban areas across the country, as white majorities gave way to racial minorities toward the end of the twentieth century.

8. Tariff and tax policies in the United States that made it fiscally profitable to close domestic manufacturing plants and send production overseas also facilitated this process (Light and Bonacich 1988).

9. Characteristics include a "feeling . . . of helplessness," "present-time orientation with relatively little ability to . . . plan for the future," and "a sense of resignation and fatalism" (Lewis 1966: xlvii–xlviii).

Supporting the importance of behavior and culture as contributors to poverty, Daniel Patrick Moynihan (1965) claimed that, although African Americans continued to face discrimination, one of the major factors leading to social problems among low-income African Americans was the high occurrence of female-headed households. Also, critics of social welfare programs argued that such programs created an incentive for unemployment and single-parent families, reinforcing the culture of poverty (Murray 1984). Continuing the discussion three decades after Moynihan and demonstrating the continued appeal of the culture of poverty explanation among those who focus on individual responsibility and culture, Stephan Thernstrom and Abigail Thernstrom (1997) concluded that, even in a society characterized by racial equality, economic differences among groups would continue because of different cultural patterns among racial groups. Although some discrimination remains, the problems faced by contemporary African Americans are explained by the "level of family disorganization" (Thernstrom and Thernstrom 1997: 536).

10. As Carol Stack (1974) points out, however, social scientists who attempt to shift the explanation of poverty from culture to structure accept the label of pathology attached to the behavior and family structure of poor racial minorities. Stack (1974: 24) notes that William Ryan (1971: 78) states that "economic stress" and "discrimination" are causes of poverty but also believes that "social pathology and broken homes are twin results." Stack explains that the African American families that she studied developed strong ties among members of their extended family and developed supportive, kinlike networks among friends. Rather than exhibiting signs of pathology, these female-headed households formed strong and mutually beneficial networks.

With the publication of his *Truly Disadvantaged* (1987), Wilson brings back culture with a discussion of values and role models, even though he contends that he emphasizes class and structure. See also Bonacich (1972, 1980) for a discussion of the interaction of race, class, and social structure.

11. City zoning ordinances enforced racially segregated residential areas until they were declared unconstitutional by the 1917 Supreme Court decision in *Buchanan v. Warley*. Restrictive covenants in housing deeds that excluded racial minorities from

purchasing homes then came into widespread use, with strong support from the federal government's home mortgage programs. Although the Supreme Court found restrictive covenants unconstitutional in the 1948 *Shelley v. Kraemer* decision, the use of restrictive covenants continued into the 1950s (Massey and Denton 1993; Sides 2003).

12. The 1862 Homestead Act and the 1866 Southern Homestead Act provided millions of acres of free or low-priced land, but this land primarily went to whites. Major policies of the New Deal covered whites but excluded racial minorities. The Social Security Act of 1935, for example, covered occupations held by whites and excluded domestic and agricultural workers, the domain of Asians, Latinos, and African Americans.

These advantages are multiplied by the "lower tax rates on capital gains" compared to taxes on income, because whites are more likely to have additional assets than African Americans with comparable incomes (Oliver and Shapiro 1995: 43). Given the history of access to home ownership for whites, the tax deductions that home owners receive on property taxes and mortgage interest are additional benefits that flow unequally in society.

13. The model minority stories continued in the 1980s, and in a 1984 issue, *Newsweek* contributed to the disparate views of African and Asian Americans in a pair of articles in the same issue. The article on African Americans, "A Look Back at Anger," continued the theme that African Americans focus on attacking society rather than improving themselves. The article examined the students who had participated in protests against racism at Cornell University and had carried "rifles, shotguns" in their seizure of the student union (Starr et al. 1984: 36). In contrast, the article on Asian Americans, "A Formula for Success," focused on the high educational achievement of that group (Williams et al. 1984: 77). Several years later, *Time* magazine's cover story, "The New Whiz Kids" (Brand 1987), reinforced the theme of Asian Americans as stellar scholars.

The ideological battle between explaining race through culture and individual behavior and explaining it through structure and systemic racism, which surfaced in white ethnicity, represented changing racial politics. Rather than the disappearance of ethnic differences through assimilation, differences among groups within a racial category could be recognized. The use of culture to explain success or failure in the model minority image and the emergence of ethnic distinctions converged in discussions of West Indians as the "black model minority." When West Indians entered the United States from the Caribbean in the early decades of the twentieth century, race dominated the way Americans thought about groups and shaped how West Indians fitted into American society. As Philip Kasinitz (1992) explained in his study of West Indians in New York City, "Race . . . structured their life chances. Being black determined where they lived and could not live, where they could and could not go to school, what type of job they could get" (p. 8). Nathan Glazer and Daniel P. Moynihan (who would follow with the publication on the "Negro Family" in 1965) differentiated between the cultural characteristics of African Americans from the South who migrated north and West Indians living in New York City. Glazer and Moynihan (1970) wrote that in 1963 "the ethos of the West Indians, in contrast to that of the Southern Negro, emphasized saving, hard work, investment, education" (p. 35). See also Mary Waters (1999) for her discussion of culture, structure, and the racialization of West Indians and Ivan Light (1972) for a discussion of the importance of culture and ethnic entrepreneurship.

14. The model minority image also ignored the problems of Asian Americans, or, if non–Asian Americans acknowledged problems such as poverty, the assumption was that Asian Americans could take care of their own problems without government assistance. As a result, the model minority image separated the group from other racial minorities and required that Asian Americans had to document their problems and why they needed government assistance as they lobbied for aid to address issues such as poverty, employment discrimination, political disenfranchisement, and hate crimes (APALC 2006; S. Lee 1996; Osajima 1988; Suzuki 1977).

Of the critiques of the model minority image that emerged in the 1970s through the 1990s, Paul Ong and Suzanne Hee (1994) provided one of the most comprehensive analyses. Although Ong and Hee (1994) certainly recognized the economic and educational successes achieved by Asian Americans, they also pointed out the problems with some of the indicators used to establish the model minority label. Median household income was a primary factor commonly cited, and as Ong and Hee (1994: 34) noted, Asian Americans did have a higher household median income than whites. However, when Ong and Hee took into account that Asian Americans tended to have larger households with more workers per home and were concentrated in urban areas with higher living costs, they found that Asian Americans actually had lower median household and per person incomes than whites. In fact, the poverty rate for Asian Americans in major metropolitan areas with large Asian American populations was nearly twice that of whites.

Examining the high educational attainment figures for Asian Americans, Ong and Hee explain that an overlooked factor in the model minority myth is the high number of Asian immigrants who come to the United States with advanced degrees or who come as students and remain in the country. Ong and Hee (1994: 39) estimate that this population makes up 65–75 percent of the "highly educated" Asian American population. Another overlooked issue in the discussion of the model minority is that highly educated Asian American men receive about 10 percent less in salary and wages than their white male counterparts (Ong and Hee 1994: 40). Although part of this difference is due to the problems of transferring their educational credentials and skills acquired in a foreign country to the U.S. market and their limited English skills, Ong and Hee (1994) suggest that race continues to play a part in the lower income figures. An important issue is that a racial glass ceiling limits the entrance of Asian Americans into the managerial and executive level ranks (U.S. Commission on Civil Rights 1992).

15. The 1998 resolution stated that "admissions motivated by concern for financial, political or other such benefit to the university do not have a place in the admissions process. If chancellors elect to admit students outside of established criteria, the Academic Senate should be consulted" (Weiss 1998: A3). The issue reappeared in 2007 when an investigation by the UCLA student newspaper showed that the dental school admitted relatives of wealthy donors to the highly competitive orthodontics program ahead of better-qualified applicants (Faturechi 2007).

16. Examples of exclusion include immigration policies that controlled entrance into the United States, such as the Chinese Exclusion Act of 1882 and the 1907 Gentlemen's Agreement, both explicitly enacted to ban Asian laborers (Chan 1991; Hing 1993; Takaki 1989); land use ordinances aimed at Asians, such as those passed in the 1800s by the San Francisco Board of Supervisors in the failed attempt to drive Chinese residents and Chinese-owned laundries out of the city (McClain 1994); California alien land laws passed in the early 1900s that prevented Asian immigrants from owning property (McClain 1994); restrictive covenants governing residential segregation that prevented a range of groups, such as African, Asian, Jewish, and Mexican Americans from buying homes in white neighborhoods (Flammang 2005; Jackson 1985; Massey and Denton 1993; Sides 2003; U.S. Commission on Civil Rights 1973, 1975); naturalization regulations that governed citizenship requirements for immigrants and were challenged repeatedly by Asian immigrants, such as the U.S. Supreme Court cases *Ozawa v. United States* of 1922 and *United States v. Bhagat Singh Thind* in 1923 (Okihiro 2001); and the history of redistricting and the fragmentation of minority neighborhoods, which diluted the political power of minorities (Davidson 1984; Grofman 1998; Kousser 1999).

Three explanations are commonly used to account for the supposed lack of political activity among immigrants: (1) the idea of immigrants as sojourners, viewing themselves as temporary residents and unwilling to involve themselves in local issues; (2) the problems of economic survival in their new country, which dominate the lives of immigrants, leaving no time to get involved in politics; or (3) new immigrants' lack of knowledge of U.S. politics and how to become involved (Lien et al. 2004).

17. New York City and Los Angeles, as exemplars of urban locales with large numbers of immigrants and a majority of people of color and as the major metropolitan regions on opposite coasts, have generated a number of comparative studies, especially on electoral politics and race relations (Halle 2003; Kaufmann 2004; Logan and Mollenkopf 2003; Wong 2006).

18. Contemporary anti-immigrant activities echo California's history as one of the major sites for anti-Asian immigration in the late 1800s and early 1900s (Saxton 1971) and anti-Mexican movements, such as the forced deportation and repatriation

of Mexican immigrants and Mexican Americans in the 1930s and 1950s (Grebler et al. 1970; Sanchez 1993).

Chapter 2

An earlier version of parts of this chapter appeared as "Reclamation and Preservation: The San Diego Chinese Mission, 1927 to 1996," *Journal of San Diego History* 49(1) (2003): 1–20.

1. As indicators of downtown's decreasing importance, the population of San Diego grew 47.8 percent from 1950 to 1957, but the downtown population contracted by 8.6 percent during the same period; downtown pedestrian traffic dropped nearly in half, from 94,155 in 1948 to 58,588 in 1957; and property values fell (Hof 1990: 2). In the four decades after World War II, all the major department stores abandoned downtown and relocated in the new suburban malls (Gordon 1985: 3), and from 1945 to 1975, "no major new development went to the south of Broadway" in the downtown area (Gordon 1985: 12). A 1967 office space study noted that in 1958 "there was little, if any, class A office space in this area. This is to say that there really were no new, modern in design, sizeable high rise air conditioned office buildings downtown. The newest of the then existing high rise office buildings were at least 30 years old" (Hippaka 1967: 6).

2. The rating of the Chinese Mission in Brandes's (1986a: 2) report was as follows: historical significance, 7/10; architectural integrity, 3/10; how docs building function in relation to current Chinese population in the area, 0/10; likely to cause concern within Chinese community if demolished, 5/10; degree to which original exterior remains intact, 3/10; total, 18/50.

3. The "Historical Landmarks Designated by the San Diego Historical Resources Board" list began including the "Designation Criteria" in 1994, allowing for a more detailed analysis of how the board determined the historical importance of sites. In 2001, the Clermont/Coast Hotel (discussed in Chapter 3) was the first site added to the list pertaining to African Americans. Using 2001 as a reference point and examining the 192 sites listed in 2000 and 2001, one can see that the emphasis is on whites, either explicitly in the case of people or implicitly in the case of neighborhoods. For the criterion "Historical Persons," forty individuals and two families are listed. Based on a name analysis, I conclude that the individuals and families were all white. The list included two historic districts of neighborhoods established in the 1920s, when restrictive covenants and racial steering by real estate agents meant that these neighborhoods allowed only white residents (Harris 1974).

4. Lia later denied any conflict of interest between her earlier position as the CCDC special counsel dealing with historic preservation and her position representing Tyson, noting that she disclosed the information necessary to avoid a conflict of interest (Jarmusch and Wilson 1992).

5. Developer Dan Pearson also submitted a proposal, with a plan to reconstruct the Chinese Mission as part of the planned Horton Grand Hotel in the historic district, but he had stated earlier that he would defer to the plans of the Chinese community. Pearson explained, "I'm not fighting them (the Chinese community). If they can come up with a better proposal, I'll back off. I think they'll give it a real try. Tom Hom . . . is a close personal friend of mine and I'll do anything I can for the group" (Hathcock 1987).

6. For an in-depth discussion of the establishment of the Asian Pacific Thematic Historic District Advisory Committee and the Lincoln Hotel discussed later in this chapter, see Vo (2004). I draw heavily from Vo's work for my discussion of these two issues.

Chapter 3

An earlier version of parts of this chapter appeared in "African Americans and Historic Preservation in San Diego: The Douglas and Clermont/Coast Hotel," *Journal of San Diego History* 54(1) (2008): 15.

1. Studies of African Americans in downtown San Diego have described Robert Rowe as both African American and white, although most list his racial identity as African American. Considering that antimiscegenation views at the time were strong and that Robert married Mabel Rowe, an African American woman well known in the community because she ran a prostitution business, it is likely that Rowe was African American; a white man married to an African American woman at the time would have generated more discussion in the press among those interviewed about their memories of Robert and Mabel Rowe. In their study of African American history in downtown San Diego, Richard L. Carrico and Stacey Jordan (2004) describe Robert Rowe as white, stating that "Mr. Ramsey had developed a business relationship with Robert Rowe, a white businessman and husband of Mabel Rowe, a Black or possibly mulatto woman" (p. II-16). Local historian Micheal Austin categorized Rowe as African American, stating that "Rowe and Ramsey were 'aggressive black entrepreneurs who exemplified a bold, self-confident spirit . . . during a period of insufferable segregation in the United States'" (Krueger 1991: 1). Newspaper articles described Rowe as African American, with an article in the *Los Angeles Times* on the Douglas Hotel noting that "two black men . . . built and owned it, Bob Rowe and George Ramsey" (Parker 1984: J1) and the *Voice and Viewpoint* explaining that "African American entrepreneurs, Robert Rowe and George Ramsey, built the hotel in 1924" (Picou 1996: C9).

2. Austin explained that he spelled his name "Micheal" rather than "Michael" because that was the way his grandmother back in Alabama had shown him how to

write it and he retains that spelling because it is a link to her and a way to "keep that connection to my family" (Krueger 1991: 1).

3. Twenty-nine units would be reserved for "very low income" residents and would be rented at 30 percent of the tenant's income, eleven units would go to low-income individuals, and the remainder would rent at market rates (Bernstein 1987: 2-1). Displaced tenants from the Douglas Hotel would have priority to rent one of the affordable units. The building was complete and ready for renters on August 1, 1987. The developer sent letters to the former tenants in June and again in early August; as of late August, 10 former Douglas Hotel residents were set to move in and 300 others had applied for the affordable housing (Bernstein 1987: 2-1).

4. The contemporary economic and cultural revitalization of Harlem, marked by the movement of African American and white professionals into the neighborhood and increased capital investment in its residential and commercial areas, was given added visibility when former president Bill Clinton located his office in Harlem in 2001. The day after speaking at the annual United Nations General Assembly in New York City in September 2006, Hugo Chavez, the president of Venezuela, went to Harlem to an-nounce that he was increasing to 100 million gallons the amount of discounted heating oil that his country would send to the low-income residents of the United States (James 2006). Chavez's presence in the neighborhood is a recognition of the fact that even as Harlem experiences gentrification, it is an important symbol not only of African American and Latino communities but also of racial inequality in the United States.

5. Also working to preserve their civil rights history, Memphis residents formed the Martin Luther King Memorial Foundation and raised funds to buy the Lorraine Motel, where Martin Luther King Jr. was assassinated in 1968. With government sup-port, the foundation created the National Civil Rights Museum in the motel. The museum opened in 1991 and expanded in 2002 (NCRM 2006).

6. A change appears to be occurring in Atlanta as new development is mixed with historic preservation. The Los Angeles Times reported in 2006 that "gentrification is coming to the crumbling district around Martin Luther King Jr.'s grave" (Fausset 2006: A18) and that one of the largest new projects is the Renaissance Walk, a mixed-use project with condominiums and retail space. The Renaissance Walk project il-lustrates the conflict among community members with different visions for the area. Big Bethel AME Church, located on Auburn Avenue and one of the oldest African American congregations in the city, and the African American development com-pany Integral Group are partners in the Renaissance Walk project and have designed the project to take into account the history of the area and the need for affordable housing. The project includes the "facades of four original businesses on the block" (Fausset 2006: A18), a suggestion put forward by Tom Hom in his effort to keep the San Diego Chinese Mission Church in its original location but dismissed by the owner

of the Chinese Mission. The Renaissance Walk will include space for historical exhibits and reserve 20 percent of the housing "at below market rate" (Fausset 2006: A18). Shirley Franklin, mayor of Atlanta, praised the project for providing housing close to downtown: "Projects like this help ensure that people who work hard every day in Atlanta will also be able to live in Atlanta. . . . It is especially exciting because it is located in one of our most treasured neighborhoods" (Post 2006). Kwanza Hall, city council member, also supported the project. Speaking about the new development in and future prosperity of the area, he stated, "This is the beginning for many new projects in the area that will result in affordable housing, retail opportunities and residential units. . . . At the same time, Renaissance Walk will respect the history and heritage on Auburn Avenue. . . . Auburn Avenue will become the cultural anchor of the city" (Post 2006). Noting the neglect the area has faced, Hall continued, "We can't afford to waste another moment" (Fausset 2006: A18).

Critics of the Renaissance Walk include staff of the Historic District Development Corporation (HDDC), a nonprofit group that began in 1980 "to rehabilitate and revitalize the residential and commercial properties" on Auburn Avenue with an emphasis on historic preservation (HDDC 2006). Speaking about the historic importance of the area and its connection to Martin Luther King Jr., the HDDC vice chair, Mtamanika Youngblood, stated that "it means we have to be smarter, more creative, more thoughtful" (Fausset 2006: A18). Youngblood expressed dismay that the Palamont Motor Lodge, a 1950s-era motel, was demolished for the project. As with the struggle over the Clermont/Coast Hotel in San Diego, described later in this chapter, Youngblood believed that the Palamont Motor Lodge should have been preserved because it served African Americans during the segregation era. The president of the HDDC, Joan Garner, expressed her concern about the effect on independent local businesses if national chain stores move into the new project. "The challenge is, how do you weave the old and the new in a way that's representative of the historic aspect of the community?" (Fausset 2006: A18).

7. The Bethel African Methodist Episcopal Church is one of the still-standing structures documented by the Mooney report that has attracted the attention of the GBHS but has not yet been placed on the city's list of historic sites. Designed in 1911 by one of San Diego's most prominent architects, Irving Gill, the church members relocated in 1939. The Mooney report cites the *San Diego Union-Tribune* and states that the building "was thought to have been demolished in 1962 for the construction of Interstate 5, but a portion of the church was moved two miles away and is now owned by a motorcycle club" (Carrico and Jordan 2004: V-39).

8. As of 2007, the complete Mooney report is available on the CCDC website at http://www.ccdc.com/index.cfm/fuseaction/projects.history. I served on the Mooney team during its presentation to the CCDC during the consultant selection process and in the early stages of the research process. The GBHS (now called the Black Histori-

cal Society) website, located at http://www.blackhistoricalsociety.org, also contains information on the history of African Americans in San Diego.

Chapter 4

Earlier versions of parts of this chapter appeared as "Asian Americans and Multiracial Political Coalitions: New York City's Chinatown and Redistricting, 1990–1991," in *Asian Americans and Politics: An Exploration*, edited by Gordon H. Chang (Stanford, CA: Woodrow Wilson Center Press and Stanford University Press, 2001); "The Political Significance of Race: Asian American and Latino Redistricting Debates in California and New York City," in *Racial Transformations: Latinos and Asians Remaking the United States*, edited by Nicholas De Genova (Durham, NC: Duke University Press, 2006); and, coauthored with Edward Park, "Multiracial Collaborations and Coalitions," in *The State of Asian Pacific Americans: Transforming Race Relations*, edited by Paul Ong (Los Angeles: LEAP/UCLA Asian Pacific American Public Policy Institute, 2001).

1. Two Spanish-surnamed supervisors were elected in 1872 and served until 1875. Although records are not clear on the matter, it appears that no women or members of ethnic groups were elected during the 1900s until the election of Molina in 1991 (Ferrell 1991; Simon 1991).

2. Data used included the following elections and Asian American candidates: 1985 City Council, 2nd District, Virginia Kee; 1986 Judicial Race, Democratic Primary, Dorothy Chin Brandt; 1987 Judicial Race, Democratic Primary, Peter Tom and Dorothy Chin-Brandt; 1986 and 1988 Senate Committeewoman, 61st Assembly District, Democratic Primary, Margaret Chin (D. Koo 1990a).

3. From field notes and Takeshi Nakayama (1990). In Los Angeles—December 8, 1990—members of the Asian American community held a fund-raising event for Robert Matsui's 1992 bid for the U.S. Senate. He later withdrew from the race because of a serious illness in the family.

Willie Brown, an African American who served as a California state assemblyman for three decades and as mayor of San Francisco for two terms, advised African Americans that they "have to fight against the perception that you are only a specialist on black matters," and he had to convince "white power brokers" and white voters that the expertise of African Americans covered a range of issues (Brown 2008: 47).

Chapter 5

Earlier versions of parts of this chapter appeared as "Asian Pacific Americans and Redistricting Challenges in 2001," in *National Asian Pacific American Political Almanac 2001–02*," edited by Don T. Nakanishi and James S. Lai (Los Angeles: UCLA Asian American Studies Center, 2001); and "The Sedimentation of Political Inequality:

Charter Revision and Redistricting in New York City's Chinatown, 1989–1991," *UCLA Asian Pacific American Law Journal* 8(1) (2002): 123–145.

1. I rely heavily on Mollenkopf's (1992, 2003) work on New York City politics to write this section on the 1989 mayoral election. Racial issues during this period included an assault by white men on three African American men with car problems in Howard Beach in Queens, with the assault leading to the death of one of the African American men; a young African American woman fabricating a story of being kidnapped by white men; an assault of a white woman jogging in Central Park by African American men; and just a month before the primary election, a white man killing a young African American man who had gone to Bensonhurst in Brooklyn to look at a used car.

2. In 2000 in the United States, about 27 percent of Asian Americans were less than 18 years of age, and the figure for Latinos was 35 percent, compared to 23 percent for whites (J. Wong 2006).

3. *Shaw v. Reno* was a suit filed against a congressional district in North Carolina (a district created to enhance African American voting power) by white plaintiffs on the grounds that the district violated the equal protection clause of the Fourteenth Amendment of the U.S. Constitution. The U.S. Supreme Court, on a 5 to 4 vote in 1993, ruled that the plan was unconstitutional because there was no compelling evidence to use race as the primary factor to draw a district that violated traditional redistricting principles such as compactness and respect for geographic and political boundaries. Critics of the court decision note that the Court did not adequately consider the history of African American disenfranchisement in North Carolina; that other congressional districts with white majorities also did not follow the traditional redistricting principles, such as compactness, but that these districts were not challenged; and that so-called traditional redistricting practices, rather than supporting equitable practices, have long been used to disenfranchise minority voters (Kousser 1999: 366–455).

4. Voter tabulation districts are a U.S. Census Bureau geographical denomination, which represents the smallest unit that includes both entire census blocks and entire electoral districts. There are 4,368 voter tabulation districts in New York City (Gartner 1993: 45).

5. I rely heavily on the works of Anderson and Fienberg (1999) and Prewitt (2000c) for this discussion of the census undercount.

6. In 2004, the Census Bureau provided population data on Arab Americans at the neighborhood level to the Department of Homeland Security. Although no information on individuals was released and although the data were already available to the public, Arab Americans criticized the actions of the Census Bureau. Hussam Ayloush, a member of the Council on American-Islamic Relations, stated, "It's open season on all privacy rights under the pretext of national security" (Watanabe 2007: A18). Ken Prewitt explained that with the range of current methods of collecting data on indi-

viduals, other data for surveillance, such as credit card information, provide more information. Nonetheless, Prewitt suggested that "the Census Bureau has to bend over backwards to maintain the confidence and the trust of the public" (Minkel 2007).

7. "Since 1965, Chinatown has grown another 500%, as estimates since the 1980 census have placed Chinatown's population at over 100,000 people" (New York Chinatown History Project 1990). Nancy Lam, of the Chinatown Voter Education Alliance, said, "With Chinatown presently populated by more than 120,000 residents, CVEA considers any districting plan that does not keep the community intact a violation of the Voting Rights Act" (Lam 1990: n.p.). And Bill Chong, president of Asian Americans for Equality, said, "Most sources estimate its population to have reached 150,000 by 1990" (Chong 1990: n.p.).

Chapter 6

Earlier versions of parts of this chapter appeared as "The Politics of Race and Redistricting in California, 2000–2002," in *Remapping Asian American History*, edited by Sucheng Chan (Walnut Creek, CA: Altamira Press, 2003); and "The Political Significance of Race: Asian American and Latino Redistricting Debates in California and New York City," in *Racial Transformations: Latinos and Asians Remaking the United States*, edited by Nicholas De Genova (Durham, NC: Duke University Press, 2006).

1. With Latinos and African Americans, groups with larger and more concentrated populations than Asian Americans, another issue is "packing." Packing reduces the number of possible districts in which these groups have a majority population by drawing boundaries that put as many members of these groups in as few districts as possible, rather than maximizing their voting potential by spreading out their population in more districts while still maintaining a majority in each district.

2. For figures on the 1980 and 2000 Compton population, see "Table 249. Persons by Spanish Origin and Race for Areas and Places: 1980," in *1980 Census of Population*, v. 1, *Characteristics of the Population*, ch. C, "General Social and Economic Characteristics," pt. 1, "United States Summary," PC80-1-C1 (Washington, DC: U.S. Government Printing Office, 1983), 1–411; and "Table DP-1. Profile of General Demographic Characteristics: 2000. Geographic Area: Compton City, California," p. 256, available at http://censtats.census.gov/pub/Profiles.shtml (accessed September 15, 2008).

3. The nine regions in the CAPAFR network were Sacramento, Alameda, San Francisco, Santa Clara, Los Angeles Metropolitan Center, San Gabriel Valley, Los Angeles South Bay, Orange County, and San Diego (CAPAFR, n.d.).

4. See United States District Court, Central District of California, *Cano v. Davis*, CV 01-08477 MMM (RCx), Opinion and Order Granting Defendants' Motions for Summary Judgment, 12 June 2002, 22–23 (http://www.cacd.uscourts.gov/CACD/RecentPubOp.nsf/, accessed July 1, 2002).

5. The book does not list a place of publication, publisher, or publication date.

6. NAACP Legal Defense and Educational Fund, Asian Pacific American Legal Center, and the Mexican American Legal Defense and Educational Fund, "Making Our Communities Count: United for a Fair Redistricting Process," University of California, Los Angeles, May 12, 2001.

7. For a discussion of the creation of Assembly District 49 in 1990, see Keith Aoki (2002) and Leland Saito (1993, 1998).

8. http://www.assembly.ca.gov/acs/committee/c7/phr.htm, accessed September 15, 2008.

9. Descriptions of the districts can be found at http://www.sen.ca.gov/ftp/SEN/senplan/SD21.HTM, http://www.sen.ca.gov/ftp/SEN/senplan/SD22.HTM, http://www.sen.ca.gov/ftp/SEN/senplan/SD24.HTM, http://www.sen.ca.gov/ftp/SEN/cngplan/CD29.HTM, and http://www.sen.ca.gov/ftp/SEN/cngplan/CD32.HTM (all accessed June 2, 2002).

10. The lawsuit pitted MALDEF against all the state legislators who supported the redistricting plan, but I focus on the conflict between MALDEF and the Latino legislators.

References

AACR (Asian Americans for Charter Reform). n.d. "Asian American Demand Fair Access to Charter Revision." Community flier.

AAFE (Asian Americans for Equality). n.d. *Asian Americans for Equality: 1974–1994.* New York City: AAFE.

AALDEF (Asian American Legal Defense and Education Fund). 1987. "Anti-Asian Violence Project: Organizing Moves Forward." *Outlook,* winter, 1.

———. 1992. "Chinatown Exit Poll Survey Results." *Outlook,* spring, 5.

———. 2005. "Asian American Voter Disenfranchisement Persists in 2004 Elections." *Outlook,* winter, 1.

———. 2006. "AALDEF Brings Language Assistance Suit to Protect Minority Voting Rights." *Outlook,* fall, 9.

Abelmann, Nancy, and John Lie. 1995. *Blue Dreams: Korean Americans and the Los Angeles Riots.* Cambridge, MA: Harvard University Press.

Abrajano, Marisa, Jonathan Nagler, and R. Michael Alvarez. 2003. "A Natural Experiment of Race-Based and Issue Voting: The 2001 City of Los Angeles Elections." http://www.nyu.edu/classes/nagler/quant1/code/lamayor30.pdf. Accessed August 11, 2006.

Abu-Lughod, Janet. 1994. *From Urban Village to East Village: The Battle for New York's Lower East Side.* Cambridge, MA: Blackwell.

Acuna, Rudolfo. 1984. *A Community Under Siege: A Chronicle of Chicanos East of the Los Angeles River, 1945–1975.* Los Angeles: Chicano Studies Research Center, University of California at Los Angeles.

———. 1996. *Anything but Mexican: Chicanos in Contemporary Los Angeles.* New York: Verso.

Alba, Richard, and Victor Nee. 2003. *Remaking the American Mainstream: Assimilation and Contemporary Immigration.* Cambridge, MA: Harvard University Press.

Alley, Paul. 1988. "Notes on Historic Gaslamp Quarter Infill Design Study." United States Department of the Interior, National Park Service, Western Region, San Francisco. Cover letter to Diane Roberts, City Design. San Diego, November 2.

Almaguer, Tomas. 1994. *Racial Fault Lines: The Historical Origins of White Supremacy in California.* Berkeley: University of California Press.

Ancheta, Angelo N. 1998. *Race, Rights, and the Asian American Experience.* New Brunswick, NJ: Rutgers University Press.

Ancheta, Angelo, and Kathryn K. Imahara. 1993. "Multi-Ethnic Voting Rights: Redefining Vote Dilution in Communities of Color." *University of San Francisco Law Review* 27(4): 815–872.

Anderson, Kay J. 1987. "The Idea of Chinatown: The Power of Place and Institutional Practice in the Making of a Racial Category." *Annals of the Association of American Geographers* 77(4): 580–598.

Anderson, Margo J., and Stephen E. Fienberg. 1999. *Who Counts? The Politics of Census-Taking in Contemporary America.* New York: Russell Sage Foundation.

Anderson, Martin. 1964. *The Federal Bulldozer: A Critical Analysis of Urban Renewal, 1949–1962.* Cambridge, MA: MIT Press.

Aoki, Keith. 2002. "A Tale of Three Cities: Thoughts on Asian American Electoral and Political Power After 2000." *UCLA Asian Pacific American Law Journal* 8(1): 1–54.

APALC (Asian Pacific American Legal Center). 2005. *The Diverse Face of Asian and Pacific Islanders in San Diego County.* Los Angeles: Asian Pacific American Legal Center of Southern California.

———. 2006. *A Community of Contrasts: Asian Americans and Pacific Islanders in the United States: Demographic Profile.* Los Angeles: Asian Pacific American Legal Center of Southern California.

APTHD (Asian Pacific Thematic Historic District). 1995. "Asian Pacific Thematic Historic District Master Plan." Resolution 2544, Adopted by the Redevelopment Agency of the City of San Diego, August 15.

Asian American Community Letter. 1989. Letter to Frederick A. O. Schwarz Jr. Chair, New York City Charter Revision Commission, July 18, Appendix 10, 10–11.

Asian American Union for Political Action. 1991. Letter stating position of the organization on the 1991 City Council elections, August 31.

Aubry, Larry. 2001. "Senate Committee on Elections and Reapportionment, State of California. Subject: 2001 Redistricting," Los Angeles, July 17. http://www.senate.ca.gov/ftp/SEN/COMMITTEE/STANDING/EL/_home/Reapportionment/transcripts.htp. Accessed September 12, 2008.

Austin, Micheal. 1994. "Harlem of the West: The Douglas Hotel and Creole Palace Nite Club." Master's thesis, University of San Diego.

Ayon, David R. 2001. "Dirty, but Not Soiled." *Los Angeles Times,* June 10, M6.

Bailey, Thomas, and Roger Waldinger. 1991. "The Changing Ethnic/Racial Division of

Labor." In *Dual City: Restructuring New York*, edited by John H. Mollenkopf and Manuel Castells. New York: Russell Sage Foundation.

Barrett, Wayne. 1991. "Anatomy of a Smear: How a Former Reformer Set New Lows in New York City Politics." *Village Voice*, November 5, 11.

Baver, Sherrie. 1984. "Puerto Rican Politics in New York City: The Post–World War II Period." In *Puerto Rican Politics in Urban America*, edited by James Jennings and Monte Rivera. Westport, CT: Greenwood Press.

BCRI (Birmingham Civil Rights Institute). 2006. "BCRI History and Mission." http://www.bcri.org/general_information/history_and_mission/index.htm. Accessed October 24, 2006.

Benjamin, Gerald, and Frank J. Mauro. 1989. "The Reemergence of Municipal Reform." In *Restructuring the New York City Government: The Emergence of Municipal Reform*, edited by Frank J. Mauro. New York: Academy of Political Science.

Bernstein, Leonard. 1987. "Time's Running Out for Former Tenants to Get New Apartments." *Los Angeles Times*, August 21, sec. 2, 1.

Betanzos, Amalia V. 1989a. Minutes of the New York City Charter Revision Commission, May 6. NYC Mayor. CRC Submission under Section 5 of the Voting Rights Act, Appendix 5, 7–8.

———. 1989b. Minutes of Public Hearing Before the New York City Charter Revision Commission, June 27, Appendix 5, 17–17A, Exhibit 27.

Bonacich, Edna. 1972. "A Theory of Ethnic Antagonism: The Split Labor Market." *American Sociological Review* 37(5): 547–559.

———. 1980. "Class Approaches to Ethnicity and Race." *Insurgent Sociologist* 10(2): 9–23.

Bonilla-Silva, Eduardo. 2003. *Racism Without Racists: Color-Blind Racism and the Persistence of Racial Inequality in the United States*. New York: Rowman and Littlefield.

Bradley, Shannon. 2001. Interview of Karen L. Huff, chairman and historian of the Gaslamp Black Historical Society, UCSD-TV, June 7.

Brand, David. 1987. "The New Whiz Kids." *Time*, August 31, 42–52.

Brandes, Ray. 1985–1986. "Report on Market Street Square Archaeological Monitoring." Prepared for Centre City Development Corporation, San Diego.

———. 1986a. Letter to Pamela Hamilton, assistant vice president, CCDC. Attachments: Rating Sheet and Rationale for Method of Evaluations on Rating Sheet, April 21, CCDC file 32824I, Marina History and Archaeological Studies.

———. 1986b. *Research and Analysis of Buildings Within the Marina Redevelopment Project Area Known to Be Connected with Local Chinese History*. Report for the CCDC, April, CCDC file 32823I, Chinese Mission Building.

Brandes, R., K. Flanigan, K. Webster, and A. P. Cooper. 1988. "Historic Site Inventory of Centre City East for Centre City Development Corporation." Office of Marie Burke Lia, November, vols. 1 and 2.

Braun, Gerry. 1998. "Ballpark Vote Offers City a National Voice." *San Diego Union-Tribune*, November 1, A1.

Brewster, David. 1996. "Rice or Locke?" *Seattle Weekly*, September 11, 11.

Brown, Michael K., Martin Carnoy, Elliott Currie, Troy Duster, David B. Oppenheimer, Marjorie M. Shultz, and David Wellman. 2003. *Whitewashing Race: The Myth of a Colorblind Society.* Berkeley: University of California Press.

Brown, Willie L. 2008. *Basic Brown: My Life and Our Times.* New York: Simon and Schuster.

Browning, Rufus P., Dale Rogers Marshall, and David H. Tabb. 1984. *Protest Is Not Enough.* Berkeley: University of California Press.

———. 1990. *Racial Politics in American Cities*, 1st ed. New York: Longman.

———. 2003. *Racial Politics in American Cities*, 3rd ed. New York: Longman.

Bruck, Connie. 2007. "Fault Lines: Can Mayor Antonio Villaraigosa Keep Control of L.A.'s Battling Factions?" *New Yorker*, May 21, 44.

Buckley, Ron. 1986. Letter to Howard Busby, president, Centre City Development Corporation, 11 July, CCDC file 328321, Chinese Mission Building.

Bullard, Robert D. 2000. *Dumping in Dixie: Race, Class, and Environmental Quality.* Boulder, CO: Westview Press.

———, ed. 2005. *The Quest for Environmental Justice: Human Rights and the Politics of Pollution.* San Francisco: Sierra Club Books.

Bunch, Michael. 1994. "The Search for Black History." *San Diego Union-Tribune*, January 17, 3.

Bush, Valerie Chow. 1991. "Division Street: East Meets West, and the Poor Lose." *Village Voice*, November 5, 11.

CAAAV (Committee Against Anti-Asian Violence). 1996. "Police Brutality in Asian Communities." *CAAAV Voice* 8(1) (winter): 3.

———. 1998a. "RJC Uncovers Racist Efforts to Contain Chinatown." *CAAAV Voice* 10(1) (spring): 5.

———. 1998b. "Organizing Asian Communities." *CAAAV Voice* 10(2) (fall): 5.

Calavita, Nico. 1992. "Growth Machines and Ballot Box Planning: The San Diego Case." *Journal of Urban Affairs* 14(1): 1–24.

Calderon, Jose Z. 1991. "Mexican American Politics in a Multi-Ethnic Community: The Case of Monterey Park: 1985–1990." Ph.D. dissertation, University of California, Los Angeles.

———. 1995. "Multi-Ethnic Coalition Building in a Diverse School District." *Critical Sociology* 21: 101–111.

California Journal. 2002. "Redrawing California: An Incumbent Protection Plan." *California Journal*, special section, 33(1) (January): 8–46.

Camarillo, Albert M. 2004. "Black and Brown in Compton: Demographic Change, Suburban Decline, and Intergroup Relations in a South Central Los Angeles Community, 1950 to 2000." In *Not Just Black and White: Historical and Contemporary Perspectives on Immigration, Race, and Ethnicity in the United States*, edited by Nancy Foner and George M. Fredrickson. New York: Russell Sage Foundation.

Cannon, Carl M. 2002. "California Divided." *California Journal* 33(1) (January): 8–12.

Cano v. Davis. 2002. United States District Court, Central District of California, CV 01-08477 MMM (RCx), Opinion and Order Granting Defendants' Motions for Summary Judgment, June 12, 2002, 27, 85–86. http://www.cacd.uscourts.gov/CACD/RecentPubOp.nsf/. Accessed July 1, 2002.

CAPAFR (Coalition of Asian Pacific Americans for Fair Redistricting). n.d. "Fair Representation, Coalition Building, Political Empowerment." Handout published by the Asian Pacific American Legal Center and included in "CAPAFR California Assembly Redistricting Proposal 2001."

Carlton, Robert L. 1975. "Blacks in San Diego County: A Social Profile, 1850–1880." *Journal of San Diego History* 21(4): 7–20.

Caro, Robert A. 1975. *The Power Broker: Robert Moses and the Fall of New York*. New York: Vintage Books.

Carrico, Richard L., and Stacey Jordon. 2004. "Centre City Development Corporation Downtown San Diego African-American Heritage Study." Prepared by Mooney and Associates, San Diego, for CCDC. Complete report available at http://www.ccdc.com/index.cfm/fuseaction/projects.history.

Cate, Elizabeth. 1999. Letter to Beverly Schroeder, CCDC, "Re: 235 Market Project," September 30.

CAUSE (Center for Asian Americans United for Self Empowerment). 2006. http://www.causeusa.org. Accessed December 6, 2006.

CCDC (Centre City Development Corporation). n.d. "Asian/Pacific Thematic Historic District Advisory Committee." Information sheet included with application for Advisory Committee in 1996.

———. 1984. Memorandum to Chairman and Members of the Redevelopment Agency from Gerald M. Trimble, "Joint Public Hearing—Disposition and Development Agreement with Shapell Housing, Inc. and Goldrich Kest and Associates (Market Street Square Apartments)," July 30.

———. 1987a. "Centre City Development Corporation Minutes of the Regular Meeting of August 7." File CCDC Board of Directors minutes, January 1987 to December 1989.

———. 1987b. "Request for Proposals for the Relocation/Reconstruction and Reuse of the Chinese Mission Building Downtown San Diego," December 2.

———. 1988. "Marina: Urban Design Plan Development Guidelines." City of San Diego.

Chan, Elaine. 1990. Oral testimony delivered to the New York City Districting Commission, November 1, Appendix 3, v. 2, 253.

———. 1991. Oral testimony delivered to the New York City Districting Commission, March 21, Appendix 3, v. 7.

Chan, Sucheng. 1991. *Asian Americans: An Interpretive History*. Boston: Twayne.

———, ed. 2003. *Remapping Asian American History*. Walnut Creek, CA: AltaMira Press.

Chau, Hope. 2001. Phone interview with James Pusey, August 13, San Diego.

Chau, Hope, and Erika Gutierrez. 2001. Interview with Tom Hom, May 22, San Diego.

Chavez, Ernesto. 2002. *"¡Mi Raza Primero!": Nationalism, Identity, and Insurgency in the Chicano Movement in Los Angeles, 1966–1978*. Berkeley: University of California Press.

Chavez, Lydia. 1998. *The Color Bind: California's Battle to End Affirmative Action*. Berkeley: University of California Press.

Chen, Pauline. 1989. Testimony of Pauline Chen, president of the Chinatown Voter Education Alliance before the New York City Charter Revision Commission, June 6, Appendix 10, no. 9, item 14.

Chin, Ken. 1991. Transcript of July 25 New York City Districting Commission Meeting, p. 20.

Chin, Margaret. 1990. Oral testimony delivered to the New York City Districting Commission, November 1, Appendix 3, v. 2, 127.

———. 1991. Campaign fliers for 1991 City Council Campaign.

Chin, Rocky. 1971. "New York Chinatown Today: Community in Crisis." *Amerasia Journal* 1(1): 1–24.

Cho, Milyoung. 1994. "Overcoming Our Legacy as Cheap Labor, Scabs, and Model Minorities: Asian Activists Fight for Community Empowerment." In *The State of Asian America: Activism and Resistance in the 1990s*, edited by Karin Aguilar-San Juan. Boston: South End Press.

Chong, Bill. 1990. Written testimony submitted to the New York City Districting Commission, Appendix 3, v. 2. n.p.

Chuang, Alexander. 2004. "How the Museum Extension Was Born." *San Diego Chinese Historical Society and Museum* [newsletter] (fall), 1.

Chuang, Alexander, Mary Anne Lacaman, Isabelle Heyward, and Alex Stewart. 2006. *Our First Ten Years: A Retrospective of the San Diego Chinese Historical Museum*. San Diego: San Diego Chinese Historical Museum.

Chung, Angie Y. 2007. *Legacies of Struggle: Conflict and Cooperation in Korean American Politics*. Palo Alto, CA: Stanford University Press.

City Council Resolution R-270599. 1988. Adopted on March 22. San Diego Historical Resources Board, folder 207.

Clifford, Frank. 1990. "Census Count May Be Low by 4.7 Million." *Los Angeles Times*, December 28, A26.

Clifford, Jane. 1990. "Goal Is to Save What's Left of Old Chinatown." *San Diego Tribune*, August 14, D2.

CNN. 2005. "Congressman Dies of Rare Disease." http://www.cnn.com/2005/ALLPOL ITICS/01/02/obit.matsui/index.html. Accessed September 11, 2008.

Cornell, Stephen. 1988. *The Return of the Native: American Indian Political Resurgence.* New York: Oxford University Press.

Crenshaw, Kimberle, Neil Gotanda, Gary Peller, and Kendall Thomas, eds. 1995. *Critical Race Theory.* New York: New Press.

Cuff, Dana. 2000. *The Provisional City: Los Angeles Stories of Architecture and Urbanism.* Cambridge, MA: MIT Press.

Dana, Richard Henry, Jr. 1990. *Two Years Before the Mast: A Personal Narrative of Life at Sea.* New York: Penguin Books.

Daniels, Roger. 1974. *The Politics of Prejudice.* New York: Atheneum.

———. 1982. "The Bureau of the Census and the Relocation of the Japanese Americans: A Note and a Document." *Amerasia Journal* 9(1): 101–105.

Davidson, Chandler, ed. 1984. *Minority Vote Dilution.* Washington DC: Howard University Press.

———. 1992. "The Voting Rights Act: A Brief History." In *Controversies in Minority Voting: The Voting Rights Act in Perspective,* edited by Bernard Grofman and Chandler Davidson. Washington, DC: Brookings Institution.

Davidson, Chandler, and Bernard Grofman. 1994. *Quiet Revolution in the South.* Princeton, NJ: Princeton University Press.

Davis, Mike. 1990. *City of Quartz: Excavating the Future in Los Angeles.* New York: Vintage Books.

———. 2003. "The Next Little Dollar: The Private Governments of San Diego." In *Under the Perfect Sun: The San Diego Tourists Never See,* edited by Mike Davis, Kelly Mayhew, and Jim Miller. New York: New Press.

Davis, Mike, Kelly Mayhew, and Jim Miller, eds. 2003. *Under the Perfect Sun: The San Diego Tourists Never See.* New York: New Press.

Dea, Arlene. 1985. Interview with Tom Hom. San Diego Historical Society Oral History Program, January 12.

De Genova, Nicholas, ed. 2006. *Racial Transformations: Latinos and Asians Remaking the United States.* Durham, NC: Duke University Press.

DeGiovanni, Frank F. 1987. *Displacement Pressures in the Lower East Side.* Community Service Society Working Papers. New York: Community Service Society of New York.

Diaz, David R. 2005. *Barrio Urbanism: Chicanos, Planning, and American Cities.* New York: Routledge.

Donaldson, Milford Wayne. 1986. *Historic Chinese Community Buildings: Survey Analysis.* November 6 (revised December 17, 1986). Exhibit E in the CCDC Memorandum to Ad Hoc Advisory Committee from Pam Hamilton, "Recommendations Regarding Chinese Buildings in the Marina Redevelopment Project Area," February 11, 1987, CCDC file 32823I, Chinese Mission Building.

Dove, Adrian. 2001. California Legislature, Assembly, Elections, Reapportionment and Constitutional Amendments Committee, "Transcript of Public Hearing on Redistricting, Identification of Communities of Interest," Los Angeles, June 8, 2001. http://www.assembly.ca.gov/acs/committee/c7/phr.htm. Accessed June 1, 2002.

Dreier, Peter, John Mollenkopf, and Todd Swanstrom. 2001. *Place Matters: Metropolitics for the Twenty-First Century.* Lawrence: University Press of Kansas.

D'Souza, Dinesh. 1991. *Illiberal Education: The Politics of Race and Sex on Campus.* New York: Free Press.

Dubrow, Gail Lee. 1986. "Preserving Her Heritage: American Landmarks of Women's History." UCLA Urban Planning Program. Cited in Dolores Hayden, *The Power of Place* (Cambridge, MA: MIT Press, 1997), 85–86, 266n9.

Dubrow, Gail, and Donna Graves. 2002. *Sento at Sixth and Main: Preserving Landmarks of Japanese American Heritage.* Seattle: Seattle Arts Commission.

Dudziak, Mary L. 2000. *Cold War Civil Rights: Race and the Image of American Democracy.* Princeton, NJ: Princeton University Press.

Dunham, Richard S. 2006. "A Cause That Scares Business." *Business Week,* August 14, 58.

Edsall, Thomas Byrne, and Mary D. Edsall. 1992. *Chain Reaction: The Impact of Race, Rights, and Taxes on American Politics.* New York: W. W. Norton.

Egan, Timothy. 2000. "When to Campaign with Color." *New York Times,* June 20, A1.

Engle, Jane. 2004. "Bring Along the Ball Glove to San Diego." *Los Angeles Times,* March 28, L3.

Erie, Steven P. 1988. *Rainbow's End: Irish-Americans and the Dilemmas of Urban Machine Politics, 1840–1985.* Berkeley: University of California Press.

Escutia, Martha, and Gloria Romero. 2001. "MALDEF's Lawsuit Is Racially Divisive." *Los Angeles Times,* November 1, B13.

Espiritu, Yen L. 1992. *Asian American Panethnicity: Bridging Institutions and Identities.* Philadelphia: Temple University Press.

Estes, Donald H. 1978. *Before the War: The Japanese in San Diego.* San Diego: San Diego Historical Society.

Estrada, William D. 2006. *Images of America: Los Angeles's Olvera Street.* San Francisco: Arcadia.

Ethington, Philip J., William H. Frey, and Dowell Myers. 2001. *The Racial Resegregation of Los Angeles County, 1940–2000.* Public Research Report 2001-04. Race Contours 2000 Study. University of Southern California and University of Michigan Collaborative Project. http://www-rcf.usc.edu/~philipje/CENSUS_MAPS/Haynes_Reports/Contours_PRR_2001-04e.pdf.

Faturechi, Robert. 2007. "Donations Influence Admissions." *Daily Bruin,* November 13. http://www.dailybruin.ucla.edu/archives/id/42619/. Accessed November 20, 2007.

Fausset, Richard. 2006. "Dispatch from Atlanta: Preserving History, and a Legacy, in the City." *Los Angeles Times,* November 26, A18.

Feagin, Joe R. 1988. *Free Enterprise City: Houston in Political Economic Perspective.* New Brunswick, NJ: Rutgers University Press.

———. 1998. *The New Urban Paradigm: Critical Perspectives on the City.* New York: Rowman and Littlefield.

———. 2006. *Systemic Racism: A Theory of Oppression.* New York: Routledge.

Feagin, Joe R., and Hernan Vera. 1995. *White Racism.* New York: Routledge.

Feng, Kathay. 2001a. Joint Hearing, Assembly, Elections, Reapportionment and Constitutional Amendments Committee and Senate Elections and Reapportionment Committee. Transcript of Public Hearing on Redistricting. Public Comment on Proposed Redistricting Plans Hearing at the State Capitol with Interactive Testimony from San Francisco, San Jose, Monterey and Fresno, September 4. http://www.assembly.ca.gov/acs/committee/c7/phr.htm. Accessed June 2, 2002.

———.2001b. Joint Hearing, Assembly, Elections, Reapportionment and Constitutional Amendments Committee and Senate Elections and Reapportionment Committee. Transcript of Public Hearing on Redistricting. Public Comment on Proposed Redistricting Plans Hearing at the State Capitol with Interactive Testimony from San Francisco, San Jose, Monterey and Fresno, September 5. http://www.assembly.ca.gov/acs/committee/c7/phr.htm. Accessed June 2, 2002.

Feng, Kathay, Keith Aoki, and Bryan Ikegami. 2002. "Voting Matters: APIAs, Latinas/os and Post-2000 Redistricting in California." *Oregon Law Review* 81(4): 849–916.

Ferguson, Sarah. 1993. "Bucking for Realtors." *Village Voice*, September 14, 14.

Ferrell, David. 1991. "Vote Marks New Era for 1st District." *Los Angeles Times*, February 20.

Finder, Alan. 1989a. "As the Charter Vote Nears, New Yorkers Still Argue." *New York Times*, October 15, sec. 4, 24.

———. 1989b. "Charter Panel Facing More Pressure to Delay Vote." *New York Times*, June 20, B1.

———. 1989c. "Charter Panel Tilted Scales Toward Minorities and Away from Boroughs." *New York Times*, May 16, B1.

———. 1989d. "Even Approval of New Government for New York Will Not Speed Pace." *New York Times*, July 25, B2.

———. 1989e. "Next Task: Explaining and Persuading." *New York Times*, August 3, B4.

Firebaugh, Marco. 2001. Joint Hearing, Assembly, Elections, Reapportionment and Constitutional Amendments Committee and Senate Elections and Reapportionment Committee. Transcript of Public Hearing on Redistricting. Public Comment on Proposed Redistricting Plans Hearing at the State Capitol with Interactive Testimony from San Francisco, San Jose, Monterey, and Fresno, September 4. http://www.assembly.ca.gov/acs/committee/c7/phr.htm. Accessed June 2, 2002.

Fitch, Bob [Robert]. 1991. "Mauling the Mosaic." *Village Voice*, June 18, 12.

———. 1993. *The Assassination of New York.* New York: Verso.

Flamming, Douglas. 2005. *Bound for Freedom: Black Los Angeles in Jim Crow America.* Berkeley: University of California Press.

Fong, Timothy P. 1994. *The First Suburban Chinatown.* Philadelphia: Temple University Press.

———. 1995. "Asian American Redistricting in Oakland, California." Paper presented at the 1995 Association for Asian American Studies National Conference.

———. 1998. "Why Ted Dang Lost: An Analysis of the 1994 Mayoral Race in Oakland, California." *Journal of Asian American Studies* 1(2): 153–171.

Frammolino, Ralph, Mark Gladstone, and Henry Weinstein. 1996. "UCLA Eased Entry Rules for the Rich, Well-Connected." *Los Angeles Times,* March 21, A1.

Freed, Kathryn. Campaign fliers for 1991 City Council Campaign.

Frieden, Bernard J., and Lynne B. Sagalyn. 1991. *Downtown, Inc.: How America Rebuilds Cities.* Cambridge, MA: MIT Press.

Fulton, William. 2001. *The Reluctant Metropolis: The Politics of Urban Growth in Los Angeles.* Baltimore: Johns Hopkins University Press.

Fung, Margaret. 1989. Testimony of Margaret Fung, executive director, Asian American Legal Defense and Education Fund, before the New York City Charter Revision Commission, June 7, Appendix 10, v. 9, 136.

———. 1990. Written testimony delivered to the New York City Districting Commission, November 1, Appendix 3, v. 2, n.p.

———. 1991. Written testimony delivered to the New York City Districting Commission, March 27, Appendix 3, v. 7.

Furey, John. 1987. "Chinese Historic Area Favored by Board." *San Diego Tribune,* April 30, B3.

Gans, Herbert J. 1962. *The Urban Villagers: Group and Class in the Life of Italian-Americans.* New York: Free Press.

———. 1994. "Symbolic Ethnicity and Symbolic Religiosity: Towards a Comparison of Ethnic and Religious Acculturation." *Ethnic and Racial Studies* 17(4): 577–592.

———. 1995. *The War Against the Poor: The Underclass and Antipoverty Policy.* New York: Basic Books.

Gartner, Alan. 1993. "Drawing the Lines: Redistricting and the Politics of Racial Succession in New York." Unpublished. New York: City University of New York, Graduate School and University Center.

———. 1998. "New York City Redistricting: A View from Inside." In *Race and Redistricting in the 1990s,* edited by Bernard Grofman. New York: Agathon Press.

Gaslamp Black Historical Society. n.d. (a). "Harlem of the West." Informational brochure.

———. n.d. (b). "Harlem West Thematic Preservation Project (Howtipp). Black Cultural Sites List."

Gehlert, Heather. 2006. "Travelers Going Back in Time to Probe America's Deep Scar." *Los Angeles Times,* August 15, A12.

Gilmore, Ruth Wilson. 2002. "Fatal Couplings of Power and Difference: Notes on Racism and Geography." *Professional Geographer* 54(1): 15–24.

Gladstone, David L., and Susan S. Fainstein. 2003. "The New York and Los Angeles Economies." In *New York and Los Angeles: Politics, Society, and Culture*, edited by David Halle. Chicago: University of Chicago Press.

Gladstone, Mark, and Ralph Frammolino. 1996. "UC Berkeley Panel Handles Admission Requests by VIPs." *Los Angeles Times*, April 11, A1.

Glanton, A. Dahleen, and Michael Smolens. 1986. "Panel Backs Name Road for Rev. King." *San Diego Union-Tribune*, January 7, B1.

Glazer, Nathan. 1987. *Affirmative Discrimination: Ethnic Equality and Public Policy*. Cambridge, MA: Harvard University Press.

Glazer, Nathan, and Daniel P. Moynihan. 1970. *Beyond the Melting Pot: The Negroes, Puerto Ricans, Jews, Italians, and Irish of New York City*, 2nd ed. Cambridge, MA: MIT Press.

Gonzalez, Zachary. 2001. "Senate Committee on Elections and Reapportionment, State of California. Subject: 2001 Redistricting." July 17, Los Angeles. http://www.senate.ca .gov/ftp/SEN/COMMITTEE/STANDING/EL/_home/Reapportionment/transcripts .htp. Accessed September 12, 2008.

Gordon, Jacques. 1985 (December). *Horton Plaza, San Diego: A Case Study of Public-Private Development*. Working Paper 2. Cambridge, MA: Center for Real Estate Development, MIT.

Gordon, Milton M. 1964. *Assimilation in American Life*. New York: Oxford University Press.

Gotanda, Neil T. 2001. "Citizenship Nullification: The Impossibility of Asian American Politics." In *Asian Americans and Politics: Perspectives, Experiences, Prospects*, edited by Gordon H. Chang. Stanford, CA: Stanford University Press.

Gottdiener, Mark. 1997. *The Theming of America: Dreams, Visions, and Commercial Spaces*. Boulder, CO: Westview Press.

Gottlieb, Robert, Mark Vallianatos, Regina M. Freer, and Peter Dreier. 2005. *The Next Los Angeles: The Struggle for a Livable City*. Berkeley: University of California Press.

Graham, David E. 2004. "New Exhibit Goes to Bat for Ballpark Area's Past." *San Diego Union-Tribune*, September 24. http://www.signonsandiego.com/sports/padres/ball park/20040924-9999-7m24exhibit.html. Accessed September 11, 2008.

Grebler, Leo, Joan W. Moore, and Ralph C. Guzman. 1970. *The Mexican-American People*. New York: Free Press.

Greeley, Andrew M. 1971. *Why Can't They Be Like Us? America's White Ethnic Groups*. New York: E. P. Dutton.

Green, Frank. 1991. "Harlem of the West: S.D.'s Lively, Bygone Hub of Black Culture." *San Diego Union-Tribune*, February 19, C1.

Greenhouse, Linda. 2001. "Justices Permit Race as a Factor in Redistricting." *New York Times*, April 19, A1.

Griego, Andrew R. 1979. "Mayor of Chinatown: The Life of Ah Quin, Chinese Merchant and Railroad Builder of San Diego." Master's thesis, San Diego State University.

Griffin, Gil, and John Nelson. 2000. "Fit for a King?" *San Diego Union-Tribune*, January 17, E1.

Grodach, Carl. 2002. "Making a Modern City: Representations of Chinatown, Downtown Redevelopment, and the *Los Angeles Times*, 1913–1936." Paper presented at "Comparativist's Day." Los Angeles: UCLA Center for Comparative Social Analysis.

Grodzins, Morton. 1958. *The Metropolitan Area as a Racial Problem.* Pittsburgh, PA: University of Pittsburgh Press.

Grofman, Bernard, ed. 1998. *Race and Redistricting in the 1990s.* New York: Agathon Press.

Grofman, Bernard, and Chandler Davidson. 1992. *Controversies in Minority Voting: The Voting Rights Act in Perspective.* Washington, DC: Brookings Institution.

Grofman, Bernard, Lisa Handley, and David Lublin. 2001. "Drawing Effective Minority Districts: A Conceptual Framework and Some Empirical Evidence." *North Carolina Law Review* 79(5): 1383–1430.

Guinier, Lani. 1994. *The Tyranny of the Majority.* New York: Free Press.

Hacker, Andrew. 1995. *Two Nations: Black and White, Separate, Hostile, Unequal.* New York: Ballantine Books.

Hall, Stuart. 1995. "The Whites of Their Eyes: Racist Ideologies and the Media." In *Gender, Race, and Class in Media*, edited by Gail Dines and Jean M. Humez. Thousand Oaks, CA: Sage.

Halle, David, ed. 2003. *New York and Los Angeles: Politics, Society, and Culture.* Chicago: University of Chicago Press.

Hamilton, Pam. 1988. Centre City Development Corporation Memorandum from Pam Hamilton, acting executive vice president, to Centre City Development Corporation, "Relocation and Temporary Storage of the Chinese Mission," June 27.

———. 1989. Centre City Development Corporation Memorandum from Pam Hamilton, executive vice president, to Chair and Members of the Redevelopment Agency, "Joint Public Hearing—Certifying the Secondary Study of Environmental Impact, Approving Disposition and Development Agreement, Basic Concept—Schematic Drawings, Exceptions and Conditional Use Permit—Chinese Mission," July 18. CCDC binder (no number) on Chinese Mission.

Haney Lopez, Ian. 2003. *Racism on Trial: The Chicano Fight for Justice.* Cambridge, MA: Belknap Press.

Hardy-Fanta, Carol. 1993. *Latina Politics, Latino Politics: Gender, Culture, and Political Participation in Boston.* Philadelphia: Temple University Press.

Harris, Cheryl I. 1993. "Whiteness as Property." *Harvard Law Review* 106(8) (June): 1707–1791.

Harris, Leroy E. 1974. "The Other Side of the Freeway: A Study of Settlement Patterns of Negroes and Mexican Americans in San Diego, California." Ph.D. dissertation, Carnegie-Mellon University.

Harrison, Bennett, and Barry Bluestone. 1988. *The Great U-Turn: Corporate Restructuring and the Polarizing of America.* New York: Basic Books.

Harvard Law Review. 1989. "*Asian Americans for Equality v. Koch.*" *Harvard Law Review* 102(5): 1092–1099.

———. 1995. "*City of New York v. United States Department of Commerce.*" *Harvard Law Review* 108(4): 971–976.

Hasegawa, Susan Shizuko. 1998. "Rebuilding Lives, Rebuilding Communities: The Post–World War II Resettlement of Japanese Americans to San Diego." Master's thesis, San Diego State University.

Hathcock, Jim. 1987. "CCDC Searches for Solutions to Problem of Saving Mission." *San Diego Business Journal*, December 21, San Diego Historical Society, file Chinese in San Diego.

Hayden, Dolores. 1997. *The Power of Place: Urban Landscapes as Public History.* Cambridge, MA: MIT Press.

HDDC (Historic District Development Corporation). 2006. "History and Mission." Martin Luther King District. http://www.hddc.net/. Accessed September 11, 2008.

Heer, M. David, ed. 1968. *Social Statistics and the City.* Report of a Conference held in Washington, D.C. Cambridge, MA: Joint Center for Urban Studies of the Massachusetts Institute of Technology and Harvard University.

Heller, Jonathan. 2001. "Old Clermont Hotel Named a Landmark." *San Diego Union-Tribune*, December 21, B1.

Hernandez, Daniel. 2005. "Villaraigosa's Spanish Is One of L.A.'s Languages." *Los Angeles Times*, April 23, A1.

Hero, Rodney E., and Caroline J. Tolbert. 1995. "Latinos and Substantive Representation in the U.S. House of Representatives: Direct, Indirect, or Nonexistent?" *American Journal of Political Science* 39(3): 640–652.

Hester, Jere. 1991a. "Downtown Dems Shun Chin Candidacy. *Downtown Express*, May 1.

———. 1991b. "Downtown on the Chopping Block: How Downtown's Political Future Is Being Divided." *Downtown Express*, April 10, 10.

Hill, Richard Child. 1983. "Crisis in the Motor City: The Politics of Economic Development in Detroit." In *Restructuring the City: The Political Economy of Urban Redevelopment*, edited by Susan S. Fainstein, Norman I. Fainstein, Richard Child Hill, Dennis R. Judd, and Michael Peter Smith. New York: Longman.

Hines, Thomas S. 1982. "Housing, Baseball, and Creeping Socialism: The Battle of Chavez Ravine, Los Angeles, 1949–1959." *Journal of Urban Affairs* 8(2): 123–143.

Hing, Bill Ong. 1993. *Making and Remaking Asian America Through Immigration Policy, 1850–1990.* Stanford, CA: Stanford University Press.

Hippaka, William H. 1967. *The Changing Office Space Market in Downtown San Diego,*

California: 1958 to 1967. Monograph 9.5. San Diego: San Diego State College, School of Business Administration.

Hof, Reiner M. 1990. "San Diegans, Inc.: The Formative Years, 1958–63." *Journal of San Diego History* 36: 1–9. http://sandiegohistory.org/journal/90winter/sdinc.htm. Accessed January 18, 2003.

Hoffman, Lily M. 2003. "The Marketing of Diversity in the Inner City: Tourism and Regulation in Harlem." *International Journal of Urban and Regional Research* 27(2): 286–299.

Holle, Gena. 2002. "Transit in San Diego: ASCE Anniversary Project." *Journal of San Diego History* 48(1). http://sandiegohistory.org/journal/2002-1/holle.htm. Accessed January 30, 2003.

Hom, Tom. 1986. Letter to Howard Busby, president, Centre City Development Corporation, July 11. CCDC file 328231, Chinese Mission Building.

———. 1988. "Proposal on the Chinese Mission: San Diego, CA." Submitted by the San Diego Chinese Historical Society to the Members of the Board of the Redevelopment Agency, Members of the Board of Centre City Development Corporation, and the Chinese Advisory Ad Hoc Committee, February 1.

Hom Zemen, Gayle, and Donna Lee. 2000. "Dorothy Hom." *Chinese Historical Society of Greater San Diego and Baja California Inc. Newsletter,* winter, 1, 9.

Horton, John. 1995. *The Politics of Diversity: Immigration, Resistance, and Change in Monterey Park, California.* Philadelphia: Temple University Press.

HRB (Historical Resources Board), City of San Diego. 2000. Memorandum signed by Myles E. Pomeroy to the Historical Resources Board, "Historical Resources Board Agenda of July 27, 2000, Item #6, Consider the Designation of This Site as an Historical Resource," July 11.

———. 2001. "Item #7—The Clermont/Coast Hotel, Consider the Designation of the Clermont/Coast Hotel as a City Historical Landmark," Report P-01-163, September 6.

———. 2006. "Historical Landmarks Designated by the San Diego Historical Resources Board." http://www.sandiego.gov/planning/programs/historical/site/index.shtml. Accessed September 12, 2008.

———. 2007. Minutes of Regular Scheduled Meeting of January 25, 2007. Item 10—Downtown San Diego African American Heritage Study.

Hsiang, Claire. 1996. "Burned at the Ballot Box." *Outlook,* summer, 3, 6. Originally published in the *New York Times,* May 11, 1996.

Huerta, Dolores C. 2002. Declaration in Support of Senate Defendants' Motions for Summary Judgment, May 13, 2002, 1. United States District Court, Central District of California, *Cano et al. v. Davis et al.,* Case 01-084777 MMM (RCx).

Huff, Karen L. 2000. Letter to Marie Burke Lia and Scott A. Moomjian, "Request for GBHS Report on Coast Hotel," September 6.

———. 2001a. "Hotel for Colored People (a Supplemental Assessment to the Clermont/ Coast Hotel)." Gaslamp Black Historical Society, August.

———. 2001b. Letter to Beverly Schroeder, CCDC, from Gaslamp Black Historical Society, "Coast Hotel."

Huff, Karen L., Wilma Dockett-McLeod, and Lether Evans-Bullock. 2000. "Destruction of the Harlem of the West." Gaslamp Black Historical Society, February 28.

Huffman, Alice. 2001. Joint Hearing, Assembly, Elections, Reapportionment and Constitutional Amendments Committee and Senate Elections and Reapportionment Committee. Transcript of Public Hearing on Redistricting. Public Comment on Proposed Redistricting Plans Hearing at the State Capitol with Interactive Testimony from San Francisco, San Jose, Monterey and Fresno, September 5. http://www.assembly.ca.gov/acs/committee/c7/phr.htm. Accessed June 2, 2002.

Hulett, Denise. 2001. Joint Hearing, Assembly, Elections, Reapportionment and Constitutional Amendments Committee and Senate Elections and Reapportionment Committee. Transcript of Public Hearing on Redistricting. Public Comment on Proposed Redistricting Plans Hearing at the State Capitol with Interactive Testimony from San Francisco, San Jose, Monterey, and Fresno, September 4. http://www.assembly.ca.gov/acs/committee/c7/phr.htm. Accessed June 2, 2002.

Hum, Tarry. 2002. "Redistricting and the New Demographics: Defining 'Communities of Interest' in New York City." Report of a conference organized by New York University, Asian/Pacific/American Studies, and Queens College, Department of Urban Studies.

Hunter College Neighborhood Planning Workshop. 1992. *Chinatown: Land Use and Planning Study*. New York: Hunter College Neighborhood Planning Workshop.

Huntington, Samuel P. 2004. *Who Are We? The Challenge to America's National Identity*. New Haven, CT: Yale University Press.

Ichioka, Yuji. 1988. *The Issei: The World of the First Generation Japanese Immigrants, 1885–1924*. New York: Free Press.

Ingram, Carl. 2001a. "Davis OKs Redistricting That Keeps Status Quo." *Los Angeles Times*, September 28, B12.

———. 2001b. "Democrats Have Luck of Draw in Redistricting." *Los Angeles Times*, August 19, B7.

———. 2002. "Introduction" (insert). *California Journal*, January 33(1).

Ivins, Molly. 2006. "Republicans Wake a Sleeping Giant," May 4. http://www.alternet.org/story/35862/. Accessed July 23, 2006.

Jackson, Kenneth. 1985. *Crabgrass Frontier: The Suburbanization of the United States*. New York: Oxford University Press.

Jacobs, Andrew. 1997. "What a Difference Two Decades Make: Asian Americans for Equality Is Attacked as the Establishment It Once Fought." *New York Times*, January 12, sec. 13, 4.

Jacobs, Jane. 1961. *The Death and Life of Great American Cities.* New York: Vintage Books.

Jacobson, Gary. 2002. "Expert Report of Professor Gary Jacobson in Support of Senate Defendants' Motions for Summary Judgment." *Cano v. Davis,* United States District Court, Central District of California, CV 01-08477 MMM (RCx), May 13.

Jacobson, Matthew Frye. 1998. *Whiteness of a Different Color: European Immigrants and the Alchemy of Race.* Cambridge, MA: Harvard University Press.

————. 2006. *Roots Too: White Ethnic Revival in Post–Civil Rights America.* Cambridge, MA: Harvard University Press.

James, Ian. 2006. "Chavez to Discount Oil for U.S. Poor." *Washington Post* online. http://www.washingtonpost.com/wp-dyn/content/article/2006/09/21/AR2006092101163.html. Accessed September 10, 2008.

Jarmusch, Ann, and Karen Wilson. 1992. "Heritage Lost." *San Diego Union,* July 19, F1.

Jones, Gregg. 2002. "A Big Win for Farm Workers." *Los Angeles Times,* October 1, A1.

Jones-Correa, Michael. 1998. *Between Two Nations: The Political Predicament of Latinos in New York City.* Ithaca, NY: Cornell University Press.

————, ed. 2001. *Governing American Cities: Interethnic Coalitions, Competition, and Conflict.* New York: Russell Sage Foundation.

Judd, Dennis R. 1999. "Constructing the Tourist Bubble." In *The Tourist City,* edited by Dennis R. Judd and Susan S. Fainstein. New Haven, CT: Yale University Press, 35–53.

Jung, Moon-Kie. 2003. "Interracialism: The Ideological Transformation of Hawaii's Working Class." *American Sociological Review* 68(June): 373–400.

————. 2006. *Reworking Race: The Making of Hawaii's Interracial Labor Movement.* New York: Columbia University Press.

Karabel, Jerome. 2005. *The Chosen: The Hidden History of Admission and Exclusion at Harvard, Yale, and Princeton.* Boston: Houghton Mifflin.

Kasinitz, Philip. 1992. *Caribbean New York: Black Immigrants and the Politics of Race.* Ithaca, NY: Cornell University Press.

Kaufmann, Karen M. 2004. *The Urban Voter: Group Conflict and Mayoral Voting Behavior in American Cities.* Ann Arbor: University of Michigan Press.

Kee, Virginia. 1990. Oral Testimony Delivered to the New York City Districting Commission, November 1, Appendix 3, v. 2, 64.

Key, Valdimer O. 1949. *Southern Politics in State and Nation.* Knoxville: University of Tennessee Press.

Keyser Marston Associates Inc. 1984. "Re-Use Analysis: Block Bounded by G Street, Second and Third Avenues and Market Street." Prepared for Centre City Development Corporation, July 1984.

Kim, Claire Jean. 1999. "The Racial Triangulation of Asian Americans." *Politics and Society* 27(1): 105–138.

————. 2000. *Bitter Fruit: The Politics of Black-Korean Conflict in New York City.* New Haven, CT: Yale University Press.

Kirkpatrick, Maria L. 2006. "East Village Aims to Be Everyone's Downtown." *San Diego Metropolitan*, July. http://www.sandiegometro.com/2006/jul/urban.php. Accessed October 14, 2006.

Kitano, Harry H. L., and Mitchell T. Maki. 2003. "Japanese American Redress: The Proper Alignment Model." In *Asian American Politics: Law, Participation, and Policy*, edited by Don T. Nakanishi and James S. Lai. New York: Rowman and Littlefield.

Kong, Gail. 1989. Testimony Before the New York City Charter Revision Commission, June 8, Appendix 10, no. 9.

Koo, Doris. 1990a. Written Testimony Delivered to the New York City Districting Commission, November 1, Appendix 3, v. 2, map 2, figure 5.

———. 1990b. Written Testimony Delivered to the New York City Districting Commission, December 10, Appendix 3, v. 4.

Koo, Rosa. 1990. Written Testimony Delivered to the New York City Districting Commission, November 1, Appendix 3, v. 2.

Koshy, Susan. 2001. "Morphing Race into Ethnicity: Asian Americans and Critical Transformations of Whiteness." *Boundary 2* 28(1): 153–194.

Kousser, J. Morgan. 1999. *Colorblind Injustice: Minority Voting Rights and the Undoing of the Second Reconstruction*. Chapel Hill: University of North Carolina Press.

Kovner, Victor A., Joel Berger, and Judith Reed. 1991a. Letter to Richard Jerome, Esq., Department of Justice, on Behalf of the New York City Districting Commission, "Section 5 Submission for Preclearance of 1991 City Council Districts: Expedited Consideration Requested," July 26.

———. 1991b. "Submission Under Section 5 of the Voting Rights Act for Preclearance of 1991 Redistricting Plan for New York City Council." City of New York districting plans submitted to the U.S. Justice Department, June 17.

Krey, Michael, 1986. "The Chinese Want All Last Vestiges of Past Preserved." *San Diego Daily Transcript*, June 20, A1.

Kropp, Phoebe S. 2001. "Citizens of the Past? Olvera Street and the Construction of Race and Memory in 1930s Los Angeles." *Radical History Review* 81: 35–60.

Krueger, Paul. 1991. "Black Palace." *San Diego Reader*, February 21, 1.

Kwoh, Stewart. 2001. Joint Hearing, Assembly, Elections, Reapportionment and Constitutional Amendments Committee and Senate Elections and Reapportionment Committee. Transcript of Public Hearing on Redistricting. Public Comment on Proposed Redistricting Plans Hearing at the State Capitol with Interactive Testimony from Los Angeles, San Bernardino, San Diego and Santa Ana, v. 2, September 5, 2001. http://www.assembly.ca.gov/acs/committee/c7/phr.htm. Accessed June 2, 2002.

Kwong, Peter. 1996. *The New Chinatown*. New York: Hill and Wang.

Kwong, Peter, and Dusanka Miscevic. 2005. *Chinese America: The Untold Story of America's Oldest New Community*. New York: New Press.

LaGanga, Maria L., and Shawn Hubler. 2001. "California Grows to 33.9 Million, Reflecting Increased Diversity." *Los Angeles Times*, March 30, A1.

Lagnado, Lucette. 1991. "Friends in High Places: Margaret Chin's Ties to the Chinatown Elite." *Village Voice*, September 9, 17.

Lai, James S., Wendy K. Tam Cho, Thomas P. Kim, and Okiyoshi Takeda. 2001. "Asian Pacific American Campaigns, Elections, and Elected Officials." *PS: Political Science and Politics* 34(3): 611–619.

Lam, Nancy. 1990. "Chinatown Voter Education Alliance," Written Testimony Delivered to the New York City Districting Commission, November 1, Appendix 3, v. 2.

Lau, Angela. 1992. "San Diego's Racial History: Failures to Achieve Harmony." *San Diego Union-Tribune*, July 12, B1.

Lea, Diane. 2003. "America's Preservation Ethos." In *A Richer Heritage: Historic Preservation in the Twenty-First Century*, edited by Robert E. Stipe. Chapel Hill: University of North Carolina Press.

Lee, Antoinette J. 2003. "The Social and Ethnic Dimensions of Historic Preservation." In *A Richer Heritage: Historic Preservation in the Twenty-First Century*, edited by Robert E. Stipe. Chapel Hill: University of North Carolina Press.

Lee, Murray. 2007. "The Origins of the Chinese Historical Society and Museum: Part 1." *San Diego Chinese Historical Society and Museum* [newsletter], fall, 13–14.

Lee, Murray K., Jennifer Fukuhara-Good, and Alexander Chuang. 2000. "The San Diego Historical Museum." In *Chinese America: History and Perspectives*, edited by M. Hom, M. Hsu, H. M. Lai, L. W. Mclain, and R. L. McCunn. Brisbane, CA: Fong Brothers Printing, 69–76.

Lee, Stacey. 1996. *Unraveling the "Model Minority" Stereotype: Listening to Asian American Youth*. New York: Teachers College Press.

Levy, Frank. 1998. *The New Dollars and Dreams: American Incomes and Economic Change*. New York: Russell Sage Foundation.

Lewis, Oscar. 1966. *La Vida: A Puerto Rican Family in the Culture of Poverty—San Juan and New York*. New York: Random House.

Li, Wei. 1999. "Building Ethnoburbia: The Emergence and Manifestation of the Chinese Ethnoburb in Los Angeles' San Gabriel Valley." *Journal of Asian American Studies* 2(1): 1–28.

Lia, Marie Burke. 1986. Memorandum to Pam Hamilton, CCDC, "Report on Historical Chinese Buildings," April 17, CCDC file 32823I, Chinese Mission Building.

———. 1987. Letter to Chairperson Kathryn Willets and Members, Historical Site Board, May 20, CCDC file 328231I, Chinese Mission Building.

———. 2000. Letter to Karen L. Huff, Gaslamp Black Historical Society, "Request for Gaslamp Black Historical Society (GBHS) Historical Report on the Coast Hotel," August 28.

Lieberson, Stanley. 1980. *A Piece of the Pie: Blacks and White Immigrants Since 1880.* Berkeley: University of California Press.

Lien, Pei-te. 1997. *The Political Participation of Asian Americans: Voting Behavior in Southern California.* New York: Garland.

———. 2001. *The Making of Asian America Through Political Participation.* Philadelphia: Temple University Press.

Lien, Pei-te, M. Margaret Conway, and Janelle Wong. 2004. *The Politics of Asian Americans: Diversity and Community.* New York: Routledge.

Light, Ivan H. 1972. *Ethnic Enterprise in America.* Berkeley: University of California Press.

———. 1974. "From Vice District to Tourist Attraction: The Moral Career of American Chinatowns, 1880–1940." *Pacific Historical Review* 43(3): 367–394.

Light, Ivan, and Edna Bonacich. 1988. *Immigrant Entrepreneurs: Koreans in Los Angeles 1965–1982.* Berkeley: University of California Press.

Light, Ivan, and Charles Choy Wong. 1975. "Protest or Work: Dilemmas of the Tourist Industry in American Chinatowns." *American Journal of Sociology* 80(6): 1342–1368.

Lin, Jan. 1995. "Ethnic Places, Postmodernism, and Urban Change in Houston." *Sociological Quarterly* 36(4): 629–647.

———. 1998. *Reconstructing Chinatown: Ethnic Enclave, Global Change.* Minneapolis: University of Minnesota Press.

Ling, Susie. 2001. "Our Legacy: History of Chinese Americans in Southern California." In *Bridging the Centuries: History of Chinese Americans in Southern California,* edited by Susie Ling. Los Angeles: Chinese Historical Society of Southern California.

Lipsitz, George. 2006 [1998]. *The Possessive Investment in Whiteness: How White People Profit from Identity Politics.* Philadelphia: Temple University Press.

Little Tokyo Anti-Eviction Task Force. 1976. "Redevelopment in Los Angeles' Little Tokyo." In *Counterpoint,* edited by Emma Gee. Los Angeles: Asian American Studies Center, UCLA.

Liu, Baodong. 2003. "Deracialization and Urban Racial Contexts." *Urban Affairs Review* 38(4): 572–591.

———. 2006. "Whites as a Minority and the New Biracial Coalition in New Orleans and Memphis." *PS: Political Science and Politics Online.* http://www.apsanet.org. Accessed November 17, 2006.

Liu, Judith. 1977. "Celestials in the Golden Mountain: The Chinese in One California City, San Diego, 1870–1900." Master's thesis, San Diego State University.

Liu, Mini. 1991. Oral Testimony Delivered to the New York City Districting Commission, March 21, Appendix 3, v. 7, 290.

Locke, Gary. 2003. "The One-Hundred Year Journey: From Houseboy to the Governor's Office." In *Asian American Politics: Law, Participation, and Policy,* edited by Don T. Nakanishi and James S. Lai. New York: Rowman and Littlefield.

Logan, John R. 2001. "Ethnic Diversity Grows, Neighborhood Integration Lags Behind." Report by the Lewis Mumford Center, April 3 (revised December 18, 2001). http://www.s4.brown.edu/cen2000/WholePop/WPreport/page1.html. Accessed September 11, 2008.

Logan, John R., Richard D. Alba, and Shu-Yin Leung. 1996. "Minority Access to White Suburbs: A Multiregional Comparison." *Social Forces* 74(3): 851–881.

Logan, John R., and John Mollenkopf. 2003. "People and Politics in American's Big Cities." Report issued May 15, Metropolitan College of New York and Drum Major Institute, New York City.

Logan, John R., and Harvey L. Molotch. 1987. *Urban Fortunes: The Political Economy of Place.* Berkeley: University of California Press.

Logan, John R., and Todd Swanstrom. 1990. *Beyond City Limits: Urban Policy and Economic Restructuring in Comparative Perspective.* Philadelphia: Temple University Press.

Los Angeles Times. 1994. "Times Poll: A Look at the Electorate." *Los Angeles Times,* November 10, B2.

———. 1996. "Los Angeles Times Poll." Study 389. Exit Poll: The General Election, November 5, 1996. Poll information sheet published by the *Los Angeles Times.*

———. 1997. "Profile of the City Electorate." *Los Angeles Times,* April 10, A27.

———. 2001. Editorial, "The Politics of Map-Making." *Los Angeles Times,* September 7, B14.

———. 2005a. "Excerpts from Inaugural Address." *Los Angeles Times,* July 2, A36.

———. 2005b. "Poll." *Los Angeles Times,* May 19, A19.

———. 2006. "Profile of Democratic Primary Voters." *Los Angeles Times,* June 8, A10.

Louie, Ruby Ling. 2001. "Reliving China City." In *Bridging the Centuries: History of Chinese Americans in Southern California,"* edited by Susie Ling. Los Angeles: Chinese Historical Society of Southern California.

Louie, Steve, and Glenn Omatsu. 2006. *Asian Americans: The Movement and the Moment.* Los Angeles: UCLA Asian American Studies Center Press.

Lowe, Lisa. 1996. *Immigrant Acts: On Asian American Cultural Politics.* Durham, NC: Duke University Press.

Lower East Side Joint Planning Council. 1984. "This Land Is Ours: A Strategy for the Preservation and Development of Affordable Housing on the Lower East Side." Report submitted to the Joint Planning Council, March 22.

Lower East Siders for a Multi-Racial District. 1991. *Redistricting: Community Empowerment in Action.* Report submitted to the New York City Districting Commission, March.

Lowery, Brian S., Miguel M. Unzueta, and Eric D. Knowles. 2007 (April). *Why White Americans Oppose Affirmative Action: A Group Interest Approach.* Latino Policy and Issues Brief 15. Los Angeles: UCLA Chicano Studies Research Center.

Lowery, Brian S., Miguel M. Unzueta, Eric D. Knowles, and Philip A. Goff. 2006. "Concern for the In-Group and Opposition to Affirmative Action." *Journal of Personality and Social Psychology* 90(6): 961–974.

Luce, Stephanie. 2005. "The Role of Community Involvement in Implementing Living Wage Ordinances." *Industrial Relations* 44(1): 32–58.

MacPhail, Elizabeth C. 1974. "When the Red Lights Went Out in San Diego." *Journal of San Diego History* 20(2): 1–28.

———. 1977. "San Diego's Chinese Mission." *Journal of San Diego History* 23(2): 9–21.

Madyun, Gail, and Larry Malone. 1981. "Black Pioneers in San Diego: 1880–1920." *Journal of San Diego History* 27(2): n.p.

MALDEF (Mexican American Legal Defense and Educational Fund). 2001. "MALDEF Sues State of California for Violating Voting Rights Act and Constitution with Redistricting Plans." Press release, October 1.

———. 2002. "Point/Counterpoint: The Redistricting Dispute." *California Journal* 33(1) (January): 39–41.

Mariscal, George. 2005. *Brown-Eyed Children of the Sun: Lessons from the Chicano Movement, 1965–1975.* Albuquerque: University of New Mexico Press.

Martin, Hugo. 1997. "For Underground Pipeline, Risk Is Relative." *Los Angeles Times*, April 27, B1.

Massey, Douglas S., and Nancy A. Denton. 1993. *American Apartheid.* Cambridge, MA: Harvard University Press.

Matsuda, Mari. 1995. "Looking to the Bottom: Critical Legal Studies and Reparations." In *Critical Race Theory*, edited by Kimberle Crenshaw, Neil Gotanda, Gary Peller, and Kendall Thomas. New York: New Press.

Matthews, Karen. 2001. "Candidates Vying to Be the First Asian-American on New York City Council." Associated Press State and Local Wire, February 17.

Mauro, Frank J. 1989a. Minutes of Public Hearing Before the New York City Charter Revision Commission, June 27, Appendix 5, 17–17A, Exhibit 27.

———. 1989b. Minutes of the New York City Charter Revision Commission, May 6. NYC Mayor, CRC Submission under Section 5 of the Voting Rights Act, Appendix 5, 7–8.

Mauro, Frank J., and Gerald Benjamin. 1989. "*Morris v. Board of Estimate.*" In *Restructuring the New York City Government: The Emergence of Municipal Reform*, edited by Frank J. Mauro. New York: Academy of Political Science.

McAdam, Doug. 1999. *Political Process and the Development of Black Insurgency, 1930–1970.* Chicago: University of Chicago Press.

McClain, Charles. 1994. *In Search of Equality: The Chinese Struggle Against Discrimination in Nineteenth-Century America.* Berkeley: University of California Press.

McCormick, Joseph, and Charles E. Jones. 1993. "The Conceptualization of Deracialization: Thinking Through the Dilemma." In *Dilemmas of Black Politics: Issues of Leadership and Strategy*, edited by Georgia Persons. New York: HarperCollins.

McEvoy, Arthur F. 1977. "In Places Men Reject: Chinese Fishermen at San Diego, 1870–1893." *Journal of San Diego History* 23(4): 12–24.

McGreevy, Patrick. 2005. "Latinos, Flexing Political Muscle, Come of Age in L.A." *Los Angeles Times*, June 27, A1.

McGreevy, Patrick, and Jessica Garrison. 2005. "We Need to Start Thinking Big Again." *Los Angeles Times*, July 2, A1.

Mele, Christopher. 1994. "Neighborhood 'Burn-Out': Puerto Ricans at the End of the Queue." In *From Urban Village to East Village: The Battle for New York's Lower East Side*, edited by Janet L. Abu-Lughod. Cambridge, MA: Blackwell.

———. 2000. *Selling the Lower East Side: Culture, Real Estate, and Resistance in New York City*. Minneapolis: University of Minnesota Press.

Meyerson, Harold. 2000. "Primary Concerns: Race, Class, and Gumption in the March Local Elections." *L.A. Weekly*, January 14–20. http://www.laweekly.com/2000-01-20/news/primary-concerns/. Accessed September 11, 2008.

———. 2007. "The Delicate Balance of Black and Brown." *Los Angeles Times*, June 24, M1.

Millican, Anthony. 2001. "Researcher Tries to Save Once-Segregated Hotel." *San Diego Union-Tribune*, September 17, B1.

Mills, Jesse, and Ben Bunyi. 2000. Interview with Reverend George Walker Smith, San Diego.

Minkel, J. R. 2007. "Confirmed: The U.S. Census Bureau Gave Up Names of Japanese-Americans in WW II." *Scientific American* online, March 30. http://www.sciam.com/article.cfm?id=confirmed-the-us-census-b. Accessed September 11, 2008.

Mohl, Raymond A. 1993. "Race and Space in the Modern City: Interstate-95 and the Black Community in Miami." In *Urban Policy in Twentieth-Century America*, edited by Arnold R. Hirsch and Raymond A. Mohl. New Brunswick, NJ: Rutgers University Press.

Molina, Natalia. 2006. *Fit to Be Citizens? Public Health and Race in Los Angeles, 1879–1939*. Berkeley: University of California Press.

Mollenkopf, John. 1983. *The Contested City*. Princeton, NJ: Princeton University Press.

———. 1990. "New York: The Great Anomaly." In *Racial Politics in American Cities*, edited by Rufus P. Browning, Dale Rogers Marshall, and David H. Tabb. New York: Longman.

———. 1992. *A Phoenix in the Ashes: The Rise and Fall of the Koch Coalition in New York City Politics*. Princeton, NJ: Princeton University Press.

———. 2003. "New York: Still the Great Anomaly." In *Racial Politics in American Cities*, 3rd ed., edited by Rufus P. Browning, Dale Rogers Marshall, and David H. Tabb. New York: Longman.

Mollenkopf, John H., and Manuel Castells. 1991. *Dual City: Restructuring New York*. New York: Russell Sage Foundation.

Molotch, Harvey L. 1976. "The City as a Growth Machine: Toward a Political Economy of Place." *American Journal of Sociology* 82(2): 309–330.

Moomjian, Scott A. 2000. "Historical Assessment of the Coast Hotel, 501 Seventh Avenue, San Diego, California 92101." Prepared for the Centre City Development Corporation by Scott A. Moomjian, Esq., Office of Marie Burke Lia, Attorney at Law, San Diego, July.

———. 2001. "Addendum to the Historical Assessment of the Coast Hotel, 501 Seventh Avenue, San Diego, California 92101." Prepared for the Centre City Development Corporation by Scott A. Moomjian, Esq., Office of Marie Burke Lia, Attorney at Law, San Diego, February.

Morales, Ed. 1991. "East Side Story." *Village Voice*, August 20, 11.

Morgan, Neil. 2000. "Way We Were in San Diego: Black People Recall It Well." *San Diego Union-Tribune*, March 23, A3.

Morris, Aldon D. 1984. *The Origins of the Civil Rights Movement.* New York: Free Press.

Moynihan, Daniel P. 1965. *The Negro Family: The Case for National Action.* Washington, DC: U.S. Government Printing Office.

Munoz, Carlos, Jr. 2007. *Youth, Identity, Power: The Chicano Movement.* London: Verso.

Murray, Charles. 1984. *Losing Ground: American Social Policy, 1950–1980.* New York: Basic Books.

Muzzio, Douglas, and Tim Tompkins. 1989. "On the Size of City Council: Finding the Mean." In *Restructuring the New York City Government: The Reemergence of Municipal Reform*, edited by Frank J. Mauro and Gerald Benjamin. New York: Academy of Political Science.

Myrdal, Gunnar. 1944. *An American Dilemma: The Negro Problem and Modern Democracy*, v. 1. New York: Harper and Row.

Nagel, Joane. 1997. *American Indian Ethnic Renewal: Red Power and the Resurgence of Identity and Culture.* New York: Oxford University Press.

Nagler, Jonathan, and R. Michael Alvarez. 2004. "Latinos, Anglos, Voters, Candidates, and Voting Rights." *University of Pennsylvania Law Review* 153(1): 393–432.

Nakanishi, Don. 1985–1986. "Asian American Politics: An Agenda for Research." *Amerasia Journal* 12: 1–27.

Nakanishi, Don T., and James S. Lai, eds. 2003. *Asian American Politics: Law, Participation, and Policy.* New York: Rowman and Littlefield.

Nakayama, Takeshi. 1990. "Matsui Meets Supporters at L.A. Fund-Raiser Reception." *Rafu Shimpo*, December 10.

NAPALC (National Asian Pacific American Legal Consortium). 1991. *Audit of Violence Against Asian Pacific Americans.* Washington, DC: NAPALC.

Navarro, Armando. 1993. "The South Central Los Angeles Eruption: A Latino Perspective." *Amerasia Journal* 19(2): 69–85.

NCRM (National Civil Rights Museum). 2006. "About the Museum." http://www.civil rightsmuseum.org/about/about.asp. Accessed October 24, 2006.

Neuman, Johanna. 2006. "Voting Rights Act Renewal Wins House Approval." *Los Angeles Times*, July 14, A20.

New York Chinatown History Project. 1990. Written Testimony Delivered to the New York City Districting Commission, November 1, Appendix 3, v. 2.

New York City Districting Commission. 1991a. "News from the New York City Districting Commission." Newsletter, August, 2.

———. 1991b. "A Short History of the Reapportionment of the City Council." In Appendix 1 of the "Submission Under Section 5 of the Voting Rights Act for Preclearance of 1991 Redistricting Plan for New York City Council," Districting plans submitted to the U.S. Justice Department on June 17, 8–19.

New York Times. 1989. Editorial: "For Voting Rights, a Clear Triumph." *New York Times*, August 17, A22.

NFHA (National Fair Housing Alliance). 2006. *Unequal Opportunity: Perpetuating Housing Segregation in America.* 2006 Fair Housing Trends Report, April 5. Washington, DC: NFHA.

Ngai, Mae M. 2004. *Impossible Subjects: Illegal Aliens and the Making of Modern America.* Princeton, NJ: Princeton University Press.

Novak, Michael. 1996. *Unmeltable Ethnics: Politics and Culture in American Life.* New Brunswick, NJ: Transaction.

NPS (National Park Service), U.S. Department of the Interior. 2003. "Martin Luther King, Jr. National Historic Site, Georgia." Brochure.

NYC-CRC (New York City Charter Revision Commission). 1989. *Report of the New York City Charter Revision Commission: December 1986–November 1988.* New York City Charter Revision Commission, January.

———. 1990. *Final Report of the New York City Charter Revision Commission: January 1989–November 1989.* New York City Charter Revision Commission, March.

NYC Department of Planning. 1993. "Estimated Resident Illegal Alien Population: October 1992." Report, September 2.

Oboler, Suzanne. 1995. *Ethnic Labels, Latino Lives.* Minneapolis: University of Minnesota Press.

Ohnuma, Keiko. 1991. "Asian Camps Split on District Lines for Lower Manhattan." *Asian Week*, April 26, 1.

Okamoto, Dina G. 2003. "Toward a Theory of Panethnicity: Explaining Asian American Collective Action." *American Sociological Review* 68(6): 811–842.

Okamura, Raymond. 1981. "The Myth of Census Confidentiality." *Amerasia Journal* 8(2): 111–120.

Okihiro, Gary Y. 1994. *Margins and Mainstreams: Asians in American History and Culture.* Seattle: University of Washington Press.

————. 2001. *The Columbia Guide to Asian American History*. New York: Columbia University Press.

Oliver, Melvin L., and Thomas M. Shapiro. 1995. *Black Wealth/White Wealth: A New Perspective on Racial Inequality*. New York: Routledge.

Omatsu, Glenn. 1994. "The 'Four Prisons' and the Movements of Liberation: Asian American Activism from the 1960s to the 1990s." In *The State of Asian America: Activism and Resistance in the 1990s*, edited by Karin Aguilar-San Juan. Boston: South End Press.

Omi, Michael, and Howard Winant. 1994. *Racial Formation in the United States*. New York: Routledge.

Ong, Paul, and Suzanne Hee. 1994. "Economic Diversity." In *The State of Asian Pacific America: Economic Diversity, Issues, and Policies*, edited by Paul Ong. Los Angeles: LEAP Asian Pacific American Public Policy Institute and UCLA Asian American Studies Center.

Ong, Paul, Kye Young Park, and Yasmin Tong. 1994. "The Korean-Black Conflict and the State." In *The New Asian Immigration in Los Angeles and Global Restructuring*, edited by Paul Ong, Edna Bonacich, and Lucie Cheng. Philadelphia: Temple University Press.

Ono, Thomas. 2001. California Legislature, Assembly, Elections, Reapportionment and Constitutional Amendments Committee, Transcript of Public Hearing on Redistricting, Identification of Communities of Interest, Los Angeles, June 8. http://www.assembly.ca.gov/acs/committee/c7/phr.htm. Accessed June 1, 2002.

Osajima, Keith. 1988. "Asian Americans as the Model Minority: An Analysis of the Popular Press Image in the 1960s and 1980s." In *Reflections on Shattered Windows: Promises and Prospects for Asian American Studies*, edited by Gary Y. Okihiro, Shirley Hune, Arthur A. Hansen, and John M. Liu. Pullman: Washington State University Press.

Padilla, Felix M. 1985. *Latino Ethnic Consciousness*. Notre Dame, IN: University of Notre Dame Press.

Pagan, Antonio. 1990. Oral Testimony Delivered to the New York City Districting Commission, November 1, Appendix 3, v. 2, 213.

Pardo, Mary S. 1990. "Mexican American Grassroots Community Activists: Mothers of East Los Angeles." *Frontiers* 11(1): 1–7.

————. 1998. *Mexican American Women Activists: Identity and Resistance in Two Los Angeles Communities*. Philadelphia: Temple University Press.

Park, Edward J. W. 1996. "Our L.A.? Korean Americans in Los Angeles After the Civil Unrest." In *Rethinking Los Angeles*, edited by Michael J. Dear, H. Eric Schockman, and Greg Hise. Thousand Oaks, CA: Sage Publications.

Park, Edward J. W., and John S. W. Park. 1999. "A New American Dilemma? Asian Americans and Latinos in American Race Relations Theorizing." *Journal of Asian American Studies* 2(3): 289–309.

———. 2001. "Korean Americans and the Crisis of the Liberal Coalition: Immigrants and Politics in Los Angeles. In *Governing American Cities: Interethnic Coalitions, Competition, and Conflict*, edited by Michael Jones-Correa. New York: Russell Sage Foundation.

———. 2005. *Probationary Americans: Contemporary Immigration Policies and the Shaping of Asian American Communities*. New York: Routledge.

Park, Robert Ezra. 1950. *Race and Culture*. Glencoe, IL: Free Press.

Park, Robert Ezra, and Ernest Burgess. 1967. *The City*. Chicago: University of Chicago Press.

Parker, Paula. 1980. "Heyday of Julian Hotel." *Los Angeles Times*, February 3, sec. II, 1.

———. 1984. "Page of Black History Crumbles, Hotel Douglas Was Known as Harlem of the West." *Los Angeles Times*, April 1, J1.

Pattee, Sarah. 1988. "Creole Palace: Memories of '30s Hot Spot for San Diego Still Warm." *San Diego Union-Tribune*, January 15, D1.

Petersen, William. 1966. "Success Story, Japanese-American Style." *New York Times Magazine*, January 9, 20.

Peterson, Paul. 1981. *City Limits*. Chicago: University of Chicago Press.

Picou, Cecile. 1996. "Douglas Hotel/Creole Palace: San Diego's Harlem of the West." *Voice and Viewpoint*, February 22, C9.

Pincetl, Stephanie S. 1999. *Transforming California: A Political History of Land Use and Development*. Baltimore: Johns Hopkins University Press.

Pitkin, Hanna Fenichel. 1967. *The Concept of Representation*. Berkeley: University of California Press.

Pitt, Leonard, and Dale Pitt. 1997. *Los Angeles A to Z: An Encyclopedia of the City and County*. Berkeley: University of California Press.

Polanco, Richard. 2001. Joint Hearing, Assembly, Elections, Reapportionment and Constitutional Amendments Committee and Senate Elections and Reapportionment Committee, Transcript of Public Hearing on Redistricting, Public Comment on Proposed Redistricting Plans Hearing at the State Capitol with Interactive Testimony from San Francisco, San Jose, Monterey, and Fresno, September 4. http://www.assembly.ca.gov/acs/committee/c7/phr.htm. Accessed June 2, 2002.

Post, Cynthia. 2006. "Renaissance Walk Rise on Auburn." *Atlanta Daily World*, February 16. http://www.zwire.com/site/news.cfm?newsid=16142028&BRD=1077&PAG=461&dept_id=237827&rfi=6. Accessed September 12, 2008.

Powell, Ronald W. 2000. "Once, Part of San Diego Was 'Harlem of the West.'" *San Diego Union-Tribune*, April 25, A1.

———. 2004. "Midway Magic." *San Diego Union-Tribune*, May 31, A1.

Prewitt, Ken. 2000a. "Additional Comments by Census Bureau Director Kenneth Prewitt and the Role of the Census Bureau and the Use of Census Tabulations in the Internment of Japanese Americans in World War II." *United States Department of Commerce News*. Washington, DC: U.S. Census Bureau, March 20.

———. 2000b. "Statement of Census Bureau Director Kenneth Prewitt on Internment of Japanese Americans in World War II." *United States Department of Commerce News*. Washington, DC: U.S. Census Bureau, March 17.

———. 2000c. "The U.S. Decennial Census: Political Questions, Scientific Answers." *Population and Development Review* 26(1): 1–16.

Puerto Rican Legal Defense and Education Fund. 1988. Letter to Richard Ravitch, chair of the Charter Reform Commission, April 1, Appendix 9, no. 2, page number not legible.

Pulido, Laura. 1998. "Development of the 'People of Color' Identity in the Environmental Justice Movement of the Southwestern United States." *Socialist Review* 96(3–4): 145–180.

———. 2000. "Rethinking Environmental Racism: White Privilege and Urban Development in Southern California." *Annals of the Association of American Geographers* 90: 12–40.

———. 2006. *Black, Brown, Yellow, and Left: Radical Activism in Los Angeles*. Berkeley: University of California Press.

Purdum, Todd S. 1989. "Charter Panel Chairman Sees a Larger Role for Minorities." *New York Times*, March 25, sec. 1, 1.

Quach, Hanh, and Dena Bunis. 2001. "All Bow to Redistrict Architect: Politics Secretive, Single-Minded Michael Berman Holds All the Crucial Cards." *Orange County Register*, August 26. http://www.fairvote.org/redistricting/reports/remanual/canews4.htm. Accessed March 25, 2003.

Redevelopment Agency of the City of San Diego. 1984. Environmental Impact Secondary Study, Market Street Square Apartments, July 30, CCDC folder 32176.

———. 1992. "Redevelopment Plan for the Centre City Redevelopment Project, a Merger and Expansion of the Columbia Redevelopment Project, Marina Development Project, the Gaslamp Quarter Redevelopment Project."

Reed, Judith. 1991. Letter to Richard Jerome, attorney, Department of Justice, Civil Rights Division, July 17.

———. 1992. "Of Boroughs, Boundaries, and Bullwinkles: The Limitations of Single-Member Districts in a Multiracial Context." *Fordham Urban Law Journal* 19: 759–780.

Reichl, Alexander J. 1997. "Historic Preservation and Progrowth Politics in U.S. Cities." *Urban Affairs Review* 32(4): 513–535.

———. 1999. *Reconstructing Times Square: Politics and Culture in Urban Development*. Lawrence: University Press of Kansas.

Richland, W. Bernard. 1989. Minutes of the New York City Charter Revision Commission, May 6, NYC Mayor, CRC Submission Under Section 5 of the Voting Rights Act, Appendix 5, 7–8.

Richter, Paul. 1995. "Clinton Declares Affirmative Action Is 'Good for America.'" *Los Angeles Times*, July 20, A1.

Rieder, Jonathan. 1985. *Canarsie: The Jews and Italians of Brooklyn Against Liberalism*. Cambridge, MA: Harvard University Press.

Ristine, Jeff. 2006. "After 25 Years, the Trolley Keeps On Moving." *San Diego Union-Tribune*, July 23, B2.

Rodriguez, Emelyn. 2001. "Hilda Solis: Profile in Courage." *California Journal*, December, 26–31. http://www.house.gov/apps/list/press/ca32_solis/morenews4/cajournal .html. Accessed September 12, 2008.

Rodriguez, Gregory. 2005. "Why We're the New Irish." *Newsweek*, May 30, 35.

Roediger, David. 1994. *Towards the Abolition of Whiteness*. London: Verso.

———. 2007. *The Wages of Whiteness: Race and the Making of the American Working Class*. Verso: New York.

Rosenblatt, Robert A. 2001. "Census See No Need to Revise First Tally." *Los Angeles Times*, March 2, A1.

Ryan, William. 1971. *Blaming the Victim*. New York: Vintage Books.

Sabagh, Georges, and Mehdi Bozorgmehr. 2003. "From 'Give Me Your Poor' to 'Save Our State': New York and Los Angeles as Immigrant Cities and Regions." In *New York and Los Angeles: Politics, Society, and Culture*, edited by David Halle. Chicago: University of Chicago Press.

Saito, Leland T. 1993. "Asian Americans and Latinos in San Gabriel Valley, California: Ethnic Political Cooperation and Redistricting, 1990–1991." *Amerasia Journal* 19(2): 55–68.

———. 1996a. Interview with Angelo Falcon, April 24, New York City.

———. 1996b. Interview with Margaret Chin, May 10, New York City.

———. 1996c. Interview with Margarita Lopez, April 26, New York City.

———. 1996d. Interview with Wing Lam, April 30, New York City.

———. 1998. *Race and Politics: Asian Americans, Latinos, and Whites in a Los Angeles Suburb*. Urbana: University of Illinois Press.

———. 1999. Interview with anonymous member of the Soho Alliance, September 13, New York City.

———. 2000. Phone discussion with Esmeralda Simmons, September 28.

———. 2003a. Phone interview with Larry Malone, June 18.

———. 2003b. Phone interview with Leon Williams, July 16.

———. 2004. E-mail correspondence with Gayle Hom Zemen.

———. 2006. "The Political Significance of Race: Asian American and Latino Redistricting Debates in California and New York City." In *Racial Transformations: Latinos and Asians Remaking the United States*, edited by Nicholas De Genova. Durham, NC: Duke University Press.

Sanchez, George. 1993. *Becoming Mexican American: Ethnicity, Culture, and Identity in Chicano Los Angeles, 1900–1945.* New York: Oxford University Press.

———. 2004. "'What's Good for Boyle Heights Is Good for the Jews': Creating Multiracialism on the Eastside During the 1950s." *American Quarterly* 56(3): 633–661.

Sanders, Heywood T. 1992. "Building the Convention City: Politics, Finance, and Public Investment in Urban America." *Journal of Urban Affairs* 14(2): 135–159.

San Diego City. 1965. "Centre City: 75—A Development Plan for Centre City San Diego."

———. 1984. "Housing Development Grant, Market Street Square," August 14.

San Diego Daily Transcript. 1988. San Diego Historical Society, August 17, file Chinese in San Diego.

San Diego Planning Department. 1982. "Report to the City Council on the Proposed Redevelopment Plan for the Gaslamp Quarter Redevelopment Project, June 1982."

San Diego Union-Tribune. 2000. "Redevelopment Wiping Out Black History, Group Says." *San Diego Union-Tribune,* March 1, B3.

San Francisco Chronicle. 2001. "Bush Calls On Mineta." http://www.sfgate.com/cgi-bin/article.cgi?f=/c/a/2001/01/03/MN179016.DTL&hw=Bush+Calls+On+Mineta&sn=001&sc=1000. Accessed September 12, 2008.

Sanjek, Roger. 1998. *The Future of Us All: Race and Neighborhood Politics in New York City.* Ithaca, NY: Cornell University Press.

Santiago, John, ed. n.d. *Redistricting, Race, and Ethnicity in New York City: The Gartner Report and Its Critics.* New York: Institute for Puerto Rican Policy.

Saxton, Alexander. 1971. *The Indispensable Enemy.* Berkeley: University of California Press.

Scharlin, Craig, and Lilia V. Villanueva. 1992. *Philip Vera Cruz.* Los Angeles: UCLA Labor Center, Institute of Industrial Relations and Asian American Studies Center.

Schenker, Nathaniel. 1993. "Undercount in the 1990 Census: Special Section." *Journal of the American Statistical Association* 88(423): 1044–1046.

Schlesinger, Arthur M., Jr. 1998. *The Disuniting of America: Reflections on a Multicultural Society.* New York: W. W. Norton.

Schwartz, Joel. 1993. *The New York Approach: Robert Moses, Urban Liberals, and the Redevelopment of the Inner City.* Columbus: Ohio State University Press.

Schwarz, Frederick A. O., Jr. 1989a. Minutes of Public Hearing Before the New York City Charter Revision Commission, June 27, Appendix 5, 17–17A, Exhibit 27.

———. 1989b. Minutes of Public Meeting of the Charter Revision Commission, June 15, NYC Mayor, Submission Under Section 5 of the Voting Rights Act, Appendix 5, 11–12.

———. 1989c. Minutes of the New York City Charter Revision Commission, May 6, NYC Mayor, CRC Submission Under Section 5 of the Voting Rights Act, Appendix 5, 7–8.

Schwarz, Frederick A. O., Jr., and Eric Lane. 1989. Letter to Barry H. Weinberg, acting chief, Voting Section, Civil Rights Division, United States Department of Justice, "Submission Under Section 5 of the Voting Rights Act for Preclearance of Proposed Amendments to the New York City Charter," August 11.

SDCC (San Diego Chinese Center). 1998. "Chinese New Year Food and Cultural Faire: Souvenir Program." Asian Pacific Thematic District, January 31 and February 1.

Seattle Weekly. 1996. "Endorsement." *Seattle Weekly*, September 11, 12.

Seid, David. 1986. Letter to Pamela M. Hamilton, assistant vice president, Centre City Development Corporation, June 10, CCDC file 32831.

Senate Redistricting Staff and Consultants. 2002. "Point/Counterpoint: The Redistricting Dispute." *California Journal* 33(1) (January): 38, 41–42.

Shah, Nayan. 2001. *Contagious Divides: Epidemics and Race in San Francisco's Chinatown.* Berkeley: University of California Press.

Showley, Roger. 1987. "Hopes to Save Old Chinese Mission Suffer a Setback." *San Diego Union-Tribune*, August 8, B3.

Sides, Josh. 2003. *L.A. City Limits: African American Los Angeles from the Great Depression to the Present.* Berkeley: University of California Press.

Silver, Allison. 1998. "Jon Jerde: Pioneering Architect Who Put 'Experience' into Downtowns." *Los Angeles Times*, December 20, M3.

Simon, Richard. 1991. "Molina Wins Historic Contest for Supervisor." *Los Angeles Times*, February 20.

———. 2000. "Martinez Switches to GOP in His Final Term." *Los Angeles Times*, July 27, B3.

Simon, Richard, and Antonio Olivo. 2000. "Two Incumbent Congressmen Facing Tough Challenges." *Los Angeles Times*, February 23, B1.

Sites, William. 1994. "Public Action: New York City Policy and the Gentrification of the Lower East Side." In *From Urban Village to East Village: The Battle for New York's Lower East Side*, edited by Janet L. Abu-Lughod. Cambridge, MA: Blackwell.

———. 2003. *Remaking New York: Primitive Globalization and the Politics of Urban Community.* Minneapolis: University of Minnesota Press.

Skerry, Peter. 2000. *Counting on the Census? Race, Group Identity, and the Evasion of Politics.* Washington, DC: Brookings Institution Press.

Smith, Icy. 2000. *The Lonely Queue: The Forgotten History of the Courageous Chinese Americans in Los Angeles.* Manhattan Beach, CA: East West Discovery Press.

Smith, Neil, Betsy Duncan, and Laura Reid. 1994. "From Disinvestment to Reinvestment: Mapping the Urban 'Frontier' in the Lower East Side." In *From Urban Village to East Village: The Battle for New York's Lower East Side*, edited by Janet L. Abu-Lughod. Cambridge, MA: Blackwell.

Solomon, Alisa. 1990. "Ravitch Sues Districting Panel." *Village Voice*, November 13, 12.

Sonenshein, Raphael J. 1993. *Politics in Black and White: Race and Power in Los Angeles.* Princeton, NJ: Princeton University Press.

Spivak, Sharon. 1985. "Downtown Hotel Yields to Progress." *San Diego Union-Tribune,* August 3, C1.

Sridharan, Priya. 2001. California Legislature, Assembly, Elections, Reapportionment and Constitutional Amendments Committee, Transcript of Public Hearing on Redistricting, Identification of Communities of Interest, Los Angeles, June 8. http://www.assembly.ca.gov/acs/committee/c7/phr.htm. Accessed June 1, 2002.

Stack, Carol B. 1974. *All Our Kin: Strategies for Survival in a Black Community.* New York: Harper Torchbooks.

Starr, Mark, Dennis A. Williams, and ARIC Press. 1984. "A Look Back at Anger." *Newsweek,* April 23, 36.

Steele, Shelby. 1990. *The Content of Our Character: A New Vision of Race in America.* New York: St. Martin's Press.

Stepner, Michael. 1977. "San Diego's Gaslamp Quarter." *Journal of San Diego History* 23(2): 24–33.

———. 1987. Memorandum to CCDC regarding the Chinese/Asian Thematic Historic District, July 17. Cited in Linda Trinh Vo, *Mobilizing an Asian American Community* (Philadelphia: Temple University Press, 2004), 261–262n16.

Stolz, Martin. 2005. "Black Historical Society Seeks Court Order to Halt Construction." *San Diego Union-Tribune,* April 28, B4.

Stone, Clarence N. 1989. *Regime Politics: Governing Atlanta, 1946–1988.* Lawrence: University Press of Kansas.

Sullivan, Mark T. 1987a. "Owners Not Thrilled Their Property Listed in Historic Register." *San Diego Tribune,* July 18, A1.

———. 1987b. "Your Move, Says Centre City to Mission Backers." *San Diego Union-Tribune,* August 8, C1.

———. 1989. "Talks on Fate of Famed Downtown Chinese Mission Building Put on Hold." *San Diego Union-Tribune,* February 16, B7.

Sutro, Dirk. 1991. "Time Is Now to Keep S.D.'s Past Alive." *Los Angeles Times,* September 12, E1.

Suzuki, Bob H. 1977. "Education and the Socialization of Asian Americans: A Revisionist Analysis of the 'Model Minority' Thesis." *Amerasia Journal* 4(2): 23–51.

Takagi, Dana. 1998. *The Retreat from Race: Asian American Admissions and Racial Politics.* New Brunswick, NJ: Rutgers University Press.

Takaki, Ronald. 1989. *Strangers from a Different Shore: A History of Asian Americans.* New York: Penguin Books.

Taylor, Monique M. 2002. *Harlem: Between Heaven and Hell.* Minneapolis: University of Minnesota Press.

Tchen, John Kuo Wei. 1999. *New York Before Chinatown: Orientalism and the Shaping of American Culture*. Baltimore: Johns Hopkins University Press.

Telles, Edward E., and Vilma Ortiz. 2008. *Generations of Exclusion: Mexican Americans, Assimilation, and Race*. New York: Russell Sage Foundation.

Thernstrom, Abigail M. 1987. *Whose Votes Count? Affirmative Action and Minority Voting Rights*. Cambridge, MA: Harvard University Press.

———. 1995. "More Notes from a Political Thicket." *Emory Law Journal* 44(3): 911–941.

Thernstrom, Stephan, and Abigail Thernstrom. 1997. *America in Black and White: One Nation, Indivisible*. New York: Simon and Schuster.

Tocqueville, Alexis de. 1969. *Democracy in America*. New York: Anchor Books.

Tom, Maeley. 2001. "APIA . . . Making Gains in the Highest Stake Political Game-Redistricting." Unpublished paper included in the information packet at the Coalition of Asian Pacific Americans for Fair Redistricting Wrap-Up Meeting, Los Angeles, December 14.

Trimble, Gerald M. 1984a. CCDC Memorandum to Chairman and Members of the Redevelopment Agency from Gerald M. Trimble. "Joint Public Hearing—Disposition and Development Agreement with Shapell Housing, Inc. and Goldrich Kest and Associates (Market Street Square Apartments)," July 30.

———. 1984b. "Making Better Use of Urban Space, Local Redevelopment Initiatives, the New Downtown San Diego: Horton Plaza." San Diego: CCDC.

———. 1986. CCDC Memorandum to Chairman and Members of the Redevelopment Agency from Gerald M. Trimble. "Findings of Research and Analysis of Chinese Buildings, Marina Development Project," April 29, CCDC file 32823I, Chinese Mission Building.

———. 1987. CCDC Memorandum to Centre City Development Corporation from Gerald Trimble, executive vice president. "Recommendations Regarding Chinese Buildings in the Marina Development Project Area," February 9, CCDC file 32823I, Chinese Mission Building.

Tseng, Yen-Fen. 1994. "Chinese Ethnic Economy: San Gabriel Valley, Los Angeles County." *Journal of Urban Affairs* 16: 169–189.

Tuan, Mia. 1998. *Forever Foreigners or Honorary Whites?* New Brunswick, NJ: Rutgers University Press.

Tumulty, Karen. 2001. "Courting a Sleeping Giant." *Time Magazine*, June 11. http://www.time.com/time/covers/1101010611/flatin.html. Accessed July 24, 2006.

Tyson, Charles Parry. 1987. Letter to Chairperson and Members of the Historical Site Board, May 20, Historical Resources Board, folder 207.

Umemoto, Karen. 1989. "'On Strike!' San Francisco State College Strike, 1968–69: The Role of Asian American Students." *Amerasia Journal* 15(1): 3–41.

Underwood, Katherine. 1992. "Process and Politics: Multiracial Electoral Coalition

Building and Representation in Los Angeles' Ninth District, 1949–1962." Ph.D. dissertation, University of California, San Diego.

———. 1997. "Ethnicity Is Not Enough: Latino-Led Multiracial Coalitions in Los Angeles." *Urban Affairs Review* 33(1): 3–25.

Upton, Dell. 1986. *America's Architectural Roots: Ethnic Groups That Built America.* Washington, DC: Preservation Press.

U.S. Census Bureau. 2000. "State and County Quick Facts, California." http://quickfacts .census.gov/qfd/states/06000.html. Accessed July 30, 2002.

———. 2006. "Table 3: Annual Estimates of the Population by Sex, Race and Hispanic or Latino Origin for the United States, April 1, 2000, to July 1, 2005 (NC-EST2005-03)." Population Division, U.S. Census Bureau, May 10. http://www.census.gov/popest/national/asrh/. Accessed July 25, 2006.

U.S. Commission on Civil Rights. 1973. *Understanding Fair Housing.* Washington, DC: U.S. Government Printing Office.

———. 1975. *Twenty Years After Brown: Equal Opportunity in Housing.* Washington, DC: U.S. Government Printing Office.

———. 1992. *Civil Rights Issues Facing Asian Americans in the 1990s.* Washington, DC: U.S. Government Printing Office.

U.S. News and World Report. 1966. "Success Story of One Minority Group in U.S." *U.S. News and World Report,* December 26, 73.

Valle, Victor M., and Rodolfo D. Torres. 2000. *Latino Metropolis.* Minneapolis: University of Minnesota Press.

Vanderleeuw, James, Baodong Liu, and Gregory Marsh. 2004. "Applying Black Threat Theory, Urban Regime Theory, and Deracialization: The Memphis Mayoral Elections of 1991, 1995, and 1999." *Journal of Urban Affairs* 26(4): 505–519.

Vargas, Joao H. Costa. 2006. *Catching Hell in the City of Angels: Life and Meanings of Blackness in South Central Los Angeles.* Minneapolis: University of Minnesota Press.

Velez, Amadis. 2001. Joint Hearing, Assembly, Elections, Reapportionment and Constitutional Amendments Committee and Senate Elections and Reapportionment Committee. Transcript of Public Hearing on Redistricting. Public Comment on Proposed Redistricting Plans Hearing at the State Capitol with Interactive Testimony from San Francisco, San Jose, Monterey and Fresno, September 4. http://www .assembly.ca.gov/acs/committee/c7/phr.htm. Accessed June 2, 2002.

Villa, Raul Homer. 2000. *Barrio-Logos: Space and Place in Urban Chicano Literature and Culture.* Austin: University of Texas Press.

Virasami, Bryan. 2001. "Groundbreaking Win for Asian." *Newsday,* November 8, A56.

Viteritti, Joseph P. 1989. "The Tradition of Municipal Reform: Charter Revision in Historical Context." In *Restructuring the New York City Government: The Reemergence of*

Municipal Reform, edited by Frank J. Mauro and Gerald Benjamin. New York: Academy of Political Science.

Vo, Linda Trinh. 1996. "Asian Immigrants, Asian Americans, and the Politics of Economic Mobilization in San Diego." *Amerasia Journal* 22(2): 89–108.

———. 2004. *Mobilizing an Asian American Community*. Philadelphia: Temple University Press.

Voice and Viewpoint. 1979. "Drive Starts to Save Douglas Hotel." *Voice and Viewpoint*, September, A5.

Waldinger, Roger. 1986. *Through the Eye of the Needle: Immigrants and Enterprise in New York's Garment Trades*. New York: New York University Press.

———. 1996. *Still the Promised City? African-Americans and New Immigrants in Postindustrial New York*. Cambridge, MA: Harvard University Press.

Waldinger, Roger, and Yenfen Tseng. 1992. "Divergent Diasporas: The Chinese Communities of New York and Los Angeles Compared." *Revue Européene des Migrations Internationales* 8(3): 91–115.

Wallace, Amy, and Dave Lesher. 1995. "UC Regents, in Historic Vote, Wipe Out Affirmative Action." *Los Angeles Times*, July 21, A1.

Wallsten, Peter, and Johanna Neuman. 2006. "Voting Rights Act Renewal Divides GOP." *Los Angeles Times*, July 12, A15.

Washington, Geraldine. 2001. "Statement of Geraldine Washington Read into the Record by William Monroe Campbell." Senate Committee on Elections and Reapportionment, State of California, 2001 Redistricting, July 17, Los Angeles. http://www.senate.ca.gov/ftp/SEN/COMMITTEE/STANDING/EL/_home/transcripts.htp. Accessed June 1, 2002.

Watanabe, Teresa. 2003. "Chinese Take to U.S. Politics." *Los Angeles Times*, August 4, B9.

———. 2007. "In 1943, Census Released Japanese Americans' Data." *Los Angeles Times*, March 31, A18.

Waters, Mary. 1990. *Ethnic Options: Choosing Identities in America*. Berkeley: University of California Press.

———. 1999. *Black Identities: West Indian Immigrant Dreams and American Realities*. New York: Russell Sage Foundation, and Cambridge, MA: Harvard University Press.

Waugh, John C. 1968. "Both a 'Promise' and a 'Problem.'" *Christian Science Monitor*, April 17, 5.

Weintraub, Daniel M. 1991. "Incumbents Come First in Redistricting, Speaker Says." *Los Angeles Times*, August 30.

Weiss, Kenneth R. 1998. "UC Regents Decry but Keep Entrance Favors." *Los Angeles Times*, July 17, A3.

Wild, Mark. 2005. *Street Meeting: Multiethnic Neighborhoods in Early Twentieth-Century Los Angeles*. Berkeley: University of California Press.

William C. Velasquez Institute. n.d. "Fair Redistricting in the 2000's: A Manual for Minority Groups." Unpublished paper handed out at the Community Redistricting Workshop sponsored by the William C. Velasquez Institute, MALDEF, and the National Association of Latino Elected Officials, February 6, 2001, National City, California.

Williams, Dennis A., Dianne H. McDonald, Lucy Howard, Margaret Mittelbach, and Cynthia Kyle. 1984. "A Formula for Success." *Newsweek,* April 23, 36.

Wilson, William J. 1980. *The Declining Significance of Race: Blacks and Changing American Institutions.* Chicago: University of Chicago Press.

———. 1987. *The Truly Disadvantaged: The Inner City, the Underclass, and Public Policy.* Chicago: University of Chicago Press.

———. 1990. "Race-Neutral Policies and the Democratic Coalition." *American Prospect* online. http://www.prospect.org/cs/articles?article=raceneutral_policies_and_the_democratic_coalition. Accessed September 12, 2008.

Winant, Howard. 2001. *The World Is a Ghetto: Race and Democracy Since World War II.* New York: Basic Books.

Winton, Richard. 2001a. "Asian Americans Flex Growing Political Muscle." *Los Angeles Times,* September 12, B1.

———. 2001b. "Campaigning Across Ethnic Lines." *Los Angeles Times,* May 12, sec. II, 4.

Wolfley, Bob. 2001. "A Bat, a House, a Cabinet, a Life's Story." *Milwaukee Journal Sentinel* online. http://www2.jsonline.com/sports/brew/mpark/apr01/sptsday07040601.asp?format=print. Accessed November 20, 2006.

Wong, Frank. 1986a. Letter to Howard Busby, president of Centre City Development Corporation, June 27, CCDC file 32823I, Chinese Mission Building.

———. 1986b. Letter to Pamela Hamilton, CCDC, July 7, petitions attached to letter, CCDC file 32823I, Chinese Mission Building.

Wong, Janelle S. 2006. *Democracy's Promise: Immigrants and American Civic Institutions.* Ann Arbor: University of Michigan Press.

Wong, K. Scott. 1995. "Chinatown: Conflicting Images, Contested Terrain." *MELUS* 20(1): 3–15.

Wu, Frank H. 2002. *Yellow: Race in America Beyond Black and White.* New York: Basic Books.

Yoo, David K. 2003. "Testing Assumptions: IQ, Japanese Americans, and the Model Minority Myth in the 1920s and 1930s." In *Remapping Asian American History,* edited by Sucheng Chan. Walnut Creek, CA: AltaMira Press.

Yu, Judy, and Grace T. Yuan. 2001. "Lessons Learned from the 'Locke for Governor' Campaign." In *Asian Americans and Politics: Perspectives, Experiences, Prospects,* edited by Gordon H. Chang. Stanford, CA: Stanford University Press.

Yu, Nancy W., and Daniel K. Ichinose. n.d. "Twenty Faster Growing Counties Based on

Numerical Population Change." Unpublished handout included with information packet in 2001 for the San Diego region of the California Asian Pacific Americans for Fair Redistricting Coalition.

Zhou, Min. 1992. *Chinatown: The Socioeconomic Potential of an Urban Enclave*. Philadelphia: Temple University Press.

Index

Italic page numbers indicate figures, maps, or tables.